Developing Creative Economy Through Disruptive Leadership:

Emerging Research and Opportunities

Kristin Joyce Tardif
University of Arkansas - Fort Smith, USA

A volume in the Advances in Business Strategy and Competitive Advantage (ABSCA) Book Series

IGI Global
DISSEMINATOR OF KNOWLEDGE

Published in the United States of America by
IGI Global
Business Science Reference (an imprint of IGI Global)
701 E. Chocolate Avenue
Hershey PA, USA 17033
Tel: 717-533-8845
Fax: 717-533-8661
E-mail: cust@igi-global.com
Web site: http://www.igi-global.com

Library of Congress Cataloging-in-Publication Data

Names: Tardif, Kristin Joyce, 1955- author.
Title: Developing creative economy through disruptive leadership : emerging research and opportunities / by Kristin Joyce Tardif.
Description: Hershey, PA : Business Science Reference, [2020] | Includes bibliographical references and index. | Summary: "This book explores the development of a creative economy through disruptive leadership"-- Provided by publisher.
Identifiers: LCCN 2019053031 (print) | LCCN 2019053032 (ebook) | ISBN 9781799834168 (hardcover) | ISBN 9781799834175 (paperback) | ISBN 9781799834182 (ebook)
Subjects: LCSH: Cultural industries. | Creative ability in business. | Leadership.
Classification: LCC HD9999.C9472 T37 2020 (print) | LCC HD9999.C9472 (ebook) | DDC 658.4/092--dc23
LC record available at https://lccn.loc.gov/2019053031
LC ebook record available at https://lccn.loc.gov/2019053032

This book is published in the IGI Global book series Advances in Business Strategy and Competitive Advantage (ABSCA) (ISSN: 2327-3429; eISSN: 2327-3437)

British Cataloguing in Publication Data
A Cataloguing in Publication record for this book is available from the British Library.

All work contributed to this book is new, previously-unpublished material.
The views expressed in this book are those of the authors, but not necessarily of the publisher.

For electronic access to this publication, please contact: eresources@igi-global.com.

Advances in Business Strategy and Competitive Advantage (ABSCA) Book Series

ISSN:2327-3429
EISSN:2327-3437

Editor-in-Chief: Patricia Ordóñez de Pablos, Universidad de Oviedo, Spain

MISSION

Business entities are constantly seeking new ways through which to gain advantage over their competitors and strengthen their position within the business environment. With competition at an all-time high due to technological advancements allowing for competition on a global scale, firms continue to seek new ways through which to improve and strengthen their business processes, procedures, and profitability.

The **Advances in Business Strategy and Competitive Advantage (ABSCA) Book Series** is a timely series responding to the high demand for state-of-the-art research on how business strategies are created, implemented and re-designed to meet the demands of globalized competitive markets. With a focus on local and global challenges, business opportunities and the needs of society, the **ABSCA** encourages scientific discourse on doing business and managing information technologies for the creation of sustainable competitive advantage.

COVERAGE

- Business Models
- International Business Strategy
- Tacit Knowledge
- Co-operative Strategies
- Competitive Strategy
- Cost Leadership Strategy
- Innovation Strategy
- Ethics and Business Strategy
- Value Creation
- Joint Ventures

IGI Global is currently accepting manuscripts for publication within this series. To submit a proposal for a volume in this series, please contact our Acquisition Editors at Acquisitions@igi-global.com or visit: http://www.igi-global.com/publish/.

The Advances in Business Strategy and Competitive Advantage (ABSCA) Book Series (ISSN 2327-3429) is published by IGI Global, 701 E. Chocolate Avenue, Hershey, PA 17033-1240, USA, www.igi-global.com. This series is composed of titles available for purchase individually; each title is edited to be contextually exclusive from any other title within the series. For pricing and ordering information please visit http://www.igi-global.com/book-series/advances-business-strategy-competitive-advantage/73672. Postmaster: Send all address changes to above address.

Titles in this Series

For a list of additional titles in this series, please visit:
http://www.igi-global.com/book-series/advances-business-strategy-competitive-advantage/73672

Knowledge Management, Innovation, and Entrepreneurship in a Changing World
Murray Eugene Jennex (San Diego State University, USA)
Business Science Reference • ©2020 • 463pp • H/C (ISBN: 9781799823551) • US $215.00

Developing Entrepreneurial Competencies for Start-Ups and Small Business
Jarmila Šebestová (Silesian University in Opava, Czech Republic)
Business Science Reference • ©2020 • 316pp • H/C (ISBN: 9781799827146) • US $225.00

Leadership and Followership in an Organizational Change Context
Sajjad Nawaz Khan (University Malaysia Sarawak, Malaysia) and Abdul Halim Busari (University Malaysia Sarawak, Malaysia)
Business Science Reference • ©2020 • 300pp • H/C (ISBN: 9781799828075) • US $225.00

Digital Marketing Strategies and Models for Competitive Business
Filipe Mota Pinto (Polytechnic Institute of Leiria, Portugal) and Teresa Guarda (Universidad Peninsula de Santa Elena (UPSE), Ecuador)
Business Science Reference • ©2020 • 300pp • H/C (ISBN: 9781799829638) • US $225.00

Recent Advancements in Sustainable Entrepreneurship and Corporate Social Responsibility
Amulya Gurtu (Cofrin School of Business, University of Wisconsin-Green Bay, USA)
Business Science Reference • ©2020 • 219pp • H/C (ISBN: 9781799823476) • US $215.00

Challenges and Opportunities for SMEs in Industry 4.0
Noor Hazlina Ahmad (Universiti Sains Malaysia, Malaysia) Qaisar Iqbal (Universiti Sains Malaysia, Malaysia) and Hasliza Abdul Halim (Universiti Sains Malaysia, Malaysia)
Business Science Reference • ©2020 • 271pp • H/C (ISBN: 9781799825777) • US $215.00

For an entire list of titles in this series, please visit:
http://www.igi-global.com/book-series/advances-business-strategy-competitive-advantage/73672

IGI Global
DISSEMINATOR OF KNOWLEDGE

701 East Chocolate Avenue, Hershey, PA 17033, USA
Tel: 717-533-8845 x100 • Fax: 717-533-8661
E-Mail: cust@igi-global.com • www.igi-global.com

Table of Contents

Foreword

I had the pleasure of working with Dr. Kristin Tardif and Steve Clark from the nascent conversations of how university leaders and business leader could collaborate to change the trajectory of a regional economy dependent on legacy manufacturing. How could we create the catalyst for change? What role could the university play? How are we educating the next generation of leaders to navigate in this new world of disruption?

Having worked in the aerospace and technology industries as a management consultant for years before moving to higher education, I recognized the incredible potential of Dr. Tardif's work to drive the conversation on leadership development in a creative economy. Now that I have served as a leader of a public university in two rural states, I am even more convinced of how valuable her work is for higher education. We are beginning to recognize the shift in market labor needs for college graduates from purely technical expertise to a capacity for creativity and an appetite for disruption. While historically higher education has been slow in responding to the markets they serve, in the post Great Recession economy, higher education must be more creative in order to remain relevant. As public higher education leaders, we must recognize that the days of the ivory tower have faded. We must recognize that public higher education is a mechanism for social mobility and an engine for regional economic development. These are the demands of our stakeholders. These are the expectations of parents, students, legislators, and business. Dr. Tardif's work highlights three critical roles higher education must serve to support the creative economy.

First, the leaders of public universities must evolve to fit Dr. Tardif's description of a disruptive leader. In order to fully achieve their potential in the new economy, universities must be led by boundary-spanning leaders capable of building networks, communicating an inspiring vision, and embracing ambiguity. The next generation of university leaders must look beyond the traditional boundaries of the campus and challenge the status quo that has eroded the public's confidence in our mission. We must be bold, risk takers.

Secondly, we also have a charge to educate leaders who can thrive in this new economy. Future leaders must not be bound by the archaic dogma of the industrial age. We must develop leaders who can recognize and create value, who can thrive in ambiguity, who can lead in new ways. We must look to cross-disciplinary delivery that leverages the liberal arts in teaching creativity, risk taking, team work, and other skills that will be valuable in the new creative economy. We have an obligation to be good stewards in educating the next generation of leaders.

Finally, universities serve a vital role in regional economic development. As anchor institutions in rural states facing an aging and declining population coupled with the decline of traditional agricultural and manufacturing economies, we must act as a catalyst and engine for creative industry development in the communities we serve. For public universities to truly serve the public good during periods of economic disruption, we must better integrate ourselves into the fabric of our regions.

We have our work cut out for us, but Dr. Tardif's work is a critical resource in the evolution that is taking place in public higher education to support the creative economy. Higher education has been entrenched for too many years, has been too risk averse, and created organizational structures that are not conducive to innovation. This work is a must read for both educational and business leaders committed to developing a healthy ecosystem of talented leaders who can thrive in the new disruptive economy.

Edward A. Serna
University of Maine at Farmington, USA

Preface

Our modern times are often referred to as times of turbulence. In these times, organizations and communities often navigate on autopilot, failing to see unintended circumstances and implications. However, every time a decision is made there is a trade-off. A true understanding of the trade-off may determine success or failure. Either failure could mean very high cost monetarily or the organizations share of the marketplace. For communities the future will be determined by their re-development and re-vitalization.

With change being a constant, and with turbulence possibly being the new norm, disruptive creative leadership will be needed to ignite the creative economy, which will lead to the development of new technologies that enable the building of a sustainable community, quality of life, and a healthy socio-economic society. The role of higher education in igniting the creative economy and contributing to the sustainable community may have been ignored or understated. In times of turbulence, higher education will be forced to change. A modernization of higher education is needed. A renewal of faith, trust that higher education is non-biased, and truly researching and teaching truth base on higher order thinking and decision-making. A new commitment for a modern world where disruptive creative leadership in universities is the norm.

Collective societies are on one hand intimately connected to one another via the internet and social media. However, on the other hand, rapidly changing events and the flood of incorrect information competing with accurate information significantly influences local communities as well as the global society. Governance has become more difficult in a turbulent changing world. New structures and systems may have to be implemented for success. The management guru Peter Drucker surmised, "Turbulent times can be analyzed, predicted and managed" (Drucker, 1980), however, leaders who seek stability might be surprised to learn that they might never arrive at stability. In this new modern world, previous concepts of stability could be antiquated. Furthermore, current management and leadership skills may be inadequate. Ultimately, some unstable, shifting finish line means that leaders will have to change or be outpaced (Volker's & Skeet, 2016).

With the advent of the third stage of singularity and turbulence associated with the coming Fifth and Sixth Industrial Revolutions may bring about the need for leaders to expand from transformational and authenticity to a disruptive creative leader. The future may be a new enlightenment focusing on the need for the personal mastery of lifelong learners, who live continually in the fundamental state of leadership. Such mastery enables leaders to become higher functioning leaders, where divergent decisions can recognize "wicked" opportunities in the mist of "wicked" problems.

Social media presents new problems and has changed social norms. The young are being diagnosed with ADHD and other communication disorders. Social media bullying is leading to teen suicide and self-harm. We have become addicted to social media, often picking up our phones several times a day. Many only correspond by social media or texting. Mindfulness is becoming non-existent. Research is needed to determine how this affects our own creativity. Further research is needed to determine if our need of media, reality T.V. and our fascination with Hollywood and public figures has had an effect on individual creativity. Our need to be constantly entertained has eliminated our mindfulness, which is needed to enhance and develop our individual creativity. Our new social norms may actually be eliminating our ability to innovate and be creative at a time it is needed most to thrive in a new and turbulent world.

The new love of fairytales and advanced graphics play out in shows such as Marvel Universe, Game of Thrones, Vikings, Outlander, and Percy Jackson and the Olympians' The popularity of these shows conveys the need to escape the pressures of the modern world, taking us to a far off places where we dream and our imagination blooms. This could mean our society is ready for a new enlightenment, and if this is the case, it can happen in all disciplines as long as we develop our heightened creativity, institution and understand the importance of mindfulness.

We might ask the question, does this heightened creativity come from change? Creative leadership and the creative economy is based on building our self-awareness, self-worth and developing a sense of place; and by focusing on this, we might prevail and prosper in modern turbulent times. Could this be the redeeming feature of our culture and socio-economic systems? Technology and the modern world has moved us further away of these social systems that were once so important, however, the creative economy can bring us back to those important social systems so important to our quality of life.

The creative economy and disruptive leadership transcends all countries, all states, and all communities. The creative economy is based on capitalizing on one's own unique culture. Traveling to many countries and meeting many government officials and higher education scholars, who all have advocated building the creative economy is a pathway to rebuilding the rich tapestries of our everyday culture and at the same time building our economies. As we build our economies, we rebuild our social networks that once bound our communities to a common moral ground.

Currently, we are seeing urban outward migration and rural towns experiencing inward migration. Research has determined that younger generations are sacrificing the high salaries they once coveted, and now just want to realize a quality of life even at a financial loss. They still want the many programs once only found in the city, however, because of the creative economy they are now found in rural towns. The experience once found in cities, is now a lovely experience in states like South Dakota.

States, communities and business is looking to relocate to a more profitable area will be interested in the findings of this publication. This publication is informational, and a guide to how successful people undertook revitalizing their local and state economies. In addition, many Native American Nations are leading the way and creating vibrant economies based on their own unique culture. This is not a movement solely grounded to the U.S., this is a global initiative. The Prime Minister of India Modi has spoken of the importance of the creative economy to the growth and stability of India. In Ireland at the University of Ireland Galloway, groups of scholars are working to collaborate with industry and government to build a stronger creative economy. Creative problem solving and our heightened creativity is what has helped us in the past, and will in future. This book gives hope, an update on where we are at with the creative economy, and shows a pathway to changing higher education, government, and business to develop the creative economy, a sense of place and quality of life in our communities.

Disruptive leaders possess a deep understanding of the nonobvious, developing solutions with a heightened creativity, solving problems and addressing risks, finding the right tradeoffs, and essentially recognizing the opportunities in the problems. These disruptive leaders are able to scan the environment, identify trends, and envision the future. Often this is done by finding superior solutions, products and services.

The word disrupt means to cause something, to be unable to continue in the normal way, and to interrupt the normal progress or activity of something. It is much more than a modern buzzword. The disruptive leader is seen as the leader that "shakes it up", wakes up an organization from its slumber, and helps them compete in the modern world. There are many case studies about organizations that woke up too late, to the surprise of their employees; they no longer had employment, such Sears and K-mart. For this reason alone leaders must continually challenge what they hold sacred.

Public culture embodies a number of principles. One is that art and innovation can be experienced in a public way, not just private or in specific groups. Public culture identifies uniquely social functions of a specific culture, goals shared across society that our worthy to pursue. In 1982 Kevin Mulcahy, (Mulcahy, 1982), determined five dominant justifications of public culture: 1) economic 2) social 3) educational 4) moral 5) political arguments. In addition, public culture is thought to serve private interest, so the support of public culture is necessary for public interest as well.

Branding builds off the public culture of a community or organization by depicting the heart of the culture. In essence, what are the overlaying beliefs, values, traditions and stories of the community or organization? The majority has to agree that the brand reflects these overlaying beliefs and values. When the community can stand together on their culture, they can build their brand. This is not a marketing ploy or for advertisement. This is the life-blood of the community, organization, region or state. Many states have re-branded for tourism, and cultural tourism is part of the creative economy. Arkansas uses the tag line the *Natural State* that reflects the beautiful lakes, forest and rivers that are enjoyed by many tourists. Maine uses the tag line *It Must Be Maine.* Kentucky's tag line is *Unbridled Spirit;* New Mexico's tag line is *Land of Enchantment.* New York's famous tag line *I Love New York* is known by the distinct logo with love being replaced by the heart. For the creative economy to be strong and sustainable, it is necessary to build a strong brand. The strong brand will elevate and attract people to your community, region or state.

Cluster groups are those organizations or individuals who have similar businesses and relationships. Clusters usually form organically due to the nature of the economic activity. Regional and local economies grow and decline based on their ability to specialize in high-value industries and then evolve those specializations over time. Cluster groups aim to embrace advantages of productive, innovative and creative mechanisms by sharing knowledge, infrastructure, resources and suppliers.

The term "Tool Kit" has various meanings. Most definitions state that Tool Kit is usually a set of tools, and a set of documents, such as informational summaries and form letters, that we use to inform others about a topic of interest. The tools are designed to be used together or for a particular purpose. Often the Tool Kit provides a fixed set of procedures, guidelines, and criteria to established a desired outcome and prevent oversights (Harper Collins, 2014).

It could be said that one of the foundations of leadership studies is higher order thinking and decision-making or divergent learning. Higher-order thinking skills (HOTS) is a concept popular in American education, and its roots lie in Blooms Taxonomy.

Benjamin Bloom created bloom's Taxonomy (1956), as a classification of learning outcomes and objectives. The Classification was based on a sequence of cognitive skills: Knowledge, Comprehension, Application, Analysis, Synthesis, and Evaluation. The framework was revised in 2001 by Lorin Anderson and David Krathwohl in which 'Synthesis' was removed and 'Creation' was added as the highest-level of Bloom's Taxonomy. The highest level being the most complex or demanding cognitive skill, or at least the representation of a pinnacle for cognitive tasks (Krathwohl, 2002). A major transformation is needed in education. Education is seen as behind, not trusted and stagnant. Education needs to modernize, re-develop and be trusted in our communities and states. The most elite schools are seen as not rewarding achievement but breeding. Top schools are under fire for elitism and ending opportunity, but there is more to the overall dissatisfaction. Parents perceive higher education as a place where scholars practice indoctrination, and not developing critical thought. Perhaps educators need to drop preconceived ideology, and regain the ability to reason, and become life-long learners themselves. Simply teach students to think and make decisions on a higher level.

For this research, fifteen state agencies were interviewed and studied. They are a mixture of rural, semi urban and urban agencies, all quite different in culture and diversity. Some states have been successful in developing and implementing the creative economy, some are still working toward a goal, but all have dedicated professionals leading the charge and no doubt, they will be successful. They have a tireless energy and passion to build state programs, even some on limited funding, but still their accomplishments are great. Talking to state agencies and looking at existing research, the economic environment gives a clearer picture of where the state stands, and if the creative economy is existing or flourishing.

Michael Rendell's team at Price Waterhouse (2007) along with the James Martin Institute for Science and Civilization at the Said Business School in Oxford, UK, looked at the future of work and identified three possible worlds of business. By examining the ways organizations might operate in the future, related to societal changes, the environment, and what is needed in the workplace they came up with a new theme. First, being that business models will dramatically change. Second, leadership will be a skill needed to meet the challenges. Leadership studies is a discipline of the future, and disruptive leaders will be the ones to thrive.

Disruptive creative change is often driven by need, and the need to be competitive. In recent years, problems with the depletion of nature resources, pollution, natural disasters, traffic, nuclear risk, energy and water shortages have given way to the need for more advances in technology to solve these problems on a global scale. At the same time, the global society is demanding that companies develop and innovate to accommodate the demands of sustainability. Several disruptive leaders and companies have risen to the challenge, and technology is currently being invented. This is based on science not politics. The truth will create a new world.

Our future may be as simple as our own ability to be disruptive, and disruptive with a heightened creativity. This work promotes the field of leadership studies and economic development with a fresh look at what is happening on the ground in states striving to develop their creative economies. This work takes a close look at what has happened from 2017 to 2019 that could re-define how we perceive the U.S. today. This could not only re-define communities and states, but also totally re-define voting districts that could alter elections. Success may be coming from an un-defined pathway; this book highlights the specific instructions and learnings that will develop disruptive leaders and the creative economy.

Case studies and models are presented to give further explanation to the material. Real life experiences of those in trenches doing the work, gives one the right perspective of how to be successful and avoid pitfalls. A major shift in economic development is happening across the U.S. and globally. A new enlightenment has started with the creative economy, and maybe the greatest savior of our cultures and civilizations.

REFERENCES

Drucker, P. F. (1980). Managing in Turbulent Times. Harper Collins.

Krathwohl, D. R. (2002). A Revision of Blooms Taxonomy: An Overview. *Theory into Practice*, *41*(4), 212–218. doi:10.120715430421tip4104_2

Mulcahy, K. V. (1982). The Rationale of Public Culture: In Public Policy and the Arts. Westview Press.

Volker, J., & Skeet, P. (2016). Leading in Turbulent Times. *ILA*. Retrieved from http://www.ila-net.org/Conferences/2017/theme.html

Acknowledgment

To Steve Clark who is my inspiration for the Disruptive Leader. To John McIntosh whose counsel and friendship over many lunches provided the sounding board and inspiration to keep me going. To my Dean Dr. Ken Warden for the best support system a person could ask for.

I owe a special debt to Dr. Sally Rood with the National Governors Association whose knowledge and advice was greatly appreciated. A special thank you to the state directors of agencies working tirelessly to build the creative economy in their states, and whose work is creating a paradigm shift that could possibly lead to a new enlightenment. These great people are listed below: Joseph Donovan, Desiree Brothe, Andrew Reinartz, Jim Speirs, Patrick Baker, Joel Gavin, Yellow Light Beam.

To my family for letting pursue my dream. A special thank you to my husband, L. VanOsdol and Linda Blair, for your wonderful input and edits.

Introduction

My interest in the Creative Economy began in the late 1990's when the National Governors Association launched this initiative in all fifty states. This was a popular initiative in many states. However, I seriously started researching the creative economy four years ago when I moved to an area where a disruptive leader, by the name of Steve Clark, was actively developing collaborations and initiatives that were very successful in developing the local creative economy. The creative economy is described in a variety of ways and each state perceives the creative economy in their own unique way. However, since 2017 many states have changed the way they are doing business and implementing the creative economy. In the past, States saw the implementation of the creative economy as based on the work of nonprofits and cultural tourism. Today the creative economy encompasses technology as well, and the states that have recognized this have built a new vibrant creative economy that is driving social change and inward migration. The creation of micropolitan areas are changing the face of America.

The most successful creative economy movements have started with a Disruptive Leader.

Disruptive leaders possess a deep understanding of the nonobvious, developing solutions with a heighten creativity, solving problems and addressing risks, finding the right tradeoffs, and essentially recognizing the "wicked" opportunities in the"wicked" problems. These disruptive leaders can scan the environment, identify trends, and envision the future. Often this is done by finding superior solutions, products and services.

Many of the creative economies are based on entrepreneurism, culture, cultural districts and cluster development. These have a decentralized nature that can benefit residents of areas often thought to lack economic strength—such as rural areas and the urban core. The heart of the creative industries are entrepreneurs, inventors, individual artists and micro businesses who are typically well-connected to the communities where they reside. Linking these entrepreneurs, inventors, artist and technology experts with opportunities both inside and beyond their regions offers many economic development possibilities. A state's cultural resources can be economic assets, providing jobs, attracting investments through cultural events and tourism, crafts with retail and trade opportunities.

Perhaps more significantly, technology creates opportunities for a contemporary workforce, and creates an appeal to a young skilled workforce. When states combine the technology opportunities with revitalization and the arts, transformation is taking place across rural America. Young people are moving to rural areas for a quality of life, jobs, and a safe community that is revitalizing. They are not finding this is in urban areas that are experiencing decay or states where high taxes and little opportunities impact quality of life.

In May of 2018 The Walton Family Foundation published "Micropolitan Success Stories from the Heartland" by Ross DeVol and Shelly J. Wisecarver. The U.S. Census Bureau defines a micropolitan statistical area as a geographical area of one or more counties with one city containing at least 10,000 but less than 50,000 in population. There are currently 551 micropolitan areas in the country, and this geographic classification is growing in relevance. The importance of this work should not be underestimated. Furthermore, the success of these communities are directly related to the creative economy, and since 2015 these communities are on the rise. Since 2017 a change has occurred and these communities are experiencing inward migration of young professionals and retirees. Featured in the report are five communities in the Heartland, who with authenticity overcame many challenges and are now experiencing economic growth, and inward migration of young professionals looking for quality of life.

Our future may be as simple as our own ability to be disruptive, creative and persistent. Not to allow failure to define one but define ourselves by our ability to shift our life path and alter our paradigm through a heightened creativity. Local communities and state governments can pass laws, enact programs, award grants, and collaborate with local and state economic development agencies to encourage disruptive creative entrepreneurs; but it is in recognizing the benefits of the creative economy a community and state can revitalize and attract young professionals and families seeking a quality life.

Kristin Joyce Tardif
University of Arkansas – Fort Smith, USA

Chapter 1
The Turbulence of Our Times

ABSTRACT

We are full swing into the era of turbulence, and at this time, our creativity is more important than ever. We have heard many scholars and business leaders ask the question, "Can we invent and innovate effectively to keep up with the fast changes happening around us?" This chapter explores how to develop a heightened creativity and help weak economic areas by using technology, the arts, and our unique cultures to ignite economic development. Attracting tourism; young, talented people; and entrepreneurs to rural and urban cores is essential to thrive in turbulent times. In times of turbulence, organizations often navigate on autopilot, failing to see unintended circumstances and implications. However, every time a decision is made there is a trade-off. A true understanding of the trade-off may determine success or failure. Failure could mean very high cost either monetarily or the organizational future in the marketplace.

INTRODUCTION

Turbulence is life force. It is opportunity. Let's love turbulence and use it for change-Rosemary Clark

As turbulence becomes the new normal, organizations will find it necessary to build their organizations' agility and absorption. Agility being a company's ability to consistently identify and capture business opportunities at a faster pace than that of their competitors. This agility allows them to relocate resources,

DOI: 10.4018/978-1-7998-3416-8.ch001

including cash and talent, from less promising initiatives into more creative initiatives. Absorption is a complement to agility. Absorption is the ability to build resources, both in talent, cash flow and products/services. Together agility and adsorption allow an organization to adopt and move quickly in turbulent times, and to withstand the punishment of tough times, even if size could hinder their dexterity (Whalen, 2016).

With change being a constant, and with turbulence possibly being the new norm, disruptive creative leadership or self-disruptive leaders will be needed to ignite the creative economy; which will lead to the development of new technologies that enable the building of a sustainable community, quality of life, and a healthy socio-economic society. The case studies at the end of this chapter and through the book highlight self-disruptive leaders who are developing organizations that are disruptive and through heightened creativity, they are igniting economic development that is not only sustainable but is attracting many young professionals from across the U.S. and globally. This, a new model of business through disruptive leadership and the creative economy, is our future.

The future could be determined by seeing the wicked opportunities in turbulence instead of the wicked problems. When addressing those wicked problems, an organization's agility and absorption may determine their ability to sustain (Whalen, 2016).

Collective societies are on one hand intimately connected to one another via the internet and social media. However, rapidly changing events, and the flood of incorrect information competing with accurate information, significantly influences local communities as well as the global society. Governance will be more difficult in a turbulent changing world. New structures and systems may have to be implemented for success. The management guru Peter Drucker surmised, "Turbulent times can be analyzed, predicted and managed" (Drucker, 1980, pp 45-60), however, leaders who seek stability, will be surprised to learn that stability is not achievable.

In this new modern turbulent world, previous concepts of stability are antiquated. In addition, current management and leadership skills are inadequate. The new unstable, shifting finish line means that leaders will have to change or be outpaced (Volkers & Skeet, 2016). In addition, with the advent of the third stage of singularity adds a new dimension to turbulence associated with the coming Fifth and Sixth Industrial Revolutions, turbulence is the new norm, thus, bringing about the need for leaders to expand from transformational and authenticity to being "Self-Disruptive Leaders". The future could influence a new enlightenment, focusing on the need for the personal mastery of lifelong learners, who live continually in the fundamental state of leadership as self-disruptive leaders. Such mastery enables leaders to become higher functioning leaders, where divergent decisions can recognize wicked opportunities in the mist of wicked problems.

The New Era of Turbulence

The cause of this turbulence goes beyond singularity and the new industrial revolutions, to new problems that have changed our social norms such as social media. The young are being diagnosed with ADHD and communication disorders. Children with a diagnosis of ADHD are more likely to feel rejected and neglected by other children (Grygield, et al, 2014). This new surge in ADHD is being blamed on screen time and is creating a young society that cannot survive a world that can be full ambiguity. Strong social skills build strong societies. In addition, social media bullying is leading to teen suicide (Grygiel, et al, 2014).

We have become a global society addicted to social media, often checking our phones several times a day. Many only correspond by social media or texting. Mindfulness and listening are becoming non-existent (Treasure, 2017). In his research, Treasure sees listening as a lost art, which not only affects are ability to communicate, but the ability to speak so that others will want to listen. Not only does this influence our ability to handle situations, this impacts our ability to make decisions and develop a heightened creativity needed in a turbulent world (Treasure, 2017). We end up with social media halting one's ability to listen, communicate, and are isolating people who cannot thrive in a turbulent world, and cannot solve their own problems. A society very much unprepared for the workforce and complex problems ahead of them. Disruptive leaders radically change traditional ways of doing business, but do so with a commitment to really listen. By listening, they know what to challenge and change.

In a world of turbulence, business cannot afford not to hear accurately and listen intently to what others are saying, what the market is saying, and what is happening in the world. Treasure calls this the "The Golden Rules of Sound", (Treasure, 2011, pp. 112-116). Surviving turbulence is to take responsibility for sound by developing deep knowledge on intensive research, and heightened creativity. Drinking deep of knowledge is how to develop the self-disruptive leader within you. These ambitious leaders push the boundaries. In a world of turbulence where boundaries and past norms mean extinction, these self-disruptive leaders are in small supply. Most disruptive leaders have no problem thinking outside the box, and many actively push the boundaries. Great leaders know when change is needed, they are open-minded, and replace ego with confidence (Furth, 2018).

Ray Williams, in his article "Anti-Intellectualism and the "Dumbing Down" of America found a growing and disturbing trend of anti-intellectual elitism in American culture. A dismissal of fact, science, art and the humanities; which has been replaced with entertainment, self-righteousness, and ideology. The trend is to ignore facts and be deliberately gullible (Williams, 2014). This transcends political parties and the modern media, where journalism is now opinion shows, not based on facts but someone's ideology and opinion. This blind ambition coupled with ego is the result of the unrelenting drive to get what they want, even if it sacrifices their own ethical conduct (Furth, 2018); the results are the lowest ratings the media has ever suffered, and the loss of respect from the American people.

However, the result of this unethical behavior and goal of high profits has created the need to be constantly entertained, and a fascination with celebrities. This need to be constantly entertained has eliminated our mindfulness and created the rise of the "Idiot American" (Williams, 2014). Our new social norms may be eliminating our ability to innovate and be creative at a time it is needed most to thrive in a new and turbulent world. In addition, Mark Bauerlein, in his book, "The Dumbest Generation" reveals how an entire new generation is being dumbed down by their aversion to reading anything of substance and their addiction to digital media and social media. He warns that this will affect the democracy and culture of America (Bauerlein, 2009). According to the recent report by the National Endowment of the Arts most young people in the United States do not read literature, visit museums or vote (2019). In a turbulent world where changes are happening constantly, we are challenged as never before. Our young need to develop skills that come from literature, art and history. Civics is no longer taught in our schools, and our young do not understand how our own government works. Most are concerned with having the latest fashion or gadget.

This not only effects the new workforce, and overall society, but individual growth. The Japanese are stressing Kakeibo, which is a manual way of tracking one's finances. Kakeibi revolves around four key questions:

- How much money do you have available?
- How much do you want to save?
- How much money are you spending?

- How can you improve?

The concept is credited to Hani Makoto, the first female journalist in Japan, who published one of the first magazines targeted at the homemaker audience in Japan. The total concept is based on mindfulness, and by tracking your money manually, you are more likely to achieve them. You are more focused! In addition, you are building your individual absorption, which will increase your agility. This helps the individual thrive in the age of turbulence (Freeman, 2020). When one has the freedom that absorption and agility gives, they are on the path to heightened creativity and disruption.

Creativity and Modern Fairytales

Fairy tales come from changes within our culture. They can inspire, and be inspired from creativity in the arts, technological advancement, new science and business innovation and modern artistry. This inspired creativity may lead to new societal norms (Schnelbach, 2014). Fairytales may warn us that we have not produced creative work on a scale, as past periods, or that we are not ready for times of great change and turbulence. However, changes of existing fairytales, and the creation of new fairytales will often reflect those changes. These fairytales let us know the overall ambience of society.

If we look at the remaking of existing fairytales and the creation of new ones, we can begin to understand the uncertainty, fear, and the assumption that we may not have the power to overcome all obstacles. The use of modern technology can be seen in fairytales, because they present a new outlook on folklore, current and past. Today's empowerment of women in fairytales is prominent. Modern versions do not depict the woman who needs to be saved by her prince, but the strong woman who saves herself, her community and her prince.

Tim Burton's take on Hansel and Gretel took elements of old and mixed it with new to produce a new exciting look at the fairytale. This new version of an old fairytale depicted the changes occurring in our society, where modern pop culture works to empower the powerless, and the new strong empowered modern woman. A fearless warrior woman who can face great evil without fear of failure (Schnelbach, 2014).

Furthermore, popularity of the hit television show "Once Upon A Time" has brought about a new vision, created a (new adolescence), and took old fairytales, which were primarily meant for children, into the modern edgy adult fairytale. Fans enjoy the romanticism now felt in times past. Most importantly this show is an example of how modern artist provided the building blocks to creating something new from something old (Schnelbach, 2014).

Harry Potter has taken the world to the realm of muggles, witchcraft and good overcoming evil. One cannot dismiss the synergy and potential of friends working to fight evil. Add new computer animation, and the world of Hogwarts comes alive and is enjoyed by all age groups. The Harry Potter franchise has made $24, 851,000,000 (Statistic Brain, 2017).

This new love of fairytales and advance graphics play out in shows such as Game of Thrones, Vikings, Outlander, and Percy Jackson and the Olympians'. The popularity of these shows conveys the need to escape the pressures of the modern world, taking us to a far- off place where we dream and our imagination blooms. A new enlightenment can happen in all disciplines, if we develop our heightened creativity, intuition, understand the importance of mindfulness and most all be self-disruptive.

Heightened Creativity

We might ask ourselves, does this heightened creativity come from change and turbulence? What is the importance of disruptive and creative leadership, the creative economy, and developing a sense of place? How does this influence the quality of life and one's ability to thrive in the modern world full of complexities where turbulence may be the new norm? Creative leadership and the creative economy are based on building our self-awareness, self-worth and developing a sense of place; and by focusing on this; we might prevail and prosper in modern turbulent times. Could this be the redeeming feature of our culture and socio-economic systems? If it is, then we need more disruptive leaders to accomplish this.

Furthermore, we must analyze and investigate if turbulence is really the new normal in the advent of the fifth and sixth industrial revolutions. How will these future industrial revolutions change societal norms, and will this produce even more turbulence? Will we have the disruptive creativity to produce the technology to save our planet and ourselves?

In the fourth industrial revolution, we have come into the age of the internet, broadband, high-speed computation, robotics, nanotechnology, and now we are on the cusp of singularity. It is important to fully understand what the modern age has done for us, and most importantly, how do our very important human assets survive and thrive in the advent and advance into the fifth and sixth industrial revolution. The importance of keeping our talented young professionals in our communities or attracting them to our communities will be determined by the development of self-disruptive leaders, and new creative technologies.

If turbulent times cannot be analyzed, predicted and managed, then everything we currently know, all the theories and practices of leading, governance and societal norms are destined to be altered as we transition to the fifth and sixth industrial revolutions. We will have to depend on our ability to adapt and to effectively lead in great times of turbulence, to adapt across structures and boundaries we have never known before, and our constantly shifting, our trade- offs, agility and absorption may even determine our very existence. The collaborative and technological demands will form new organizations, groups, governments, non-governmental organizations and individuals. Therefore, those who are successful and live in a perpetual state of heighten creativity may determine the socio-economic condition of societies globally. This new norm will be based on self-disruptive leadership, entrepreneurism, creative endeavors, collaboration, micro businesses based on a new creative economy and creative class, with a new financial system, and societal norms.

The discipline of Leadership Studies and Organizational Behaviors will have to adjust and change in this new modern world. Modern theories of leadership have not effectively segmented disruptive creative new age leadership into its' own category. However, it is time to embrace this as a new theory of leadership. The self-disruptive leader may need to be defined and developed as a core leadership concept. Creative leadership has currently been defined as:

The ability to deliberately engage one's imagination to define and guide a group toward a novel goal-a direction that is new for the group. By guiding the group to a novel goal or direction, this creativity has made a profound impact of the overall success of the group (Puccio, Mance, Murdock, 2011, pp. xvii).

Creative Economy

Currently, creative economies are described in a variety of ways, depending on the composition and character of businesses, nonprofits, individuals, and venues that exist in any given area. The creative industries and the creative class have broad definitions; however, they contribute directly to jobs, tax generation, and wealth for the local economies they operate within. States have been studying the creative economy by looking at the work of nonprofits and cultural tourism. This may not be accurate; however, the creative economy encompasses technology as well.

Many creative economies are based on culture and cultural districts. These have a decentralized nature that can benefit residents of areas often thought to lack economic strength—such as rural areas and the urban core. The heart of the creative industries are individual artists and micro businesses who are typically well connected to the communities where they reside. Linking these artists and technology experts with entrepreneurial opportunities both inside and beyond their regions offers many economic development possibilities. According to Dunn & Bradstreet data analyzed by Americans for the Arts, a national arts advocacy group, there are 673,656 businesses involved in the creation or distribution of the arts. They employ 3.48 million people across the U.S. This represents 4.01% of all U.S. businesses and 2.04% of all U.S. communities. Art businesses and the creative people they employ stimulate innovation, strengthens the U.S. competitiveness in the global marketplace, and play an important role in building and sustaining economic vibrancy (Dunn & Bradstreet, 2017).

A state's arts and cultural resources can be economic assets. The arts and cultural industries provide jobs, attract investments, and stimulate local economies through events, tourism, consumer purchases, and tax revenue. Perhaps more significantly, new technology creates opportunities for a contemporary workforce, and creates an appeal to a young skilled workforce.

Cluster groups are those organizations or individuals who have similar businesses and relationships. Clusters usually form naturally and organically due to the nature of the economic activity. Cluster analysis is a tool used to understand their performance to economic development. Cluster analysis benchmarks clusters on the relative growth or decline of employment (National Governors Center, 2019).

Small clusters such as the arts often lack industry classification and are hard to measure; traditional analyses often do not account for self-employment or nonprofit organizations. By not accounting for small clusters, not only is the impact of the creative sector underestimated, but also communities and states miss the opportunity to help ignite the competitiveness of this significant industry. Therefore, in chapter five, analysis has been performed of state clusters supplemented with case studies, self-identification by businesses and associations, chamber business directories, and local cultural knowledge for identification of micro-clusters necessary to develop effective creative economic efforts.

Figure 1. Understanding Cluster Groups

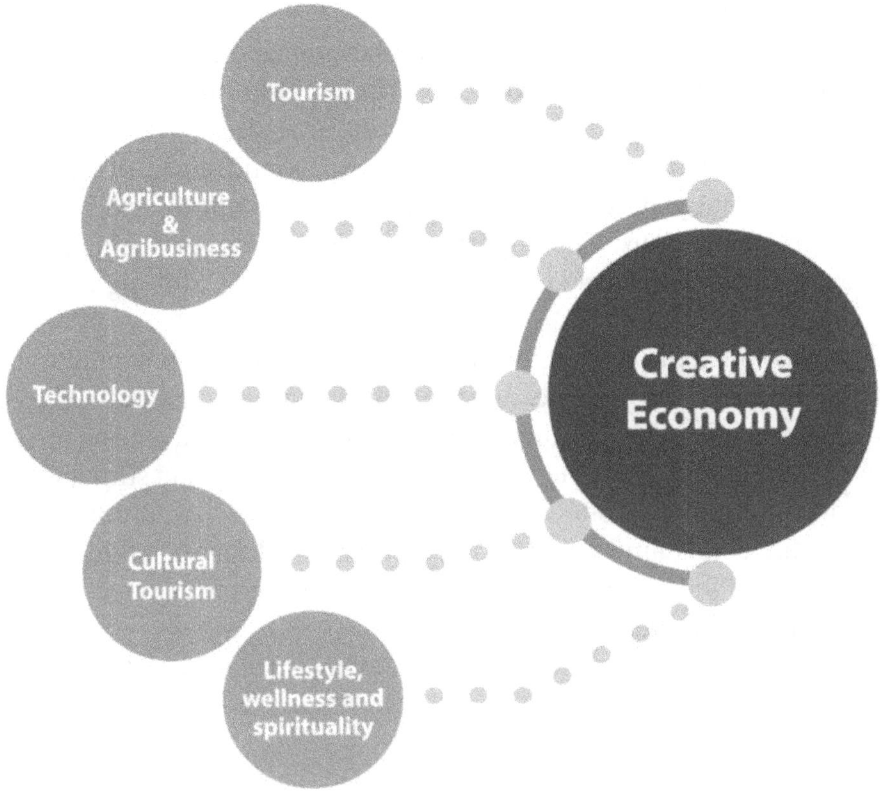

Currently, creative economies are described in a variety of ways, depending on the composition and character of businesses, nonprofits, individuals, and venues that exist in any given area. The creative economy may include human, organizational, and physical assets with many types of cultural institutions, artistic disciplines, and business pursuits. Industries that comprise the arts and culture sector may include advertising, architecture, the art and antiques market, crafts, design, fashion, film, digital media, television, radio, music, software and computer games, the performing arts, publishing, graphic arts, and cultural tourism.

The creative industries and the creative class have broad definitions; however, they contribute directly to jobs, tax generation, and wealth for the local economies they operate within. An example of this is the creative economy in Arkansas, which employs nearly 27,000 individuals and generates $927 million in personal income for Arkansas citizens. The creative economy in Arkansas is the third largest employer, after transport and logistics of food products (Arkansas State, 2015).

States have been studying the economic contributions of the creative economy by looking at the work of nonprofits and cultural tourism. However, this might not be an accurate picture of the true creative economy. The research in chapter three determined the socio-economic impact of the creative economy regionally affects one's quality of life, the future, and influences the younger generations. The importance of developing or keeping a sense of place in a turbulent world could be the difference of thriving in the new fifth industrial revolution.

Creative leadership and the creative economy have the potential to offer numerous benefits to the socio-economic health, and builds a sense of place in a thriving community. Through the creative industries, states have an opportunity to create jobs, attract investments, generate tax revenues, and stimulate local economies through tourism and consumer purchases. In addition, creative industries are contributing to the contemporary workforce, making creative contributions to industries' products and services, and infusing culture into community development.

Theoretically, there are eleven core characteristics needed to succeed in the creative economy. They are:

- Self-worth
- Self-efficacy
- Interpersonal intelligence
- Emotional intelligence
- Personal mastery
- Vision
- Ethical inclusion
- Business knowledge
- Creative leadership
- Service leadership
- Global citizenship

In addition to the core characteristic, the modes of developing the creative economy are through collaborative platforms with cluster development such as micro business development, incubators with toolkits, cyber laboratories, new technology development, and creative maker spaces.

Figure 2. Theoretical Concept (Tardif, 2017).

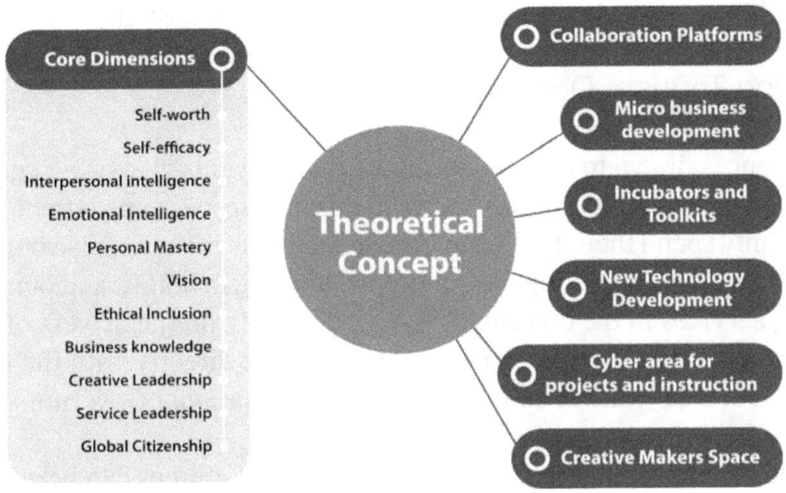

Helping Weak Economic Areas

Entrepreneurs are usually the drivers of disruption. Powerful disruptions can appear drastically different from the past, and often can cause confusion. However, the decentralized nature of the creative industries can benefit residents of areas often thought to lack economic strength—such as rural areas and the urban core. The heart of the creative industries are individual artists who are typically well connected to the communities where they reside. For this reason, disruptive leadership partners well with the creative economy. Linking these artists with entrepreneurial opportunities, both inside and beyond their regions, offers many economic development possibilities.

State Economic Development

Recruiting and developing a skilled workforce is an important complement to community development. They provide an enhanced quality of life, enrich local amenities, and play an important role in attracting young professionals to an area. Richard Florida (2011), a leading expert on economic competitiveness, innovation, and demographic trends, is credited with coining the term "Creative Class," which describes young and talented individuals who are mobile and more likely to locate where there is a vibrant and creative environment. Attracting and retaining talented young people and companies is becoming increasingly important to regional communities. The arts and culture within an area play an important role in attracting these professionals.

Attracting Tourism Dollars

The audiences drawn to arts venues and cultural events also bring economic benefits for other businesses. A thriving cultural scene helps attract visitors who not only spend their money on the events themselves, but also contribute to local economies by dining in restaurants, lodging in hotels, and purchasing gifts and services in the community. A recent study on the drivers of tourist spending found that tourist expenditures correlate directly with the number of arts and design workers employed in a region (National Governors Center, 2019).

In this environment, a state's arts and cultural resources can be economic assets. The arts and cultural industries provide jobs, attract investments, and stimulate local economies through tourism, consumer purchases, and tax revenue. Perhaps more significantly, they also prepare workers to participate in the contemporary workforce, create communities with high appeal to residents, businesses, and tourists, and contribute to the economic success of other sectors (National Governors Center, 2019).

Where are we going?

The chapters in this book detail how to develop a strategic plan to identify development goals. The strategic plans should lay the foundation for capacity-building and economic development strategies. For example: core strategies include:

- Cultivating a creative mindset
- Developing disruptors
- Becoming self-disruptive
- Investing in research and the development of new technologies
- Supporting industries' efforts to develop and/or exploit higher-value business and marketing and strategies
- Attracting and retaining creative workers
- Strengthening the creative abilities of all workers

The National Governors Association (2019) along with states have seen the creative economy as providing a solution for changing the socio-economic landscape. Many states have implemented successful plans. However, many have failed. Whether the cause is leadership, funding or just lack of true knowledge is not known. In rural communities and our urban cores, igniting the creative economy might bring the needed changes to repressed socio-economic landscapes. In documented successful areas, each started with a self-disruptive leader who led a movement and developed other disruptive leaders and disruptive organizations.

Rural Communities

In the past, our rural economies stagnated and suffered with high poverty rates. The bestselling book by J.D. Vance, The Hillbilly Elegy (2016), is an example of what may have turned the tide in the presidential election of 2016. This rural middle-class American group feels disenfranchised, living in poverty with no hope of improvement (Vance, 2017).

Currently, fifteen states are classified by the federal government as being rural, with an additional nineteen as more rural than the U.S. average. Thirteen are less rural than average, and three states being less than ten percent rural. According to this U.S. Census, rural areas are not growing as fast as urban centers (U.S. Census, 2017). Many rural communities have suffered greatly with manufacturing going overseas. These communities struggled to keep their young and talented individuals in their communities and states.

A tipping point occurred in 2017. Outward migration out of urban centers into rural areas began. Many young professionals, disappointed with urban decay, high taxes, little opportunity, and bad schools started migrating to areas for a better quality of life. Many of these migrated into micropolitian areas. These areas are greater than 10,000 people and less than 50,000 people and many have been successful in developing their creative economy. They are thriving in the era of turbulence due to disruptive leadership. Disgruntled urbanites are flowing into states like Texas, Florida and the Carolinas (Matthews, 2019).

In January of 2019, Dr. Sally Rood, Senior Policy Analyst for the National Governors Association, and a talented group of specialists and organizations wrote a new report on "*Rural Prosperity through the Arts & Creativity: A Rural Action Guide for Governors and States*". Although the new report by the National Governors Association introduces the "Who" of the creative economy as art, art museums, fashion design, historic sites, music groups, dance troupes, theaters, national parks, zoos, interior design, graph design, and photography; the creative economy is much more. Even the STEM fields challenge this notion by introducing creative innovations and inventions. Many groups support the addition of the manufacturing of musical instruments, cameras, publishing, and broadcasting as part of the creative economy. However, cyber security, innovative new inventions with newly patented materials and ideas from the STEM fields fit the definition of the creative economy.

Rural America is rich in cultural history, but troubled by poverty, and plagued by many social and economic challenges. Their research highlighted the positive and quality-of-life outcomes associated with the creative economy. Their Rural Action Guide described several principles: (National Governors Association, 2019)

- Creative economy initiatives are most effective when assimilated with other creative assets and the needs of the community.
- Creative economy initiatives work better when being part of an overall economic development plan.
- Creative economy initiatives when integrated with other state and local programs, policies, and practices add additional value.

When interviewed for this book, Dr. Rood mentioned the collaboration of many groups such as national, state, local, county and community, all of these have been instrumental in the success of many programs. In the interview Dr. Rood was asked if there were outliers, and Dr. Rood said they were really all doing the same, working together to make the programs successful. The only outlier could be the Native Americans who often operate with a different structure. The Native Nations who are thriving are doing just this; they operate within their own cultural norms to develop their economy.

This research determined that creative economic initiatives improve and help states thrive. In many states, broadband service is under 70% coverage. Montana has the worst broadband coverage at 69.2%, with New Jersey having the highest coverage at 99%. Mississippi, Arkansas, Oklahoma, Wyoming, West Virginia and Alaska are all under 80% (U.S. Government, 2018). The broadband issue is a basic need for success in building economic development. Internet service can be the deciding factor on where new business locates. The State of Mississippi's commitment to increase their broadband service has been a vital instrument in bringing technology companies to the state with high-tech jobs. States that have committed resources to these efforts have been a turning point for many rural areas.

According to the National Governors Association rural arts organizations draw non-local audiences at a higher level than urban art organizations. In fact, the National Governors Association says that 31% of rural audiences travel beyond a reasonable distance, whereas only 19% of urban audiences travel distances. In addition, businesses that value the arts are more likely to report a market growth in products and services. The recent Rural Action Guide lists five ingredients for governors wanting to support the creative initiatives in their states: (National Governors Association, 2019).

- Leadership to promote the creative economy in their states
- Do not forget to capitalize on existing programs
- Build funding and infrastructure for support
- Develop educational programs to train local talent and invest in human capital
- Welcome the investment of creativity and innovation

Highlighted in the Rural Action Guide was the topic of *Creative Place making*, and according to the National Governors Association (2019), creative place making occurs when artist or the arts organizations, work with community development initiatives to integrate the culture and arts into the revitalization projects. This process creates a collaboration between many groups such as education, agriculture, crafters, healthcare, and governments both state and local. Combining these efforts with grant money, communities are strengthened producing economic change, physical change, social change and systems change.

CONCLUSION

After speaking to Dr. Rood and several state agencies the pathways for sustainable programs are very similar. From developing statewide certification for cultural districts, to cultural mapping, cluster development, creative place making and toolkit development states now have thorough program to develop their creative economy. Fifteen states now have a certification program for designative culture districts. The certification program is the same for rural and urban programs; they seek to "create hubs and clusters of economic activity, promote a community's unique identity, and promote rural communities as appealing places to live, conduct business and attract visitors", (National Governors Association, 2019, p. 16).

Disruptive leaders can be the drivers that develop outreach plans that will foster collaboration with large and small businesses, non-profits, schools, Native American nations, artisans, crafters, and nationally recognized artists and musicians. In addition, business leaders, government officials, non-profits, education and concerned citizens can develop incubators using cross disciplines to interface and find unique solutions. Furthermore, this unique style of leadership could advance the collaboration between groups that will help solve business issues, launch new products, develop new products, and create the possibility of micro businesses in their regions.

Case Studies

In the following case study, Wilson, Arkansas depicts how the collaboration of a community combined with disruptive leadership changed the environment of a community and took it from a stagnated repressed town to a vibrant community full of promise and thriving businesses. The second case study is about two disruptors that dared to create a multi-million-dollar business selling jams and jellies. When everyone told them, it would be impossible to create a business based on jams and jellies in today's market, they refused to listen. They created one of the most successful gourmet food lines in the last 20 years.

Case Study

Wilson, Arkansas

No town or area could have been more repressed and destitute than Wilson, Arkansas. Wilson has a unique history. Known as the town founded by Robert E. Lee Wilson, in 1886, Wilson was once the most important company town in the South. From the Wilson family story, to its authentic artisanal traditions and collections of ancient aboriginal artifacts, the town occupies an important position in the landscape of the American South and the Mississippi Delta Region (Wilson, AR, 2018). This town is an example of a micropolitan area igniting their creative economy. The self-disruptive leadership of one man has changed the face of Wilson, and Wilson is thriving in an area that seems to never make it in times of turbulence.

Among the unique historic sites are the revitalized, Tudor-inspired, town square, the historic cotton gin and the Hampson Archeological Museum, housing a rare collection of late Mississippian artifact from the nearby aboriginal "Nodena site". The community has developed an array of educational, cultural and economic initiatives. The town of Wilson has paid tribute to this heritage and brings the story of Wilson to life for its visitors (Wilson, AR, 2018).

Wilson was a company town, where people worked in one of the largest cotton plantations of the South. They lived in houses and shopped in stores owned by Wilson Company. Instead of being paid monetarily, they were paid in company coupons. They could use those coupons to buy anything they needed in the company town. Labor laws were different in those days. For one hundred and twenty-five years, the Wilson Family owned and operated the town, as well as the surrounding rich farmland. Life revolved around agriculture and diversified related businesses. By the early twentieth century, Lee Wilson & Company was one of the most significant cotton plantations and agricultural enterprises in the country. In the 1950's Wilson became an incorporated town (Wilson, AR, 2017). By 2010, the town was in ruin, many buildings in disrepair, and the economy stagnant.

In 2010, the Lawrence Group purchased Lee Wilson & Company, along with many of the town's historic buildings and neighboring agricultural land, ushering in a modern era of renewal. The change in ownership heralded a major transformation in the entire community that continues today. By focusing on the future this diverse and capable group, with the town council and citizen support, is working for a new sustainable plan, using disruptive leadership, unique creativity and innovation to build a strong community, where education, infrastructure and sustainable agriculture is bringing tourist and artisans to celebrate Wilson's success (Wilson, AR, 2017).

In Wilson, Arkansas, the Delta School is distinguished by its innovative, hands-on approach to traditional learning.

We can't be everything to everyone, so we have made bold choices about where to be the best. Our Signature Programs are ones being implemented in other schools across the country. They are research backed and our unique designs of these programs are intended to develop as national models of excellence in preparing students for success. We are more than a school—we are a whole town dedicated to creating a forward-thinking culture by interweaving the School Garden Movement, the Strengths Movement and the Maker's Movement into our shared learning and expression (Delta School, 2016).

Outcomes

Below is a timeline from when the Lawrence Group purchased Lee Wilson & Company, including many of the town buildings and the surrounding agriculture acreage (Wilson, AR, 2017).

- 2010: The Lawrence Group purchased Lee Wilson & Company, including many of the town buildings and the surrounding agricultural acreage.
- 2012: Many of the Town Square Tudor buildings were restored, along with the historic Wilson Cafe. The Lawrence Group worked with leading experts to establish an independent school, as well as new business and development strategies for sustainable growth.
- 2013: Wilson hosted Chris O'Brien in the inaugural Wilson Music Series concert. The Wilson Music series is a biweekly concert series that features artists such as Phillip Sweet, Mark Collie, Marcella & Her Lovers, Deering and Down, Cally MaRae and others.
- 2014: Wilson Gardens, a different kind of farm, opened with the mission of helping residents lead healthier lives.
- 2015: The Delta School, offering a college preparatory education, an excellent campus and a creative learning environment unparalleled in the Delta, is now open. The Grange, a destination for community and cultural events and classes, is both a community gathering spot and a learning lab.
- 2016: The town secured a historic marker for the Wilson Trade School. The Delta School also voted to add an upper school to serve grades 9–12.
- 2017: White's Mercantile opened its first location outside of greater Nashville in Wilson. The new Hampson Museum is also slated for a fall opening.

(Wilson, AR, 2017).

The Future of Wilson, Arkansas is bright. The owners and board of the Lawrence Group and the people of Wilson are a successful example of disruptive leadership leading the creative economy.

Case Study

Stonewall Kitchens

Two people with a dream of entrepreneurism who were self-disruptive leaders decided to create a thriving business, when others said you could not create a million-dollar business selling jams and jellies. It all began at the Farmers Market in Portsmouth, New Hampshire. Jim Stott and Jonathan King spent endless hours cooking, handwriting labels, taking photos, and selling products. The first product, Wild Maine Blueberry Jam, was inspired by Jim's 90-year-old grandmother. According to Jim, "He wanted to create the smell of her freshly baked pie filled with tasty ripe blueberries". Jim and Jonathan were able to do just that, for every time they opened on of their jars of Wild Maine Blueberry Jam, it smells like Jim's grandmother's blueberry pie. Soon their home business became a family affair, with nephews and nieces filling jars one-by-one. Jim's grandmother Pearl helped glue burlap onto jar lids and Jonathan's mother worked as a store clerk (Stonewall Kitchens, 2019).

As the product line grew so did the recognition. In 1995, Gourmet Foods named Stonewall Kitchens "Best in Show", and over the years, twenty-nine more awards were given to the company. In 1998, their first mass mailing catalogue produced. Today their signature store has over 500,000 visits per year. Their product is nationally and internationally recognized and sold in specialty stores, kitchen stores, and major retailers. They have gone from making a few dozen jars for the Farmers Market to making 75,000 jars a day. Along with other product lines that are as equally successful (Danley, 2019).

What makes Stonewall Kitchen so successful is that they have built a thriving business on their love for food, and only select the best ingredients. They have stringent quality standards and only use pure cane sugar in their products. To Jim and Jonathan, every jar of jam they sell is as important as the first. They believe they are crafters, making a craft product. This is complex, but the result is one of the best products on the market that has captured a mixture of unique natural ingredients. In addition, all the artwork for their products is original artwork; even the special thick glass for the jams and jellies was specially crafted. They have based their business on the culture and heritage they grew up in, and Jonathan's signature is on every label (Stonewall Kitchens, 2019).

There is more to their story. They give back and are known for their generosity and philanthropy. As one of Maine's largest manufacturers, they have not forgotten where they came from. In addition, they were one of the first success stories for Maine's International Trade Center. Their product is now thriving in the global market.

In August of 2019, Stonewall Kitchens was sold to a Boston Investment Firm. At the time of the sale, Stonewall Kitchens was a powerhouse brand with 8,500 worldwide wholesale accounts. In 2016, its estimated revenue was reported to be $100 million, and they are not disclosing what the company's revenue is in 2019, nor the purchase price. However, what they do say is in the last five years they have experienced unprecedented growth. Part of the negotiations was to keep the plant in Maine, and people working. Creativity, innovation, and hard work does still pay. In addition, this business was a leader in the creative economy initiatives for the state of Maine (Danley, 2019).

REFERENCES

Bauerlein, M. (2009). *The Dumbest Generation*. Penguin Random House.

Danley, S. (2019). Audax acquires Stonewall Kitchens. *Food Business News*. Retrieved from, https://www.foodbusinessnews.net/articles/14227-audax-acquires-stonewall-kitchen

Delta School. (2016). Developing curiosity, capabilities and character in a vibrant learning environment. *Delta School.* Retrieved from, http://www.thedeltaschool.org/

Drucker, P. F. (1980). Managing in Turbulent Times. Harper Collins.

Florida, R. (2011). *The Rise of the Creative Class.* Basic Books.

Furth, J.F. (2018). *Owning Tomorrow: The Unstoppable Force of Disruptive Leadership.* Indie Books.

Grygiel, P., Humans, G., Switaj, P., Rebisz, S., & Anczewska, M. (2014). Between Isolation and Loneliness: Social Networks and Perceived Integration with Peers of Children Diagnosed with ADHD in Regular Classrooms. *Bulgarian Comparative Education Society*. Retrieved from http://search.ebscohost.com/login.aspx?direct=true&db=eric&AN=ED598009

Matthews, M. (2019). The Blue-state exodus gains momentum. *The Hill.* Retrieved from, https://thehill.com/opinion/finance/477754-the-blue-state-exodus-gains-momentumamp

National Governors Association. (2009). *Arts and the Economy: Using Art and Culture to stimulate the economy.* National Governors Center. Retrieved from, http://www.nga.org/cms/center/publications?begin7736bde9-79fd-493d-be2b-0f62416085cd=180&end7736bde9-79fd-493d-be2b-0f624160 85cd=189&pagesize7736bde9-79fd-493d-be2b-0f62416085cd=10&

National Governors Association. (2019). *Rural Prosperity Through The Arts & Creative Sector: A Rural Action Guide for Governors and States.* National Governors Association.

Puccio, G.J., Mance, M., & Murdock, M.C. (2011). *Creative Leadership: Skills That Drive Change.* Sage Publications, Inc.

Schnelbach, L. (2014). Happily Re-Mixed and Mashed-Up Ever After: Modern Fairy Tales. *Fairytales-Tor.* Retrieved from, http://www.tor.com/2014/10/21/fairy-tale-remix/

Statistic Brain. (2019). *Total Harry Potter Franchise Revenue.* Statistic Brain Institute. Retrieved from, https://www.statisticbrain.com/total-harry-potter-franchise-revenue/

Stonewall Kitchens. (2019). *The History of the Company.* Stonewall Kitchens. Retrieved from, https://www.stonewallkitchen.com/

Treasure, J. (2011). Sound Business. Management Books.

Treasure, J. (2017). *How to be Heard: Secrets for Powerful Speaking and Listening.* Mango Publishing Group.

U.S. Government. (2010). Urban/Rural Census. *U.S. Government Census.* Retrieved from, https://www.census.gov/geo/reference/ua/urban-rural-2010.html

Vance, J.D. (2016). *Hillbilly Elegy.* Harper Collins.

Volker, J., & Skeet, P. (2016). Leading in Turbulent Times. *ILA.* Retrieved from http://www.ila-net.org/Conferences/2017/theme.html

Whalen, S. A. (2016). Creating Effective Team. Sage Publications.

Williams, R. (2014). Anti-Intellectualism and the Dumbing Down of America. *Psychology Today.* Retrieved from, https://www.psychologytoday.com/blog/wired-success/201407/anti-intellectualism-and-the-dumbing-down-america

Wilson Arkansas. (2019). *History of Wilson Arkansas*. Retrieved from, https://www.arkansas.com/wilson

Chapter 2
Developing the Disruptors

ABSTRACT

Disruptive leaders possess a deep understanding of the nonobvious. Developing solutions with a heightened creativity, solving problems and addressing risks, finding the right tradeoffs, and recognizing the wicked opportunities in the wicked problems, disruptive leaders scan the environment, identify trends, and envision the future. Often, this is done by finding superior solutions, products, and services. However, this is done with a strategic process and plan. In our current business environment, right when we get comfortable, we find ourselves having to adjust to a major change that requires us to shift time, energy, and resources to solve a problem or stay ahead of the market, or change our market. Every change that we encounter creates winners and losers. If we are disruptive in our leadership, these changes can bring about fabulous innovation and create new technologies that benefit humankind. Building a disruptive organization is the best way to thrive. This chapter explores developing the disruptors.

INTRODUCTION

If you don't like something change it; if you can't change it, change the way you think about it. Mary Englebright, Graphic Artist and Children's Book Illustrator

The word *disrupt* means to cause something to be unable to continue in the normal way and to interrupt the normal progress or activity of something.

DOI: 10.4018/978-1-7998-3416-8.ch002

Disrupt is much more than a contemporary buzzword. The disruptive leader is seen as the leader that "shakes it up", wakes up an organization from its slumber and helps them compete in the modern world. Many case studies describe organizations that woke up too late, to the surprise of their employees, and soon did not exist. Furthermore, this disruption must come from the top management. Leaders must continually challenge what they hold sacred. "Change and disruption is about what needs to be done, not what has to be done" (Hoque, 2015).

Disruptive leaders pursue the truth and are always analyzing their strategies for effectiveness. Disruptive leaders must have tremendous self-worth and faith in their ability to face reality, but at the same time recognize opportunities in chaos. Decisiveness is paramount, even if it involves intuition. By the time you achieve team consensus, the opportunity can pass. Disruptive leaders break the rules and write new ones, but always listen and explain. In other words, normal does not exist for them, and they have the willingness to break the rules when embracing the new normal. Leading disruptive innovation means the new normal is facing high levels of uncertainty. By taking risks, modifying assumptions, and adapting plans, disruptive leaders allow innovation to occur. This is not new. Zen masters have used the tactics of disruptive leadership to bring out the best in the followers. Every industry and culture has trends where innovation is always the focus, and this is led by disruptive leaders. Disruptive leadership is not a fad. In fact, it is a way of being (Hoque, 2019).

When writing this, I thought of my own path as a young manager, when I had great leaders and bad ones. How many times as a single mother of four, I went home overworked and deflated by someone's arrogance and lack of appreciation. The difference when my boss appreciated me, complimented me on my hard work, and rewarded me affected my attitude and home life for the better. One boss was a catalyst is building my self-confidence and self-worth, even though he had a big ego, he never let it get in the way of doing what was right by his reports or the company. He was a disruptive leader, and constantly influenced others to be disruptive. I have often thought about his support system, which seems often weak, but he was able to stay above this, and be a self-disruptive leader. It modeled the way for me to rise above an unsupportive leader and make my own way. His influence served me well, throughout my entire career and in my personal life.

Our personal and professional journey lies within us. Our lives are formed from the minute we are born. We constantly learn new information that changes who we are as we travel on our life path. Our ability to have the courage to be disruptive changes our life-path drastically. In leadership, these disruptive changes often lead to moments of greatness. As a young 26-year-old mother of four small children, I was forced to work in a bank during the day and a steel mill at night. The owner of the steel mill liked my gumption and work ethic. During a round of golf, he told a friend about me, and the friend hired me to be the plant manager of a small ice plant. This led to building a new plant, which led to working for the world's largest food company. It was not always easy; I moved three times across the country as a single mother and faced many challenges. I realized later in life, that I was a natural disruptor. I sought change and embraced it. It took years and one big failure to embrace my self-worth but I also learned to pick myself up and succeed.

Driving Disruption

In his book *Owning Tomorrow,* John Furth (2018)), points out that thousands of years ago, humans started creating order from chaos. They did this by using heightened creativity, innovation, and developing new technology. Society began being comfortable with these new societal norms until a new disruptive way changed our old beliefs and systems. Overtime societies began to see disruption as upheaval. However, new processes and systems made it cheaper, faster and more convenient. This gave way to greater access to education and travel. It gave way to the knowledge economy.

Clayton Christensen (2010), a Harvard professor asked his class three questions: 1) How can I be assured I will be happy in my career; 2) How can I be assured my relationship with my wife and family will be a source of lifetime happiness; 3) How can I be assured I will stay out of jail. According to Christensen, the last question is very real, because 2 of 32 of his Rhodes Scholar students spent time in jail. They started out good people, but somewhere along the way, they lost their moral compass. Christensen goes on to explain, that the best in life are not making money but building people up. How we lead determines the quality of life of those that follow. True self-worth and self-confidence lead to greatness.

Furth (2018) warns of unproductive mindsets. This is when people want to stick with what they know, and do not want to take advice. This happens in academia frequently. I have heard from numerous institutions, scholars and staff. They complain about unproductive, rude and incompetent people that are never let go. His or her standard comment, "nobody gets fired in education." It is time for education to be disruptive, really start performing, and give our children the education they deserve.

The opposite of unproductivity are organizations that fall into disruptive fatigue, where the constant changes are constantly replacing everything with something new. This condition rarely leads to success or sustainable business models. Every organization can always come up with more ideas, but it is important to blend these ideas into deliberate structures and mechanisms toward the new creativity that develops products and services not thought of before. When conceptual constraints and mindsets are truly challenged, then disruption occurs. This disruptive thinking helps leaders create real value in new ways to support long-term success. Rachel Lebeaux, with Deloitte (2018) Insights states, "It's critical to get the dynamic and balance right, because changes in consumer behavior are going to conflict with deeply held convictions about the way industries are meant to work."

Business disruption author John Furth has found that disruptive leaders have eight basic traits in common: (Furth, 2018).

- While some well-known business disruptors never finished college, many received PhDs from the highest-ranked universities in the world, and they all have the same commitment to lifelong learning.
- They often push accepted behavioral, cultural, legal, and ethical boundaries to the limit.
- They have learned how to disrupt their own frames of reference and unproductive mindsets. This behavior helps them increase their focus, ability to innovate, and to stay one-step ahead of would-be competitors.
- They look for information, insights, and inspiration in unexpected places. They recognize that the usual or "traditional" sources of data are by nature backward looking and hence of limited value in a world that is being re-created. Great disruptors ask excellent questions and listen carefully to the answers because they never know when someone else might have an insight that could be useful to them and the business.
- Their businesses – regardless of whether they are B2C or B2B – deliver on at least one of three fundamental value propositions:
  - Provide goods, services and experiences that were previously only available to the most privileged members of society to a much larger percentage of the population more easily and affordably.
  - Give customers what they want, when they want it and how they want it.
  - Eliminate or reduce the things in people's everyday lives they do not want, from everyday annoyances like wasted time, boredom,

complexity or unhappiness as well as life-threatening situations like poverty and disease.

- They understand that disrupting an existing eco-system or process on a regional or even global scale can cause significant short-term negative consequences. Entrenched and inflexible companies are driven out of business, and many individual careers are adversely affected. However, the value created for billions of people far outweighs such negative incidents.
- At some point, they learn the ultimate paradox of disruption: "More stays the same than changes." Like all successful companies, disruptive enterprises need the funding necessary to execute their plans, the right people doing the right jobs and the wherewithal and commitment to push through many breakdowns and hurdles.
- They generate unimaginable wealth for themselves, their investors, their employees, and others connected to their companies.(Furth, 2018)

Disruptive leadership is needed more today than in the past. Korn Ferry's recent (2019) research has determined that the skills needed in today's increasing turbulent and disruptive environment will help organizations to adapt, collaborate, and thrive in turbulent times. A new future ready leader must take priority. Transformation leadership is part of this change, but something more is needed. The new model of disruptive leadership builds on existing concepts of agile, digital and inclusive leadership, but it also highlights the importance of future disruptive leaders who are experts in the creation of opportunity and capitalize on knowledge. In this model, the new source of competitive advantage is a leader who can connect resources and people to build an innovation ecosystem (Korn Ferry, 2019).

In Korn Ferry's research (2019), 795 business professionals analyzed the current supply of high-performance behaviors and the market's demand of them. This research revealed the shortage globally for disruptive leaders. This research further determined that 67 percent of those interviewed insisted that the pool of current leadership is not fit for the future. This is troubling because it is felt business leaders are not able to adapt to the changing environment; and may not survive. Interestingly, the pursuit of disruptive leaders means finding them in unusual places or on the fringes.

According to Furth (2018), leaders fall into three categories. The first group (young leaders) are entrepreneurs, where the second and third are experienced leaders. The second group (accidental leaders) are the one who suddenly find themselves propelled into leadership positions when they did not plan it. They are often lacking in experience and skills. Often fail at delivering the desired goals. The third is (developed leaders) they represent the majority of CEO's and top leadership. These leaders worked hard, studied hard, and successfully achieve goals (Furth, 2018, p. 21).

In 1993, the futurist Joel Barker determined that creativity and innovation come from the fringes of a discipline (Barker, 1993). This has proven to be true. Disruptive leaders come from different disciplines and may not come from traditions paths. Diversity and inclusion will be more important in the talent pool with insight, objectivity, and intuition being vital for success. Success will be determined on anticipation, the contextual intelligence and intuition to make quick decisions, to provide direction, and to unify collective efforts even when some are disoriented. Disruptive leaders must have the ability to energize others, foster a sense of purpose, and manage the mental and physical energy of themselves and others nurturing a positive ecosystem with hope, faith and motivation. Disruptive leaders must possess the ability to accelerate the flow of knowledge to constant innovation and desired business outcomes by being agile and quick to assimilate and change if need be. They must collaborate with others. Most important, they are trust builders. They embrace their own vulnerabilities and help others find a sense of being. They protect the powerless and do the right action. Disruptive leaders are self-directed disruptive leaders.

Disruptive Innovation

The theory of disruptive leadership comes from the theory of disruptive innovation. Both have been thought to prepare for the turmoil of creative destruction. Joseph Schumpeter, the famous economist wrote about this as being a time in history of great change within organizations or environments. As stated in Chapter 1, this may be the new normal, as we go forth into the third stage of Artificial Intelligence (AI) and enter the fifth industrial revolution, stability may never come, and turbulence may become daily. It is important to learn to listen to customers, invest in the opportunities, and build distinctive capabilities. (King & Baatartogtokh, 2015).

The Economist defined the theory of disruptive leadership as "one of the most influential of the modern era". Despite the theory's widespread use and appeal, it has not been tested thoroughly. The initial research was based mainly on the hard disk drive industry in the 1970s and 1980s. Scholars have published discussions of related case examples (notably about Polaroid Corp.,

Smith Corona, and the disk drive industry), but few quantitative tests have been performed. The ones that have been published fail to provide evidence for the theory, suggesting instead that full-blown disruptions are rare and that most managers respond effectively to potentially disruptive threats. More case analysis shows that the theory of disruptive leadership explains the failure of leading businesses, time after time and industry after industry (Christensen, 2003).

King and Baatartogtokh, identified four key elements of the theory of disruptive leadership: 1) leadership which improves products and services along a sustained pathway; 2) leaders who worked beyond their customer's needs; 3) leadership that possess the intuition to meet and overcome disruptive threats; 4) leaders who end up floundering as a result of the disruption (Christensen, 2003).

Figure 1. Performance is based on Customers and Time

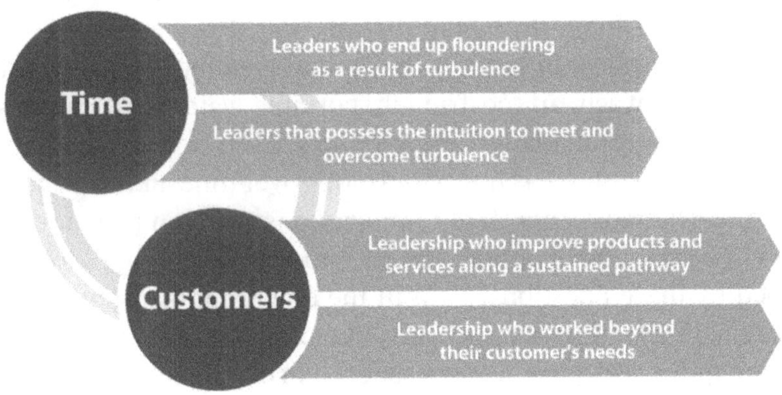

There are no substitutes for careful analysis and divergent decision-making. When experiencing turbulence an organization will have to analyze the tradeoffs; and understand how to build agility and absorption to either leave, stay, or re-invent their marketplace. These choices are heart wrenching but may make the difference of seeing opportunity or risk especially in emerging markets.

Emerging Markets

Disruptive leaders drove the economic development in Japan after World War II. By offering inexpensive products that were initially inferior in quality to their competitors, they captured the low-end segment of the market. Furthermore, as the quality of their products improved, their market changed and so did the profitability of their products. Quality improvement led to the Japanese capturing most of the market segments and pushed their products to the high end (Markides, 2012).

Japan's industries became disruptive, often causing turmoil. In the 1970's a young Swiss engineer designed the quartz technology in watch making. However, the top management of the Swiss watch making industry turn the idea down. Wanting to stay true to the old ways, they wanting nothing to do with anything new. During an international technology fair, the young engineer displayed the technology, and the Japanese took it and almost bankrupted the Swiss industry, putting 60,000 people out of work. The Swiss had to change if they wanted to survive. In 2017, Japan now is considered the Swiss watching businesses' greatest customer, with several high-profile watch boutiques opening in Tokyo in 2017 (Gomelsky, 2017).

The last twenty years have been a time of disruption in emerging markets such as China and India. In China the new car, Roewe RX8 is slated for high international sales. In India with the Nano, an inexpensive car by Tata Motors and Tata Swach, an eco-friendly portable water purification system. These are just three of many new products from new companies. What makes a product disruptive is how it develops over time and how incumbents respond to it. The most important implication is that you may never tell if a product will be disruptive or not. The potential of emerging innovations are determined by these questions: 1) Will the emerging disruptive innovation continue to have a significant price advantage over competitors? In addition, 2). Will emerging disruptive leaders succeed in closing the performance gap in advanced societies where these products are seen of good quality?

Self-disruptors must begin with a price advantage, be invested in improving performance, and have several options in how they go about closing the performance gap. Closing the gap may mean mergers, developing technology, investing in research and development, or entering into partnerships and building alliances with other organizations or governments. By focusing on a products or service's existing value and raising that to a higher value, disrupters can market the product or services as a higher product. Self-disruptors are trying to move toward the current and future benefits of the product or service. In addition, they understand that their future depends solely on them and the actions they take. Often this wins the product and service war (Markides, 2012).

Disruptors and Road Mapping

Looking back, the self-disruptor saw the Internet as having incredible business opportunities. In fact, it was thought the Internet would change the face of all organizations. The ability to see the potential, develop strategies, and execute them required foresight. Seeing what is next requires intuition and a vision of the future that others do not yet possess, and it requires a unique view of the problems that will need to be solved in the mid-term or distant future. To have the intuition and develop the vision of a future of great change means a shift of decision-making, and an overall understanding of the technology (Petrick & Martinelli, 2012).

Through strategic road mapping, organizations find new understandings about the future and how to create solutions that can reshape their own market. Road mapping is not new; however, it encompasses more technology, planning, execution, and coordination across disciplines. By encouraging employees to develop strategic sensitivity, they will grow in awareness of trends and competition that automatically creates an open dialogue across disciplines. Strategic road mapping provides a framework for facilitation and the development of opportunities.

CONCLUSION

All the strategies in this chapter goes beyond the normal planning and execution. Most often, this is a vision of a disruptive leader who is making a call to action that is often driven by turbulence (Petrick & Martinelli, 2012). The Call to Action is the problem ðnding phase and begins with the development of a collective understanding of the primary strategic challenge facing an organization. This first step is critical, as it helps frame the discussions and output generated in the following steps. Petrick and Martinelli (2012) found this step to be the most difðcult, as it was not unusual to have a team of senior leaders and strategic thinkers who each have a different view of the critical strategic challenge. By encircling a singular call to action, it created an appetite for change and the team developed a collective vision, which they called the strategic imperative, to guide innovative solutions. Petrick and Martinelli (2012) went on to develop a process for problem finding:

- Call to Action: Often a visionary leaders or external competitive threat that creates the need for change.
- Environmental Scan: Survey of environment for events that may occur to capture key aspects that determined the call to action.
- Walking the Wall: A discussion of events to identify key trends and underlying assumptions about the environment. Determined beliefs that run counter to the majority opinion that may identify important areas of uncertainty.
- Trend Filtering: Distinction of a few critical trends from many interesting ones via group consensus.
- Storytelling and Problem Finding: Construct alternative views of the future and identify problems in those futures from all stakeholders.

In the problem-solving phase of the process, the team must analyze all potential future scenarios, solutions, and actions. At this junction in the process, the team starts to conceptualize solutions and reduce them to whatever is to be executed. Solutions are often technology, repair or building ecosystems, developing new partners, or deploying new business structures and models. The problem ðnding teams carry over to the problem-solving activities. Typically, a subset of more technically oriented experts participates in problem solving (Petrick and Martinelli, 2012).

No strategic road map is the same; it must be organic to be successful. The uniqueness is what makes it work. However, several key factors have led to success. These are:

- Strong self-disruptive leadership is critical because it is the commitment to driving the process and getting participants to appreciate the importance of rethinking and envisioning the future.
- Embrace the outside-in view means re-drawing different viewpoints. Emphasizing a solution for all stakeholders and consider alternative approaches.
- Creating and delivering disruptive innovation. Changing technology and market space to deliver true innovation.
- Keeping the process organic may be one of the hardest. The plans developed need to fit the trends and assumptions identified. Willing to adjust their actions when the environment is changing.

Disruptive leaders desire to initiate disruptive innovation. Working from a convergent knowledge means overlooking exciting opportunities; however, working divergently changes biases, encourages an outside-in view, and helps participants identify critical needs before exploring alternative paths to meet those needs.

Case Study

IDEXX and David Evans Shaw

What started as a tiny start-up on the Portland, Maine waterfront that is now a global company employing over 7,000 people, IDEXX is an example of an organization whose founder is a disruptive leader, who hired disruptive leaders to create a truly inspirational company, which is an example of entrepreneurial excellence. The culture, founded on creativity, innovation, and true teamwork, had no clear job descriptions; the entire company became a family where each person worked to make the company a success by just doing what was needed. As founder David Shaw created an organization where people were passionate, and totally bought in to the company's ideals. His philosophy of cordiality, kindness, and truly respecting everyone's contribution is what built a highly successful company.

IDEXX transformed the work of animal care with creativity and innovation, diagnostics, new equipment, and testing procedures. This extraordinary company whose leadership possessed great confidence was able to launch a novel idea and new approach to animal care. In addition, they had a team of highly motivated people, who were never complacence, remained humble, but eager to accomplish the mission.

Shaw created exceptional long-term value to benefit employees, customers, shareholders, and other stakeholders. With confidence, a global vision, and a mission to be the best the leadership team created a family of great minds. They challenged traditions, worked harder and smarter than their competition, unified to solve problems and made success happen. This extraordinary organization changed and transformed an entire industry, animal health. IDEXX literally transformed the State of Maine from a natural resource-based economy to an advanced technological economy. The IDEXX team demonstrated what is possible for a business (Shaw, 2018).

Having just turned 30, Shaw was commuting every week from Maine to Agribusiness Associates, an international management-consulting firm in Boston, Massachusetts. Shaw found the commute draining. In the 1980's, he began thinking of another way to earn a living. In 1983, IDEXX was incorporated, and soon afterward, the new company started operations with a talented group of employees. IDEXX was in a growing biotechnology field and a competitive market. Where IDEXX had, the advantage was that their products were for veterinary and agricultural markets rather than human use. Therefore, approval processes from the U.S. Food and Drug Administration were minimal.

In the 1980's and 1990's, IDEXX developed numerous inexpensive test kits for veterinarians to detect diseases common among household pets, such as heartworm disease, feline immunodeficiency virus, feline leukemia, and canine parvovirus. Since veterinarians recommended regular testing for many of these diseases, these products became profitable. In addition to these tests, IDEXX developed a test for equine infectious anemia, which is important because federal law required that horses be tested for this disease before they can be transported across state lines. Adding to their product line, they developed a wide variety of more costly instrument-based testing systems: one to analyze enzyme levels in animals' blood; a second to measure electrolytes; a third to evaluate blood components; and a fourth to measure hormones. IDEXX created the software that linked these four tests, which allowed veterinarians to produce a profile in their offices instead of relying on a commercial laboratory.

Due to the expertise, creativity, and innovation of IDEXX and their founder (Shaw), Portland, Maine is now the global center for animal care. Where Maine's economy once centered on natural resources, IDEXX drove Maine's economy to shift to science, technology and innovation. Many new business ventures have spun off from IDEXX, and many entrepreneurs were inspired from this success story. Shaw's ability and his vision the future is what inspired the company to innovate and find superior solutions, products, and services.

Disruptive leaders need to have tremendous self-worth and faith in their ability to face reality, but at the same time recognize opportunities. These unique leaders have decisiveness with a high level of intuition. Disruptive leaders break the rules while writing new ones. Normal did not exist for Shaw and by having a willingness to break the rules, he is able to see and embrace a new normal. Leading disruptive innovation is not easy. A self-disruptive leader requires a tremendous amount of passion and energy.

In addition to IDEXX, Shaw has founded Covetrus, and Ikaria Pharma. He co-founded Cyteir Pharma, Vets First Choice, and Skinetics. He is a director/investor in numerous companies. He is a short-form filmmaker, and has received honorary doctorate degrees from Colby College, Bates College,

The University of Southern Maine and the Maine College of Art. Currently, Shaw is also a managing partner of Black Point Group.

Shaw is a servant leader and social entrepreneur who focuses on changing the way we honor our planet; he has been able to influence conservation directly with his work. Shaw has served as Senior Fellow at Harvard's John F. Kennedy School of Government, the advisory board of the school's Center for Public Leadership, and the selection committee for America's Best Leaders. Shaw was named Patron of Nature by the International Union for Conservations of Nature and International Sea-Keeper of the year in 2013. He served as co-chair of the Aspen Institute High Seas Initiative and on the Leadership Council of Service Year Alliance. He has served as treasurer of the American Association for the Advancement of Science (AAAS), a director of the U.S. National Park Foundation, and founding chair of the Sargasso Sean Alliance (ocean conservation).

He has been Chair of the Jackson Laboratory, a member of the Executive Committee of the U.S. Israel Science and Technology Commission, a member of the Council on Foreign Relations, a member of the leadership Council for Service Nation, a member of Young Presidents Organization and CEO (Chief Executives Organization), a member of the Science advisory board to Discovery Communications, Curiosity Stream, a trustee of Maine Medical Center, Hurricane Island Outward Bound, and many other non-profits.

In addition, Shaw was inducted into the Teddy Roosevelt Society, the UNH Entrepreneurship Hall of Fame, and IDEXX was inducted into the Life Sciences Foundation's Biotech Hall of Fame in 2008. Additionally, Shaw was the recipient of the 2013 Leslie Cheek Medal from the College of William & Mary and was honored at the 2017 New York Restoration Project Hulaween Gala. Recently, the U.S. Olympic & Paralympic Museum elected Shaw to the Board of Directors. The amount of accomplishments that David Shaw has is the sign of a disruptive servant leader, someone who has spent their life in the service of others.

The primary goal of successful leaders is to create other successful leaders. David Shaw is this leader. More than 200 people, including founders, aspiring entrepreneurs, investors, and mentors packed the University of Southern Maine's Hannaford Hall when David Shaw was the keynote speaker extending his congratulations to all participants in the Maine Center for Entrepreneurs 2019 Top Gun Showcase. David sponsors a $25,000 prize for one of the two winners. The award was established to support local entrepreneurship, to coincide with the public offering for Covetrus, and to celebrate the 35th anniversary of the founding of IDEXX Laboratories. The Top Gun Showcase is the capstone event for the Maine Center for Entrepreneurs training program. The Top Gun Showcase launched in 2009 with a dozen Portland, Maine, based entrepreneurs, that service 47 start-ups from across Maine. To date, the Showcase has supported more than 200 entrepreneurs.

Every David Shaw endeavor demonstrates depth and his true heart, from saving Gorillas in Rwanda with advance animal care, to protecting oceans, state parks, and more of our beautiful planet. Shaw's short films are truly transformational. The films re-set our priorities and give us pathways to direct our passions. David Shaw achieves this with cordiality, humbleness, life-long learning, kindness and fun. David is a true *gentleman* that not only transforms business and culture, but people.

"Entrepreneurial businesses are the engine of our economy — driving growth, innovation, and opportunity locally and across the world," David Evan Shaw.

Case Study

The Disruptors of Oxford

A remarkable group of disruptive leaders led the Oxford- Lafayette County Mississippi Economic Development Foundation. Because of the hard-passionate work of these disruptive leaders, Oxford, Mississippi is touted as the "Cultural Mecca of the South". Writers flock to Oxford to find inspiration in the rich history and world of William Faulkner. Musicians and artists abound, and the culinary experiences do not disappoint. Of course, the world of the University of Mississippi (Olde Miss) adds to the Southern Charm of the small town. Oxford is a community rooted in history, where people are as passionate about sports as they are their favorite author. Diversity is the norm, along with Southern Culture and hospitality that make Oxford unique. Oxford is in the county of Lafayette, in the mist of rolling hills of beauty. The town is filled with boutiques, galleries, and historic landmarks. Oxford is an experience!

John Maynard, Allen Kurr and their associates have a philosophy based on the book, "The Geography of Jobs", by Enrico Moretti. Moretti lays out how policy makers can learn how to lift Americans out of poverty by changing the geography of jobs. By stepping back and looking at the big picture, it is creativity and innovation that will drive change. It is the entrepreneurs that will create wealth, and this is the magical economics of job creation

(Moretti, 2012, p. 1). This group of disruptors have taken the plan outlined in Moretti's book, and adapted it to their unique situation and have come to some interesting conclusions.

They see themselves in an ocean of tropical fish attracting others to the reef. The real value is to attract entrepreneurs to the reef. Then once they are there, they give back to them with support such as money, mentorship, and community support. By collaborating with the local Arts Council, they host the "Big Bad Business Series", which are workshops providing the tools for success. These workshops resulted in 33 events with over 100 entrepreneurs. In partnership with the University of Mississippi, they are creating the workforce needed for economic development to occur. They have embraced a strategy with five commitments: (Kurr, 2019)

- Focus on people and attracting people (what do they want)
- Making sure to support their own people and their ventures
- Communicate effectively, talk about problems and how to fix them
- Everything they do is data driven. Look at the metrics to make decisions
- Give "Damn" factor. If you care, it shows in the community.

In May of 2018, The Walton Family Foundation highlighted Oxford as one of the fastest-growing communities in the nation. They gave credit to the Oxford-Lafayette County Economic Development Foundation and Chamber of Commerce for the "diversified and thoughtful strategic economic development planning", which has led to a 455 percent increase in personal income.

The U.S. Census Bureau defines a micropolitan statistical area as a geographic area of one or more counties with one city containing at least 10,000 but less than 50,000 in population. There are 551 micropolitan areas in the U.S. However, this classification is growing in relevance (DeVol & Wisecarver, 2018) and may be part of a paradigm shift on rural inward migration. Oxford, Mississippi is one of these micropolitan areas. Their growth was not random events, but strategic development planning where creativity and innovation were the foundation for entrepreneurship and efficient management. This group of disruptive leaders had the foresight to see how altering your philosophy and decisions are key components for a thriving community.

Instead of recruiting large business, Oxford took a different approach. They started recruiting firms by using a portfolio approach to economic development, firms with an organic indigenous expansion and entrepreneurial spirit. They closely monitored the environment for business retention and recruitment, regulatory and tax policies, technical assistance and strategies for workforce development. They offered incentives such as training grants and tax incentives, items that a large business would not want or require. Due to the multifaceted approach that relied on both a bottom-up, entrepreneurial-led strategy, as well as a top-down, more traditional recruitment strategy, Oxford has thrived.

In Oxford, many of these new entrepreneurial businesses are homegrown. A former University of Mississippi Vice Chancellor founded New Media Labs. Allen Kurr's family started a small business "No Time to Cook", where they offer home cooked Cajun and Southern casseroles. Karen Kurr created economic history when from her home kitchen she prepared frozen food and sold them at the local farmers market. This business grew, and now they have an industrial plant serving large chains such as Kroger and Walmart.

Oxford has low business and housing costs along with the culture, recreation, quality education, excellent healthcare, and quality of life for which young professionals are looking. Oxford retains families and attracts new families with young children. They have done this by having authenticity, examining their assets, and being strategic in their economic development. According to the U.S. Census, Oxford's Lafayette County has a population of 53,796 in 2016, was an increase of 38.8% from 2000 to 2016. Inward migration into the Oxford region accounted for 77% of the total population. In terms of economic performance, the U.S. Department of Commerce and the Bureau of Economic Analysis indicate Oxford's population increased 122% and employment rose from 9,292 to 33, 875 from 1970 to 2016. The employment growth of Oxford has been in two major areas: The University of Mississippi and tourism-related industries.

The University of Mississippi has inspired many businesses that have assisted in diversifying Oxford's economy. The university helped to form new entrepreneurial projects that contributed to the micropolitan community. Corelogic is a leading provider of consumer, financial and property information, analytics and services to business and government. Corelogic decided to stay in Oxford by establishing an innovation center that stands to bring 600 additional jobs to the city.

An entrepreneur Garret Gray has established a new start-up call Next Gear Solutions. Next Gear Solutions works to address the lack of workflow management. This firm utilizes new technology to create highly efficient online management systems for contractors and consulting services. Recently Next Gear has announced expansion in Oxford (DeVol & Wisecarver, 2018).

The tourism sector in Oxford attracts thousands on an annual basis, and the bar is set high for cultural experience. Tourist spent $156.6 million in Oxford in 2016, a gain of 13.9%. Along with this growth, wages rose from $30.1 million in 2001 to $96.6 million in 2016. Oxford has experienced another sector of growth with retirees moving to the area. Oxford has become a baby boomer magnet. With the great weather, low cost of living, and great amenities, Oxford has been named as one of the top small-town retirement destinations in the country (DeVol & Wisecarver, 2018).

REFERENCES

Christensen, C. M. (2003). The Innovator's Dilemma: When New Technologies Cause Great Firms to Fail. Harper Collins.

Christensen, C. M. (2010, July). How Will You Measure Your Life. *Harvard Business Review*.

Furth, J. F. (2018). *Owning Tomorrow: The Unstoppable Force of Disruptive Leadership*. Indie Books.

Gromelsky, V. (2017). Japan Becomes a Rising Star for the Swiss Watchmaking Industry. *New York Times*. Retrieved from, https://www.nytimes.com/2017/01/17/fashion/watches-japan-swatch-group.html,web

King, A. A., & Baatartogtokh, B. (2015). How useful is the theory of disruptive innovation? *MIT Sloan Management Review*, *57*(1), 77–90. Retrieved from https://0-search-proquest-com.libcat.uafs.edu/docview/1719426267?accountid=14481

Korn Ferry. (2019). Self-Disrupt Or Be Disrupted. *Korn Ferry*. Retrieved from, https://www.kornferry.com/self-disrupt

Lebeaux, R. (2018). Disruptive Leadership: A Recipe for Success. *The Wall Street Journal*. Retrieved from, https://deloitte.wsj.com/cio/2018/07/09/disruptive-leadership-a-recipe-for-success/

Markides, C. C. (2012). How disruptive will innovations from emerging markets be? *MIT Sloan Management Review*, *54*(1), 23–25. Retrieved from https://0-search-proquest-com.libcat.uafs.edu/docview/1115278036?accountid=14481

Petrick, I. J., & Martinelli, R. (2012). Driving disruptive innovation: Problem finding and strategy setting in an uncertain world. *Research Technology Management*, *55*(6), 49–57. doi:10.5437/08956308X5506902

Chapter 3
Institution and Governmental Support

ABSTRACT

Our great academic institutions have come under attack in recent years. Often accused of being biased, unethical, and producing inferior academic standards, our universities are a tremendous resource for community and state initiatives. Those areas where the creative economy is strong, research universities and community colleges are actively involved. Our academic institutions create wealth and a sense of place. Many state universities and community colleges have seen the need and have responded with unique specialized programs, not just in the U.S. but globally. The same can be said of local, state, and national governmental agencies, who have supported the creative economy with programs and funding. The most successful creative economies happen when a group of state holders come together to collaborate and network to build a unique disruptive initiative. There are small disruptors who are building disruptive communities and companies globally. This chapter explores institution governmental support.

INTRODUCTION

Education is the Most Powerful Weapon Which you can Use to Change the World- Nelson Mandela

Society now expects the universities it funds to work with citizens and communities to enable them to flourish in economic development. In particular, the support for small and medium-sized businesses is expected and needed to

DOI: 10.4018/978-1-7998-3416-8.ch003

help them be innovative and creative in a new global marketplace. Successful university outreach programs have driven holistic inter-disciplinary teams involved with starting entrepreneurial projects with profound outcomes (Powell, 2012). The importance and role of universities in igniting the creative economy and creating the environment of divergent learning and decision-making cannot be underestimated, and they must be looked at and explored. Universities may be the key to the future of our nation's wealth creation and improved quality of life.

Professor of media studies and author Catherine Liu argues that universities have stopped educating people and are just training them to get jobs (Williams, 2014). In his article, "Anti-Intellectualism and the Dumbing Down of America," Ray William's points to the reason for rising anti-intellectualism can be found in the declining state of U.S. education compared to other developed countries (2014). Universities may find it necessary to become externally focused by consciously analyzing their own distinct identity as a leading enterprise. By re-directing resources, modernizing curriculums, changing managerial levels of the institution, and establishing new academic norms institutions could produce a new modern Renaissance or Enlightenment (Powell, 2012).

The World Economic Forum ranked the U.S. 52nd among 139 nations in the quality of its university math and science instruction in 2010. The American Association of State Colleges and Universities (ASCU) report on education indicates the U.S. ranks second among all nations in the proportion of the population aged 35-64 with college degrees, but 19th in the percentage of those aged 25-34 with an associate or high school diploma. For the first time, the young in the U.S. will have less education than their parents. Furthermore, National Geographic-Roper found that nearly half of Americans between the ages of 18 and 24 do not think it is necessary to learn the culture of other countries or a foreign language (Williams, 2014). Mark Beuerlein's book, "The Dumbest Generation", reveals the addiction to social media may lead to aversion to reading anything of substance (Williams, 2014), let alone learn skills such as mindfulness, reflection, and increasing cognitive and metacognitive abilities to learn. Thus, inhibiting the ability to apply oneself to create, innovate and thrive in a turbulent diverse world.

In our American schools, we praise and fund the athlete, not the athletes' grades. Intellectual and creative students commonly are openly ridiculed for their abilities. We are creating angry dummies who make sure their voice is heard above the rest and fight to drag down any opposing views through personal attacks, loud repetition, and confrontation (Williams, 2014). However, rarely do they investigate and dig deep enough to understand reality. The result is people accept without questioning, believe without weighing the choices, and join the pack when its conveniences them. Divergent thinking takes too much time because it gets in the way of having the immediate and the online experience.

Furthermore, Reality TV and pop culture claim to provide information that is supposed to enrich our lives, however what they produce is cheap to produce and designed to just make money and not provide quality viewing. The mega media conglomerates, a $795 billion industry, control the media, movies, and print while gaming is making millions while distracting people from the real issues and concerns facing the global society. Creativity is out, and cheap entertainment is in. The fact that our education system is declining when there is a trend of anti-intellectualism should be a concern for leaders and the general population. Higher education needs to take a firm look at culture and ask if universities are creating the people that can face the modern world and thrive. In addition, universities need to look at becoming more of a role model and igniting the creative economies and providing the education needed to remain a world leader.

Universities and Research Institutes

Two main areas are needed to bridge higher education to the creative sector: creative human capital and knowledge development. The human capital might have to include graduates not just in the arts, but also in all disciplines. Creativity is key in all disciplines and has the potential to build entrepreneurial outcome in business, arts, science, and technology.

Knowledge development can be embedded in all networks and with all relationships engendering new platforms and practices. Creative maker's spaces include shared workspaces such as incubators for engagement and brainstorming. However, virtual platforms or "third spaces" can be develop organically and produce research and innovation on a large scale (Gilmore & Comunian, 2016). The creative economy is an economic area based on education, art, culture, technology and science. The creative economy is developing rapidly in advanced societies where maturity and richness of the consumer is based on supply and demand of an educated workforce in an economically advanced environment. The support of this kind of economy is the ability to network by working with public sectors, universities and governments (Gilmore & Comunian, 2016). There are two distinct ways that universities contribute to the creative economy, source of knowledge and learning activities. In addition, they provide an infrastructure of essential knowledge.

The U.S. can strengthen their creative workforce by incorporating critical skills into job training programs for adults in both credit and non-credit courses and certificates of proficiency. Creativity can be cultivated through exposure to the visual, performing, arts, literary arts, technology, science, and business. States can take advantage of their public higher education system by making creative programs available to students, as well as adult degree programs for non-traditional students by offering college credit for on the job training and work experience. The integration of cross disciplines with the skills and expertise of a local workforce may alter the economic marketplace. Examples of several creative new programs have been implemented at colleges and universities across the U.S.

For example:

- College of the Redwoods in California focuses on fine furniture-making
- Community colleges in Kentucky capitalizes on the region's storytelling and folk music traditions by helping students build skill sets to create public artwork, preserve historical photographs and archival documents, and sponsor community arts residencies.
- Montgomery Community College in North Carolina has linked its renowned pottery program to the business sector by linking students with an organization that specializes in helping students start and operate entrepreneurial businesses.
- Connecticut's Film Industry Training Programs at Middlesex Community College, Norwalk Community College, and Quinnipiac University offered by the Connecticut Office for Workforce Competitiveness in partnership with the Commission on Culture & Tourism. The program is designed for individuals who want to learn the basics of feature film and episodic television production and pursue entry-level freelance work in the industry. (National Governors Center, 2009).

These are wonderful programs; however, they only focus on one segment of the creative economy. The University of Maine and Maine Arts Commission understand the totality of the creative economy and see technology as an important component. University of Maine Orono has taken an active role in igniting the creative economy in Maine. The university has two patents, one on tidal power units, and the other in bridge construction components.

Both have been implemented. New bridges have been built in Maine with the patented new light composite with over 100-year life expectancy. East Coast Maine is running on the Tidal Power units built by the university (UMO, 2017). The leadership shown by the University of Maine Orono, the ability to invest time, resources, and money into these new inventions is disruptive creative leadership. Maine being an economy primarily based on tourism and the forestry industry needed better leadership to address the future of the state's socio-economic needs.

FEDERAL GOVERNMENT

The role of government is essential in promoting economic progress if the virtues of trustworthiness, tolerance, and respect are honored as well as the encouragement of individual motivation and support for economic freedom. The very act of economic exchange for civilizing society will determine the cultural characteristics of the society. Williamson determined from society's core, institutional structure would guide all economic activity (Williamson, 2011).

Trust, the most important virtue, is needed to sustain a vibrant exchange economy. As the economy develops its markets and grows, trust becomes even more important in its sustenance (Smith, 1759) because every commercial transaction involves a level of trust. Societies with higher levels trust spend less time protecting themselves, diverting resources, leading to outcomes that are more efficient. A lack of trust creates barriers where individuals do not expand to anonymous markets. These barriers discourage innovation, creativity, entrepreneurship, and investments in both human and physical assets (Williamson, 2011).

The role of government as a leader in directing our virtues is complex, but necessary to creating and sustaining rules and regulations to support economic growth. Often governments are a source of interference rather than a productive unit providing necessary rules and policies to promote economic growth. Governments make decisions on policies more in line with politicians' interest than on public interest. Predatory behavior may alter the culture and values of those living under a corrupt government lowering the trust levels and altering society to the point where the society becomes corrupt. The result is a breakdown of democracy and economic systems including society's norms, values, and culture (Williamson, 2011).

If a government provides and enforces abstract polices that apply to everyone it may fall prey to political interest, such as rules that are targeted to special groups. A productive government will enhance society by providing regulations that allow holistic organic growth of economic development.

"The crossroads of trade are the meeting places of ideas, the attrition of rival customs and beliefs; diversities beget conflict, comparison, thought; superstitions cancel one another, and reason begins". Will Durant (2011). "The Life of Greece: The Story of Civilization", p.221, Simon and Schuster

Virtuous behavior may arise because an individual's self-interest is to discover ways of collaborating and exchanging knowledge and ideas. If government is too involved, it may lead to a breakdown of a virtuous society instead of the creation of one. A market economy provides benefits and a higher quality of life, which creates a more civilized society. The competition generated by the invisible hand walks us through economic change, the improvement of goods and services, and provides incentives for innovation and creativity (Durant, 2011).

States vary in degrees of their involvement in the creative economy and how they perceive the creative economy. A major initiative by the National Governors Association in the late 1990's has started many states on the path to building the creative economies. State governors, three territorial governors, and two commonwealth governors are part of the National Governors Association (NGA). NGA helps states develop programs and policy. The NGA determines Best Practices and with the governor's staff, they can:

- Learn about what works and doesn't, and what lessons can be learned
- Aid in designing and implementing new programs and making current programs more effective
- Receive up-to-date, comprehensive information about cutting-edge policies
- Learn about emerging national trends so governors can prepare to meet future demands

STATE GOVERNMENT

Each state, territory, and commonwealth know the importance of effectively measuring its creative economy. In 1990, Maine began a program called

"Discovery Research Program", which began a statewide inventory of cultural resources within communities and Native American Nations. This ongoing program provides funds and expert assistance for Maine communities to survey local events, artists, traditions, visual, craft, and literary arts. Included in this is new technology. When collected, this information is used to analyze local economic development strategies and initiatives. The tactic is to formulate a strategic plan to develop workforce and cultural development activities. In Maine, the program indexed assets in more than 70 percent of the state's communities.

Industry Mapping

The states of Arkansas and North Carolina have a case study program to help map the industries in their states. These case study programs are making a significant impact with local communities and building a special economic relationship with the state department of economic development. The successful relationship between businesses, universities and government leads to the development of long-term sustaining programs. Arkansas' "Ducks, Documentaries and Design: Tales from Arkansas' Creative Economy" and North Carolinas'. "Arts, Culture and Design in Rural North Carolina", are examples of successful case studies that have documented the special relationship of local economies and communities.

States have used labor and business data to create flexible indexing systems that provide some perspective on cultural activity. Washington and Oregon have both implemented Creative Vitality Index systems, which track key indicators. The Michigan Office of Cultural Economic Development has launched the Cultural Economic Development Online Tool (CEDOT) in collaboration with Michigan State University to continually monitor and provide comprehensive information about the state's creative economy. CEDOT is establishing a network of statewide partners who represent inventors, entrepreneurs, artists, libraries, educators, art retailers, historic preservation, museums, and other organizations to establish and update a database to monitor, assess, and enhance Michigan's creative economy.

The database is a collection of information on the tastes and preferences of tourists and other consumers. This information is provided to artists and tourist operators to help inform their business decisions. In addition to industry mapping, states must establish and maintain a repository of useful data on the arts, culture, and technology industries that can be used to analyze state economic development strategies. States that collect accurate, comprehensive information about the creative economy have reliable information for resource allocation and policymaking.

Stimulating State Creative Economies

Mapping state creative economies has been done with a multistate initiative in New England. The New England Council and the New England for the Arts (NEFA) have spent thirty years collecting information and conducting periodic regional economic studies of nonprofit cultural organizations. The information is used as a tool to gather resources for these nonprofit cultural organizations. To capitalize on the availability of this information, state and local organizations in the New England states funded an interactive economic modeling tool, *CultureCount* (www.culturecount.org), which uses New England Cultural Department (NECD) data to calculate the economic impact of cultural organizations. *CultureCount* data is harvested from a variety of sources, including state agencies, IRS records, commercial business listings, and ongoing surveys of the cultural field. Resources such as these can help define the intellectual and creative assets of a state's labor force. The NEFA report also allows trend analyses and comparisons of artist workforce data by state.

State Stakeholders

Identifying the right people to lead is critical to the success of planning efforts. A common strategy is to establish a special council, task force, or office charged with advancing the state's economy through the arts. Maine created a Creative Council, Vermont put the creative economic initiative into the state Rural Development Council, Michigan created the office of Cultural Economic Development, and other states created a special office or position in their state governments. However, the most successful programs have started with a disruptive community leader.

Often state-driven programs with state agencies are bogged down with policy, budgets, and the transition in state government. Disruptive leaders are entrepreneurs and business leaders who are modern in ideas and divergent in their ability to make decisions. They have agility and absorption that gives them the ability to make decisions quickly while change is taking place. They can see the wicked opportunities while facing wicked problems.

Support for Small Business

In rural states, a thriving small business sector in the arts and technology is important to state economies. States can support business development in the arts and technology by utilizing existing state networks, tapping state university systems, developing virtual networks, and supporting entrepreneurial collaborations. The development of small businesses and micro-enterprises is fostered by networks of local, state, and federal programs designed to assist small businesses and encourage entrepreneurship. These programs may provide a helpful boost to the arts and technology industries. Through its 2020 Program, for example, Louisiana is currently examining how it can leverage existing small business and entrepreneurship services for the benefit of the cultural sector. There are currently 14 Small Business Development Centers (SBDCs), 16 business incubators, several Manufacturing Extension Partnership (MEP) Centers, and other services offered across the state. The goal of these programs is to help entrepreneurs and small enterprises become more economically viable and transition, where appropriate, to the next levels of business and market maturation.

Support Individual Entrepreneurs

Inventors and artists are important producers of goods and services in every state's creative economy. Through the creativity of inventors, artists, entrepreneurs, and businesses, goods and services are produced. Small businesses are started, innovative design ideas enter the marketplace, and services are created in niche findings. Many states are using small grants to encourage entrepreneurship, new product development, and career advancement among artists and creative individuals. Numerous state agencies offer grant programs that support entrepreneurship or business development activities. For example,

- The Nevada Arts Council offers Jackpot Grants to individual artists on a quarterly basis. Forty-two received $1,000 awards to support business or product development for Nevada artist-entrepreneurs. Grants allow artists to participate in training programs, develop their portfolios, and fund special exhibitions or performances/presentations that broaden the market for their work. The state also offers several other grant awards including the Artist Fellowship Program, which provides nine fellowships of $5,000; three awarded annually in three areas: the literary arts, the performing arts, and the visual and media arts. The grants are flexible and may be used to cover time, supplies and materials, and living expenses.

- Artist Entrepreneurial Grants offer New Hampshire artists the opportunity to improve their business acumen. Administered by the New Hampshire State Council on the Arts, the grants range from $250 to $1,000 and must be accompanied by a cash match from other nonpublic sources. Forty-three recipients used the grants to enhance their business skills through classes on marketing, business-plan writing, pricing, legal issues, and financial management. Recipients may also use the grants to attend showcases and develop professional marketing materials such as Web sites and printed ads.
- The Louisiana Division of the Arts' Artist Career Advancement program provides grants of up to $3,000 to support entrepreneurship, career growth, and artistic product development among artists and creative individuals within the state. Forty-four grants were used for entrepreneurial skills training, professional development workshops, public relations or advertising efforts, portfolio development, business planning, product development, and distribution.

States can play an important role in connecting universities to networks with online outreach, credit and non-credit classes for training and development. Direct funding and assistance initiate development projects based on collaboration and resource sharing. In addition, cross-discipline collaboration stimulates new thinking, encourages new product development, and make the most of a state's collective creative and business resources.

Local Government

The creative economy of a community is a system of economic development that uses the resources and skills to create imaginative and innovate work and quality of life within the community. Individuals and groups develop a canvas on which creative and innovative acts are part of the fiber of the community. In the community, individuals continually exchange with each other, and receive information based on culture, skills and experience that create their own unique culture and community. The creative community may be broken down into six areas:

- A local system of traditions, norms, and sites of memory (such as museums and exhibitions dedicated to local crafts or skills) through which certain kinds of creative impulses are preserved and transmitted.
- A visual landscape that reflects and supports the creative ambitions of the city by projecting a distinctive image and spectacle. For example in many communities, street art represents the culture of the area.
- A system of leisure opportunities and amenities that provide relevant forms of recreation. Art walks are an example and happen in communities large and small.
- A mosaic of unique residential neighborhoods offering appropriate housing and infrastructural services for workers.
- A framework of education and training activities. These activities typically play a major role in supplying and building the skilled workforce for the local creative system.
- A series of social networks supplementing interpersonal contacts in the workplace that notifies the creative workforce of useful information and other intelligence (Scott, 2010).

These creative communities have recreated with hope and optimism. However, a clear understanding is needed of the many complexities and difficulty involved in creating an organic holistic initiative. The more structured and mechanical, the less creative and innovative the initiative may become. The creative field must remain undeveloped and unfold reflexively with the cultural system. Therefore, the disruptive leaders could be more successful in developing a movement inspired by divergent thinking and more creative than thought possible.

In an increasing global marketplace, creativity and innovation have become essential to generating the jobs that we will need in order to sustain our standard of living over the coming decades. The process of innovation itself demands new skills. Our community colleges and state universities must rise to the task of fostering creativity among students, faculty, and the broader community.

"Our standard of living is not a birthright. We have to earn it in the marketplace every day." John Young, former CEO Hewlet Packard

The United States has the highest standard of living in the world. However, the down side of this is that we also have very high labor costs compared to other countries. This high labor cost has made us unable to compete directly with countries like China and India whose labor costs are low. As other nations around the world start to become a developed society, their skilled workforces grow and will start to adopt cutting-edge technology that will allow them to compete with the U.S. The U.S. can no longer assume that we will win on quality either. A possible solution is the creative economy. What Americans do best is to innovate and create new ideas, design new products, deliver sophisticated services, and introduce new business strategies. The jobs that are most vulnerable to low-wage competition tend to be the least creative. Manufacturing, as a rule is routine, digitized and codified, which means it can be "offshored" to a location with lower labor costs (Wince Smith, 2006).

Johnson (2009) identiðed ðve distinct trends of "arts economic development" in local communities, four of which continue to this day:

- the formation of arts tourism;
- the attraction of knowledge workers;
- the stimulation of creative production; and
- the prioritization of micro-development.

In the United States, colleges and universities are some of the best in the world when it comes to encouraging creativity, innovation, risk taking, and entrepreneurship. We must do better as the rest of the world builds up capacities that were once our unique advantage. Countries from around the world have taken a cue from America's success and have realized that they must focus on innovation by investing in education, research, and infrastructure. Places like China, which was espoused against the free market system (capitalism), have now embraced it. The United States employs one third of all science and engineering researchers, creates 40 percent of global research, and accounts for 35% of all scientific articles in the world. However, our lead is narrowing (Wince Smith, 2006).

Place Making in Communities

Creative place making involves bringing together a broader array of stakeholders that differs from a more conventional, cultural policy platform. The new model brings community art, non-profits, technology centers, local governments, community colleges, state universities, and the military to develop strategic alliances (place making). The result may be unprecedented and create a speed and coordination in which policy can be adopted to meet rapid change in a rapidly changing society. Creative place making capitalizes on the history of local communities and regional efforts. These efforts are used to advance the creative economy.

New concepts, as they emerge, may be ambiguous simply because they are in the state of development. They may help to stimulate the debate of what is needed for the next steps in developing the creative economy. New concepts may mature and gain substance in the course of these debates or shrivel up under the heat of scrutiny. However, they may be addressed to different audiences, meaning something distinctly different in each forum. Creative place making, as a new set of initiatives in the U.S. cultural policy toolkit, can both inform and be informed by a broader comparative perspective and a more robust dialogue (Nicodemus, 2013).

CONCLUSION

The growing importance of innovation for our national prosperity is changing nature of innovation itself. Economic development experts also challenge existing institutional structures. The boundaries that once defined our educational institutions are now dissolving disciplinary silos. National and regional boundaries are changing due to the need of collaboration. While they have evolved significantly from their origins, professional schools, community colleges and state universities see their role as job training and placement for the communities they are in, instead of developing higher order thinking and decision making skills to live in a modern turbulent world (Wince Smith, 2006).

In the United States, our democracy and freedoms have given us many advantages when it comes to creativity. Add to this a diverse population, an open society, capital markets that quickly move to support new and exciting ideas, and a heritage of risk taking and pushing back frontiers. For these reasons, the changes in the global environment play to our strengths. We are well positioned to maintain and even increase our prosperity over the coming decades. Our diverse communities and cultures will play a critical role in building our creative economy.

In the two case studies below, two states have created their own unique creative economies through culture. Both states could not be more different in culture and economics, but both have defined their cultures for the creative economy. The Universities of Texas and Maine have been active participants in developing and supporting their states creative economic initiatives. Texas has developed well-defined cultural districts and used grant money to launch projects. This support has created long-term success in many areas of Texas. Maine does not have well-defined cultural districts; however, the entire state has a well-defined culture in which Maine has capitalize to develop their own unique creative economy.

Case Study 1: Universities of Texas

University of Texas Austin

In 2016, the University of Texas's major effort was in preparing students to enter the creative economy successfully. Two undergraduate degrees were added to the curriculum with enhanced creative problem solving and hands-on learning. Austin, Texas has become the capital of the creative economy, with high tech companies disrupting business practices', popular culture, and the traditional art world. The new programs have students working across disciplines and collaborate on hands-on projects, with the goal of providing skills that work well in the workplace (Dietrich, 2016).

"We want to break down barriers between arts and technologies and equip students from Day One with the creative technologies and skills to make new work and inventions," said Bruce Pennycook, Director of the Center for Arts and Entertainment Technologies (2016). This change is to meet the demand for design coursework among students at the university, as well as a strong demand from local and regional employers for graduates with skills in design and design thinking, and by offering a degree that allows students to combine a liberal arts degree in design with a second major, Bridging Disciplines Program, study abroad and/or intensive language study. The university hopes to set a new standard and meet the needs of employers.

University of North Texas, Dallas, TX

The University of North Texas has performed extensive research on the creative economy of Texas in comparison with the rest of the country. Their conclusion of research performed in 2016 is that the creative economy plays a valuable role in the overall economy of the region and state. In the last economic downturn, the Dallas and Fort Worth regions were unscathed due to the strong creative economy in the regions. In 2016, the creative economy was growing. Thousands of organizations are engaging in creative work in the Dallas and Fort Worth regions that provides employment opportunities, but also is an avenue for branding and marketing the creative industries. These industries produces a highly educated, a highly skilled labor pool across many disciplines. This is attracting a growing workforce and many new companies (Seman & Caroll, 2016).

Cultural Districts of Texas

Working with universities, industry leaders, and community leaders, the state created cultural districts. The creation and promotion of cultural districts was a new successful strategy for communities to rehabilitate historic neighborhoods and revitalize downtown areas. A local nonprofit arts organization usually spearheads the planning effort, coordinates events, and seeks public and private sector financial support. The success of these programs at the city level as economic development projects and as jobs creators has encouraged other states to develop programs to recognize districts dedicated to art-related activities (TXP, 2016).

In the existing Texas cultural districts, there are a variety of methodologies and metrics to measure the impact of the area. Some communities focus on job creation and capital investment within the cultural district while others conduct economic impact studies that capture the total regional effects. These studies offer an annual snapshot of the economic and tax revenue impact, but not trends or changes over time. The cultural district program can be a statewide catalyst for economic development, with state universities adding degrees and cross disciplines working together. They are setting a standard for a new workforce to fill the positions created by the cultural districts (TXP, 2016).

Case Study 2: Maine's Creative Economy

The creative economy in Maine is diverse with foundations of creative economies varying from city to city, town to town. Maine is a large state with both rural and urban areas; those variations can make an enormous impact. Maine's creative workforce represents more than 20 rural artisans and businesses afðliated under the Maine Highlands Guild., They include the nationally recognized Portland Stage Company that draws actors from New York City and beyond to Bath's Chocolate Church Arts Center to "craft communities" such as the H.O.M.E. co-op in Orland. The needs, missions, and interests of these organizations could not be more different from one another, and yet each has a role in the creative economy of Maine (University of Maine, 2018)

By using the emerging creative economy to guide development, Maine hopes to ensure that urbanization is designed to protect the quality of life in the state. Communities that make Maine unique and a favorite vacation spot are trying to expand. However, they want to keep their cultural roots that have attracted creative workers. By guiding development, cities and towns can preserve their unique culture and attract the creative business community.

The authors of “The Creative Economy in Maine” take the New England Council’s work as a starting point and look at the unique features of Maine’s creative workforce (Barringer et al. 2005). They emphasize that one of the best ways to ensure a strong creative community is to coordinate urban development with colleges and universities. Colleges are anchors for the creative economy. They build museums and theaters, hold concerts and symposia, and generally bring institutional support and structure to a variety of cultural activities. They attract students with disposable income and provide jobs for faculty and staff. A university sells a clean product, the jobs it provides generally pay well, and it contributes mightily to the long-term economic and civic well-being of a community.

Maine’s cities have had tremendous success by working with their local community colleges and state universities. The University of Maine gave downtown Bangor a boost when it built a new art museum there rather than on the main campus in Orono. The museum has hosted a range of exhibits from Persian photography to African American quilt making. In Portland, the downtown renovations spearheaded by the Maine College of Art (MECA) have transformed once-derelict storefronts into a startling showcase of local artistic talent. Those art windows, in turn, have drawn the visitors, restaurants, and businesses that make Portland one of the most satisfying cities in New England for walking its streets.

Higher education supports the creative economy in the most obvious way: by educating the creators. Technology and art programs are no longer luxuries, and art in its many forms is not the privilege of an elite. As author Daniel Pink argues (Harney, 2005), the demand for more creative ideas means that MFAs will become as valuable to companies as MBAs. Maine’s best investment could possibly be its creative economy, utilizing not only its vast natural resources, but by working collaboratively and effectively to share a philosophy of higher order thinking and decision making with as many residents as possible. This could bring about a new modern society that can thrive is a changing world (University of Maine, 2018).

REFERENCES

Barringer, R., Colgan, C., DeNatale, D., Hutchins, J., Smith, D., & Wassall, G. (2005). The Creative Economy in Maine: Measurement and Analysis. University of Southern Maine, Center for Business & Economic Research and the New England Environmental Finance Center.

Bauerlein, M. (2009). *The Dumbest Generation*. Penguin Random House.

Dietrich, A. (2016). New Degree Options in UT's Fine Arts Designed to Prepare Students for Jobs in the Creative Economy. *University of Texas*. Retrieved from https://news.utexas.edu/2016/09/02/college-of-fine-arts-launches-two-new-degree-options

Durant, W. (1930). *The life of Greece: The Story of Civilization*. Simon and Schuster.

Gilmore, A., & Comunian, R. (2016). Beyond the campus: Higher education, cultural policy and the creative economy. *International Journal of Cultural Policy*, *22*(1), 1–9. doi:10.1080/10286632.2015.1101089

Maine Policy Review. (2018). The Creative Economy in Maine. *Maine Policy Center.* Retrieved from, https://mcspolicycenter.umaine.edu/mpr/2018/09/27/creative-economy-maine/

National Assembly of State Arts Agencies. (n.d.). State Arts Agency Creative Economy Initiatives. *National Assembly of State Arts Agencies*. Retrieved from, http://www.nasaa-arts.org/artworks/creativeeconomy_initiatives.html#ar

National Governors Association. (2009). *Arts and the Economy: Using Art and Culture to stimulate the economy*. National Governors Center. Retrieved from, http://www.nga.org/cms/center/publications?begin7736bde9-79fd-493d-be2b-0f62416085cd=180&end7736bde9-79fd-493d-be2b-0f62416085cd=189&pagesize7736bde9-79fd-493d-be2b-0f62416085cd=10&

National Governors Association. (2019). *Rural Prosperity Through The Arts & Creative Sector: A Rural Action Guide for Governors and States*. National Governors Association.

New Hampshire Business Committee of the Arts. (2017). Welcome and programs. *New Hampshire Business Committee of the Arts*. Retrieved from, http://nhbca.com/

Nicodemus, A. (2013). Fuzzy Vibrancy: Creative Place-Making as Ascendant US Cultural Policy. *Cultural Trends, 22*(3/4), 213–222. doi:10.1080/09548963.2013.817653

North Carolina Arts. (2007). Creative Economy: The Arts Industry in North Carolina. *Regional Technology Strategies.* Retrieved from, www.nasaa-arts.org/artworks/nc-arts-industry.pdf

Powell, J. (2012). The university role in the innovative leadership of small to medium sized enterprises. *International Journal of Entrepreneurial Behavior & Research, 18*(4), 396-416. http://0-dx.doi.org.libcat.uafs.edu/10.1108/13552551211239465

Seman, M., & Caroll, M. C. (2016). The Economic Impacts of the Dallas/Fort Worth Creative Economy. *University of North Texas.* Retrieved from, https://economicsresearch.unt.edu/sites/default/files/DFW_CreativeIndustries%20final.pdf, web.

Texas Cultural Districts' Program (TXP). (2016). *Texas Cultural District Program: Indicators for Success.* Texas Cultural Districts' Program. http://www.arts.texas.gov/wp-

Universities of Scotland. (2010). Scotland's Creative Economy: The Role of Universities. *Universities of Scotland.* ISO 14001:2004. Retrieved from www.universitiesuk.ac.uk/publications

University of Maine Orono. (2017). Advanced Structure and Composite Center. *University of Maine Orono.* Retrieved from, https://composites.umaine.edu/research/#CompositeArchBridges

Williams, R. (2014). Anti-Intellectualism and the Dumbing Down of America. *Psychology Today*. Retrieved from, https://www.psychologytoday.com/blog/wired-success/201407/anti-intellectualism-and-the-dumbing-down-america

Williamson, C. R. (2011). Civilizing society. *Journal of Private Enterprise, 27*(1), 99–120. Retrieved from https://0-search-proquest-com.libcat.uafs.edu/docview/916797650?accountid=14481

Wince-Smith, D. L. (2006). The Creativity Imperative: A National Perspective. *Peer Review: Emerging Trends and Key Debates in Undergraduate Education, 8*(2), 12–14. Retrieved from http://search.ebscohost.com/login.aspx?direct=true&db=a9h&AN=20607607

Chapter 4
Cultural Districts

ABSTRACT

Basing the creative economy on a community's history and culture makes it unique. In addition, the community will have more buy in and participate in the changes. Often, disruptive leaders come from the fringes of our communities, seeing the uniqueness when others only want the status quo or are embroiled in just trying to make their business work. Often, local governments do not see the potential of thinking out of the box and need a push to go in a different direction. In larger communities, often there are multiple cultures living in their own ethnic areas. The need to create cultural districts to support the development of the unique creative economies of each district is a catalyst to igniting the creative economy. Capitalizing on cultural mapping, the history of a region, and getting support from local, state, and national governments can mean success or failure. This chapter explores cultural districts.

INTRODUCTION

A people without the knowledge of their past history, origin and culture is like a tree without roots - Marcus Garvey

Thriving creative economies are based on the culture that the citizens of a certain community embrace. Community culture embodies several principles. One is the art and innovation experienced in a public way, not just private or in specific groups. Community culture identifies uniquely social functions of a specific culture including goals shared across society that our worthy to

DOI: 10.4018/978-1-7998-3416-8.ch004

pursue. In 1982, Kevin Mulcahy determined five dominant justifications of community culture: 1) economic; 2) social; 3) educational; 4) moral; and 5) political arguments. In addition, community culture is thought to serve private interest, so the support of community culture is necessary for public interest as well. It is within these shared goals that the creative economy develops and thrives. The creative economy grows organically from culture. Mulcahy's 1982 research reflects today's environment today. The basic functions of community culture have not changed (National Governors Association, 2019).

Community culture provides greater social connection and increases the social capital of a community. Furthermore, it removes social barriers and allows more citizens to participate in cultural creation rather than being just customers of a marketplace. Society needs to work toward a future in which communities are actively working toward retaining and building on their own unique culture. Community culture is connected to moral worth, where high culture is in the public interest and to be used for the purpose of peacebuilding and providing a higher quality of life. The concept of merit or moral high ground is an uncritical approach in which things are just and good, in and of themselves, and should be protected. The merits of artistry and innovation produce an experience of moral worth and a "quality of life." One's culture provides opportunity where everyone has a right to the culture, and everyone shares the culture (Kidd, 2012).

The President's Committee on the Arts and Humanities (2000) determined that culture is as important as education. With this increased interest in culture, Kidd (2012) determined that government should subsidize culture as they do education. The economic rationale for community culture is that it ignites economic prosperity and improves a community's sense of place. Furthermore, there is an argument that community culture is rooted in the principles of democracy. By pursuing democracy and the creative economy, we build social capital and symbolically illustrate democratic principles. The political system and democracy are then reflected in creative content. We can expect the arts and innovation to reflect society as a whole and societal changes that occur (Kidd, 2012). As democracy is challenged and modern norms threaten communities, disruptive leaders are working in their communities to ignite the creative economy to save their unique cultures.

Community Culture

Edward Arian (1982) perceives the absence of an American cultural policy and offers the concept of "cultural democracy" as a foundation upon which to build cultural policy. Arian analyzed three cultural spheres in America. The ðrst is a "performance culture" that consists of elite art institutions and small wealthy audiences. The second is a "creative culture," a set of artists and innovators who are thinking and making decisions divergently and are responsible for most contemporary culture. This creative culture is largely autonomous from the major arts institutions. The third group is a "community arts culture" that works with local communities to generate art and innovation through small local or regional organizations. Arian argues that cultural democracy must originate in the creative culture in local communities. Americans generally have a privileged performance culture. We may have failed to bring cultural democracy into the public sphere.

The American identity started with disruptive leaders and is based on visual, symbolic material and cultural diversity. Beyond national identity, the creative economy and culture create a social solidarity. This solidarity creates a sense of trust that allows society to thrive as a cohesive group. Culture provides and determines the imaginative experience that builds a shared vision from the community's history and heritage, and where the community is going. Many have lost their way. In Fort Smith, Arkansas, the rich history is based on the launching of the West and the settling of Indian Territory. However, if you ask many citizens, they refer to Fort Smith as a manufacturing town. The citizens have forgotten the history and heritage that was based on the settlement of the Louisiana Purchase and our nation.

Richard Florida's (2002) analysis of the new creative class indicates that the arts and other creative endeavors provide a kind of research and development department for a new creative economy. The arts provide new ways of thinking and creating that can transform not only culture but also technology and the economy. Tyler Cowen (2002) argues that cultural innovation is best achieved through hybridity and cross-pollination, rather than through protectionist measures that seek to preserve traditions. Cowen's approach argues in favor of market-driven innovation, organic and holistic rather than the development of public culture.

Cultural Districts

Community leaders have started to recognize the role of creative industries in sustainable economic development. Cities and states are seeking new ways to amplify the positive effects of this sector in long-term economic development to build a sense of place. The creation and promotion of cultural districts has increasingly become a successful strategy for communities to rehabilitate historic neighborhoods and revitalize downtown areas. The establishment of a recognized and branded cultural district has traditionally occurred at the city level. Various groups spearhead the planning effort, coordinate events, and seek public and private sector financial support. The success of these programs at the community level is they are seen as economic development projects and as jobs creators. This has been encouraged in several states. With the development of creative economic programs that recognize cultural districts that are dedicated to art and technological activities, these economic development programs have been more successful than those who have not delineated cultural districts (Cowen, 2018).

The establishment of a formal cultural district may be necessary, but not enough, to ensure long-term viability of the creative economy. Successful cultural district programs have several common elements including a disruptive leader, clear and concise goals, public sector financial support, community buy in, and key performance measures that track the cultural district's progress. Because cultural districts rely on varying levels of private and public sector financial support, communicating the economic importance of culture to the overall success of the creative economy is important. In addition, many cultural organizations operate in publicly owned facilities that make measuring and evaluating the total economic and fiscal impact even more challenging.

A cultural district is most often a contiguous area of a town with a set boundary. Within these boundaries the preservation and renovation of historical buildings and complementary new construction is incentivized. Artists, cultural arts organizations, and performing arts venues often serve as anchors for the cultural district. The presence of the arts as well as increased foot traffic enhances property values, the profitability of the surrounding businesses, and the tax base in a virtuous cycle of investment and growth. Cultural districts have also proven to be a successful strategy for strengthening community identity, which in turn drives occupancy, commerce, tourism, and jobs.

In fifteen states, the governors and state legislators have established statewide cultural district certification programs that formally recognize and support locally organized zones of artistic and technological activities. These programs support the local cultural districts or creative districts with grants, tax incentives, information sharing, and branding. The cultural districts have available the information and training to build tourism, place making, and commerce. The following states have cultural district certification programs: California, Colorado, Iowa, Indiana, Kentucky, Louisiana, Massachusetts, Maryland, New Mexico, Oklahoma, Rhode Island, South Carolina, Texas, Washington, and West Virginia (National Governors Association, 2019).

Mapping

Cultural district and cultural mapping are valuable tools for identifying a community or a region's strength and resources. Communities can analyze and determine resources, efficiencies and links between cultures, culture groups, and links to the arts and technology. Building common aspirations, beliefs, visions, and values help determine economic development. However, the most valuable part of cultural mapping may be in the generation of new perspectives and preparing the ground for effective cultural planning and creative economic development.

To build cultural districts, cultural mapping provides an inventory of a region or community with an organic holistic process. Mapping can be multidimensional and broad and identify a community's profile. Through the mapping process, risks and opportunities are determined and evaluated, which is important. Mapping allows an escape from the silos and gains an overview of all inter-connected relationships that cut across discipline and constitutes informal networks. Mapping is a tool to establish new insights. Although, it is demanding, mapping takes time and money.

The development of cultural mapping and districts give workers, both inside and outside of government, the means to increase their knowledge of what is happening in their region or community. Workers discover more about an area of concern and use the learned information for specific purposes to develop their own creative economy. Most importantly, the community can tell its own unique story, brand the community, and promote tourism and economic development.

Existing cultural districts use a variety of methodologies and metrics to measure the impact on the area. Some communities focus on job creation and capital investment within the cultural district, while others conduct economic impact studies that capture the total regional efforts. While these studies offer

Table 1. Some Uses of Cultural Mapping and Cultural Districts

Increase knowledge and appreciation	Define local or regional culture. Demonstrate scope and variety of cultural activity
Identify previously unknown resources and activities	Provide concise information to government officials for policy development and to stakeholders who will advocate for drawing attention to culture districts
Fresh perspective	Look at data from different points of view, cross discipline analysis, and networking
Objectivity	Observing and finding solutions to shared viewpoints
Networking	Sharing resources, communicating, and building liaisons
Locating gaps and overlaps	Identifying duplication and scarcity in each region or community
Distribution of resources	How far a population group will have to travel, workforce, and workforce skill level
Evaluating projects	How is the population currently served, is the community open to new ideas, and are there solutions to adequately solve problems
Seeing the present and planning the future	Who are the disruptive leaders to initiate change, and what needs to happen to bring skilled labor or resources to accomplish long-term goals
Cultural planning	Mapping and the building of cultural districts in communities or regions

an annual snapshot of the economic and tax revenue impact, it is not common to monitor trends or changes over time. Additionally, not all states require cultural districts to report annual activity using a standardized scorecard or metric, which makes it difficult to compare districts from different states or programs. The goal is to identify no more than five key performance indicators that apply regardless of location or district size. Based on conversations with cultural district representatives, most districts are measuring activity-using statistics such as event attendance, spending by nonlocals, and advertising effectiveness.

These metric indicators speak to the direct impact of cultural district activity and programming, but do not fully capture the spillover effects attributable to the entire creative economy. The presence of major arts organizations, for example, serves as a magnet for many smaller arts organizations and individuals that provide scaffolding for the growth of the creative community. In addition to the overall benefits provided to the community, cultural districts stimulate the growth of tourism. Individuals visiting an area rich in the arts are likely to stay longer and spend more money than the area's residents, which in turn supports jobs at local restaurants, shops, and hotels. Because many cultural districts are centered on publicly owned or tax-exempt facilities, examining the economic impact of just these organizations does not include the activity of businesses and technology that chose to locate in proximity.

Some states have chosen not to have cultural districts but have designed other programs that help build their creative economies. In Iowa, the Department of Cultural Affairs developed a program called "Iowa Great Places" to cultivate the uniqueness of Iowa and brand them as great places to work. This program provides professional development, training and grants to support infrastructure projects. The program also recognizes communities that establish projects that add value to their communities (Iowa Department of Cultural Affairs, 2019).

History

Often the most recent culture and history prevails in a community, and the older foundational history is forgotten. However, the history is still there underneath the fabric of the community and has a long-lasting impact on the community's culture, and this history has its roots with disruptive leaders who dared to establish a new community. When the community does not capitalize on this history, it overlooks the rich unique history it can bring to the creative economy and economic development, thus sacrificing the very essence of the community.

For example, in Fort Smith, Arkansas, many residents still identify the culture as either old manufacturing or military. Elvis Presley's famous picture of his military haircut was taken at Fort Chaffee in Fort Smith, Arkansas. Fort Chaffee has a smaller presence and most of the base in now industrial and retail space. Since 1962, the 188th Air National Guard Command Wing has been in Fort Smith and consequently adds to the military culture.

As previously said, many who live in Fort Smith, Arkansas do not know its history. Fort Smith was the launch pad for the development of the West. In Fort Smith, William Clark served as the surveyor over the Territory of Arkansas from 1824 to 1825. The famous Judge Parker (the hanging judge) and other famous marshals brought law and order to the new west. Parker arrived in Fort Smith on May 4, 1875. Parker is first session as the district judge was on May 10, 1875, with court prosecutor W. H. H. Clayton, who remained the United States Attorney for the Western District of Arkansas for fourteen of Parker's twenty-one years on the court. Parker's court had final jurisdiction over the Indian Territory, which is now the state of Oklahoma, from 1875 until 1889, as there was no other court available for appeals.

The legal systems and governments of the Five Civilized Tribes and other Native American tribes in the Indian Territory covered their own citizens, while federal law applied to non-Indian United States citizens in the territory. Keeping up with continued settlement in the West, the Courts Act of 1889 established a federal court system in the Indian Territory, which decreased the jurisdiction of the Western District Court at Fort Smith.

Currently this history is being re-visited with a new U.S. Marshals Museum being built and capturing the history with murals, re-enactments, and marketing the city for tourism. The community has a sense of pride in the Five High Native American Tribes, and when citizens learn the history, they have a new appreciation of the area. A cultural district would only add to the richness of this history and have the potential to bring in tourism.

Sub-Cultures

In his book, *American Nations: The History of the Eleven Rival Regional Sub-Cultures in North America,* Colin Woodard identifies eleven regional sub-cultures that have historically existed (2011). Given the many challenges facing our country, especially being deeply in debt, a large trade deficit, and the deep divide of our political leaders. All creating a distrust of government agencies and frustrating the average American citizen. Since the founding of our nation, there has always been a deep divide between states' rights and centralized government. Sub-cultures are aligned in either of these two camps. Each feeling strong in their conviction and bound to their cultural heritage (Woodard, 2011).

Each of these eleven sub-cultures have their unique principles, values, and beliefs. Each sub-culture values its democracy and has pride in its own ethnic heritage. The sub-cultures do not care about a unified national culture; they want their individuality. They see their state and regional sub-culture as a sovereign entity, just as our nation is sovereign. All sub-cultures value and want to preserve its culture.

In addition, Woodard (2011) determined that the last forty years have set the United States back and may have changed our position in global dominance. However, it could be that the loss of manufacturing in the last forty years has really changed our position and created a trade deficit that is not sustainable for our future economic needs. Our debt is certainly not sustainable. When people of cultures come together, they forget their disagreements over political divide and come together to solve their community and regional issues. The strength in America is the passion for our way of life and our need for individualism.

In the past forty years, our regional and local culture has been challenged. The loss of manufacturing jobs going overseas and the drug culture has disseminated many areas of our country. The American spirit is much more than building wealth. Is about honoring culture. It is truly about being a free individual with opportunities. When both freedom and opportunities are in jeopardy, Americans will fight (Woodard, 2011). Data has determined that in the past forty years countries with higher income inequality had slow growth. In addition, greater income inequality is associated with lower well-being, higher levels of mental illness, obesity, and high crime statistics (Buttrick and Oishi, 2017).

Research has shown that in areas of income inequality one sees less trust of government, mistrust of community members, and a negative effect on economic growth. The lack of trust is associated with several negative behaviors. Citizens are unlikely to join social activities and to do service work in their communities. Often those who suffer the most, work the longest hours and do not rise on the social ladder. This is contrary to the American dream where hard work wins. However, Americans were okay with income inequality if they felt their children would have more and rise in social status beyond them (Buttrick and Oishi, 2017).

According to Buttrick and Oishi (2017), the biggest gap is the exploration of variation, both cross-cultural and individual. Meaning in the U.S., society sees income equality as directly linked to happiness of the individual. Furthermore, the relationship between inequality and happiness found that once the psychological effects of inequality, unfairness, and mistrust were accounted for, differences in income distribution has no effect on happiness. So, the more the community or region comes together, builds trust with each other, capitalizes on their own unique culture, they will grow and be happy. There is an overwhelming need for Americans to save their culture. It is who they are. By using culture as part of making something new, finding something that is better than what they had, but keeping the culture, the solutions to the hard problems will be a unified decision (Buttrick and Oishi, 2017).

States and Regions

When states work together to do regional planning, the work can be beneficial. Regions in a state can also work together and enhance the economic development statewide. Here are some examples.

In Michigan, fourteen regional planning offices are working together to support the creative sector. Indiana's Office of Community and Rural Affairs consults with the Indiana Arts Commission. This partnership enables the Arts Commission to work directly with communities to incorporate the arts into their economic development planning. This partnership has also increased the visibility of the arts (National Governors Association, 2019). In the west, Arizona, Nevada, Utah, and Idaho are working to together to build the creative sector in the entire region. By coming together, they can give grants to new creative businesses that support the entire region and promote tourism throughout all the states.

CONCLUSION

Collaboration and revitalization are taking place all over the United States. From small rural communities to urban centers, collaboration is empowering people from civic leaders, educators, workers, immigrants, environmentalists, artists, public servants, librarians, businesspeople, city planners, students, and entrepreneurs to come together, reach for new opportunities, and take risks in rebuilding their economy and saving their culture. Revitalization is based on disruptiveness, creativity, generosity, passion, and dreams. Americans have done this in the past, and maybe we can find that path again. The soul of America is its citizens, communities, and sub-cultures.

CASE STUDIES

The following case studies offer examples of how the creative economy is working for a region and a community that embraces their own unique culture. Disruptive leaders have taken the history and culture of their communities and have driven the creative economy to new heights. The Choctaw Nation is not just a community of people; it is now a disruptive organization. Lafayette, Louisiana is rich in Cajun roots; they have transformed their community with culture and created a vibrant creative economy.

Case Study 1: Choctaw Nation

Dr. Sally Rood, of the National Governors Association, when interviewed and asked what were the outliers when studying the creative economy of states, she could not think of one. She said if there were one, it would be in the way the Native American Nations are able to build their creative economies. The ability to capture their culture, utilize smaller centralized governments, succeed with collaborative instead of competitive dispositions, and the ability to work for the greater good of the whole community all contribute to the creative economy. In addition, these creative economies tend to develop organically, which may have more acceptance from the stakeholders.

The Choctaw Nation has developed a thriving creative economy whose brand is based on their own culture and heritage. During the 1970s, the Choctaw Nation of Oklahoma claimed their sovereign rights that lead to the nation creating a new constitution. This activity led to the development of art facilities, an economic development that the Choctaw Nation reaps the benefits today.

A division of commerce was put together to support the mission and vision of the Choctaw Nation. This division worked to provide financial sustainability through efficient and effective business development and operations. What began as a world-class gaming and hospitality business has now grown into a diverse business portfolio that has generated revenue, created jobs, and is still growing.

The Choctaw nation generates revenue to accelerate the success of the tribe. They based their mission and vision on their heritage and culture, and with determination and commitment, they developed new business opportunities that generated revenue to support tribal services. Their business portfolio has generated over 5,000 jobs. The portfolio includes 20 gaming sites, 3 resorts, 6 hotels, a KOA RV park, 6 restaurant franchises, including 2 Chili's, a multi-million dollar printing company, 16 travel plazas, the Choctaw country market, 12 ranches and farms encompassing 65,000 acres, where they manage 2,100 cattle and harvest 130,000 pounds of pecans. In all the businesses, including gaming and hospitality, the Choctaw heritage and culture are prominently woven through fabric of each business line. While this is not always the case with first nation businesses, the Choctaws have been extremely successful at their maintaining culture.

In addition, the Choctaw Nation has a business development center and a store that features packaged pecans, art, jewelry, handcrafted items, books, and history documents. All of what they do is based on their culture and historical roots. The rich culture and heritage of the Choctaw's in Oklahoma and Arkansas has been linked with the original home of the Choctaw's in Alabama, eastern Mississippi, and the Florida panhandle. The Choctaw culture and heritage are parts of the great western expansion, the beginning of western development in the 1800s. Ancestral societies such as the Choctaws grew and developed over thousands of years. The social structure of the Choctaw nation has traditionally been very personal and is threaded through every endeavor of their society, especially in economic development. It is not about money, it is about their culture.

Case Study 2: Lafayette, Louisiana

The town of Lafayette, Louisiana is in south-central Louisiana and is considered the capital of the Cajun Country. The history of the Cajun people started when the British forcibly removed them from their homes after the French and Indian War in the mid-1700s. Cajuns were originally known as Acadians. They settled along the Louisiana swamps and bayous after wandering for 10 years along the Atlantic seaboard. They established communities in Louisiana, which were ruled by France. They quickly adapted to their strange new environment and were soon harvesting crawfish, shrimp, crabs, and oysters. They built houses and boats (called pirogues) from cypress trees, trapped beaver and muskrat, grew rice, hot peppers, and okra. They developed a style of cooking that has become world-renowned, with savory, spicy meals that include crawfish pie, gumbo, jambalaya, and other delicious dishes. The Bayou state of Louisiana has more than 400,000 Cajuns. They have influenced the cultures of Lafayette and the state of Louisiana (Martin, 2007).

The Cajuns are known for the spicy cuisine and dancehall and festival music from the swamp country. The Louisiana Cajuns boast their own dialect known as Cajun French. The language is derived from the French spoken in 18th century Acadia (what is now Maine and the Canadian Maritimes), but also borrows heavily from Spanish, German, Portuguese, and the Haitian form of the French Creole language.

Several cultural organizations are represented in Louisiana, such as the Acadiana Symphony Orchestra and Conservatory of Music, Chorale Acadienne, Lafayette Ballet Theater and Dance Conservatory, Lafayette Concert Band, Performing Arts Society of Acadiana, Paul and Lulu Hillard University Art Museum, and the Acadiana Center of the Arts. In addition to the arts, Lafayette hosts three world-renowned events: The Festivals Acadian et Creoles, Festival International de Louisiane, and the second largest Mardi Gras celebration (Martin, 2007).

Festivals Acadiens et Creoles formed from many other local events. The oldest single component of this cooperative is the Louisiana Native and Contemporary Crafts Festival (then named the Louisiana Native Crafts Festival), first presented October 28, 1972. In 1977, the Lafayette Convention and Visitors Commission merged the Tribute to Cajun Music and the Bayou Food Festival. Together, these events became known as the Festivals Acadiens.

The Festival International de Louisiane is an annual music and arts festival held in Lafayette that celebrates the French regional heritage and its connection to the Francophone world. The festival was first held in 1987 and has become extremely popular, attracting musicians, artists, and craftsmen from around the world. The festival is held outdoors in downtown Lafayette the last full weekend in April. The festival is free to the public. In 2016 an estimated 400,000 people attended. The festival was voted the "Best World Music Festival" by "About.com" readers in their 2012 and 2013 "Readers' Choice Awards" (Martin, 2007).

The mission of the festival is to:

- Enrich the community with a celebration of its native cultures through the performing arts.
- Educate the public of the historical achievements and artistic expressions of related global cultures while developing an appreciation for the arts.
- Develop culture and tourism, as well as enhance economic development by expanding Louisiana's reputation as an arts center and a destination for artistic events.

Much of the traditional music by Cajun and Creole musicians utilizes French lyrics. Bi-lingual radio and television announcers underscore the prevalence of French speakers in the older, rural areas among both Cajun and Creole residents.

Lafayette is home to the state's second largest Mardi Gras celebration during carnival season, which includes eight parades consisting of floats and bands. The first parade, ten days before Mardi Gras, is the celebrity-led Krewe of Carnivale en Rio Parada featuring over 600 float riders. Parade royalty on Fat Tuesday includes King Gabriel and Queen Evangeline named for the hero and heroine of Henry Wadsworth Longfellow's epic poem *Evangeline*; and King Toussaint_L'Ouverture" and "Queen Suzanne Simonet, named for the great Haitian historical leaders. Mardi Gras parades have been an annual tradition in Lafayette since 1934.

Recent attendance on Mardi Gras day has been estimated as high as 250,000 by police spokespersons. The first formal Mardi Gras ball and parade in Lafayette dates to 1869. In 1897, King Attakapas, the first Lafayette Mardi Gras king, was crowned. He rode into town on a Southern Pacific train decorated to look like a royal throne and led the parade. After 1897, formal Mardi Gras parades and balls seemed to come and go until 1934 when the Southwest Louisiana Mardi Gras association was formed by representatives from civic and service organizations to ensure that Lafayette would always have a Mardi Gras celebration (Martin, 2007).

The University of Louisiana is in Lafayette and is embedded in the community and the culture of the area. The tag line for the university is, "We are Smart, Spirited, and Seeking Solutions." That one sentence conveys how the university and the culture are one. The phrase is not a lofty phrase intended to impress, but an authentic representation of the university culture. The phrase speaks to the desire of the university and the community to be inclusive. The attitude and beliefs of the community and university is "Everyone at the same table embracing each other and celebrating who they are." From this, a special culture and creative economy has developed (University of Louisiana, 2019).

REFERENCES

Buttrick, N. R., & Oishi, S. J. (2017). Inequality and Well-Being. *Current Opinion in Psychology*, *18*(December), 15–20. doi:10.1016/j.copsyc.2017.07.016 PMID:29221506

Cowen, T. (2018). *Stubborn Attachments: A Vision for a Society of Free, Prosperous, and Responsible Individuals*. Stripe Press.

Florida, R. (2011). *The Rise of the Creative Class.* Basic Books.

Kidd, D. (2012). Public Culture in America: A Review of Cultural Policy Debates. *The Journal of Arts*.

Mulcahy, K. V. (1982). The Rationale of Public Culture. In *Public Policy and the Arts*. Westview Press.

Martin, M. (2007). Historic Lafayette: An Illustrated History of Lafayette & Lafayette Parish. San Antonio, TX: Historical Publishing Network.

National Assembly of State Arts Agencies. (n.d.). State Arts Agency Creative Economy Initiatives. *National Assembly of State Arts Agencies.* Retrieved from, http://www.nasaa-arts.org/artworks/creativeeconomy_initiatives.html#ar

National Governors Association. (2009). *Arts and the Economy: Using Art and Culture to stimulate the economy.* National Governors Center. Retrieved from, http://www.nga.org/cms/center/publications?begin7736bde9-79fd-493d-be2b-0f62416085cd=180&end7736bde9-79fd-493d-be2b-0f62416085cd=189&pagesize7736bde9-79fd-493d-be2b-0f62416085cd=10&

National Governors Association. (2019). *Rural Prosperity Through The Arts & Creative Sector: A Rural Action Guide for Governors and States.* National Governors Association.

Texas Cultural Districts' Program (TXP). (2016). *Texas Cultural District Program: Indicators for Success.* Texas Cultural Districts' Program. http://www.arts.texas.gov/wp-content/uploads/2012/04/CulturalDistrict_MeasuringSuccess.pdf

Woodard, C. (2012). *American Nations: A History of Eleven Regional Cultures of North America.* Penguin Random House.

Chapter 5
Cluster Group Development

ABSTRACT

Cluster groups are those organizations or individuals who have similar businesses and relationships. Clusters usually form naturally and organically due to the nature of the economic activity or by disruptive leaders who see an opportunity. Regional and local economies grow and decline based on their ability to specialize in high-value industries and then evolve that specialization over time. Cluster groups aim to embrace advantages of productive, innovative, and creative mechanisms by sharing knowledge, infrastructure, resources, and suppliers. Successful cluster initiatives begin with a combination of data and analysis to identify and prioritize cluster opportunities in service of broader economic development goals. Local and regional leaders identify and prioritize potential cluster group opportunities from geographically proximate organizations in a certain field. Interdependence is complex, and it is important to have the understanding of how to design a cluster group. Cluster groups can be instrumental in developing the creative economy with their uniqueness. This chapter explores cluster group development.

INTRODUCTION

If you take a galaxy and try to make it bigger, it becomes a cluster of galaxies, not a galaxy. If you try to make it smaller than that, it seems to blow itself apart - Jeremiah P. Ostriker

DOI: 10.4018/978-1-7998-3416-8.ch005

It is best when cluster groups grow organically. Clusters are a way to understand what matters to specific environments with a goal of creating programs that achieve broader economic development goals, which might relate to overall job growth, innovation capacity, or economic inclusion. The appropriate method to identify and prioritize clusters is organic and morphs according to what a region is trying to accomplish by developing a cluster group.

In Fort Smith, Arkansas, a disruptive leader created a community festival called *The Unexpected*. This event brought international artists to Fort Smith to create public art. As of 2019, over 30 pieces of public art now exist. The festival is still a major event in Fort Smith. Something unexpected was born from the festival, and now Fort Smith has become a regional center for music. One art form has developed another, a music cluster, where musicians' across the country are locating and new venues for music have opened. This has given way for more disruptive leaders to create new businesses, and entrepreneurs are coming to Fort Smith for opportunities.

Cluster-based talent development strategies help employers to address specific skills and competencies needed in that cluster. Furthermore, these strategies enable universities, community colleges, and even the K-12 system to develop talent pipelines around in-demand occupations in the cluster. Firm learning is a foundational aspect of clusters, and non-credit classes may fulfill this (Donahue, Parilla & McDearman, 2018).

Developing Cluster Group Dynamism

Practitioners can examine at least four sources of interdependency in their regions: industry product, supply chains, occupations, and technological expertise. Moving from identification to prioritization, regional leaders can consider six factors to distinguish between many cluster opportunities (Donahue, Parilla, and McDearman, 2018).

- Specialization
- Composition of firms (e.g., one big firm, many small firms or a mixture of both)
- Development stage (potential, emerging, established, declining or re-establishing)
- Intensity of inter-firm dependence
- Reliance on complex knowledge

- Ability to create inclusive employment opportunities

Clusters may suffer from information gaps both internally and externally, and this may hinder their potential. Internally, cluster initiatives provide information and research to educate firms and other internal stakeholders about opportunities and priorities for shared action. Externally, evidence-based promotion of clusters can address information failures among firms and investors outside the cluster that may benefit from cluster dynamics (Donahue, Parilla, and McDearman, 2018).

Research and development activities within universities, other research institutions, and private sector firms may yield more impact if coordinated, which oftentimes requires overcoming different mandates, cultures, and business models between these actors. Cluster disruptors can help provide this coordination function. Infrastructure itself may be a critical precondition for cluster growth, such as a logistics facility or high-speed broadband connection. Interventions related to research commercialization or talent development may require physical investments, such as applied research labs or training facilities.

Finally, an identifiable physical presence can strengthen the cluster's brand identity. The final intervention in this framework is access to capital, or lack of it. Young firms, which research suggests are critical to driving both innovation and net job creation, need capital to grow. Yet, capital providers may suffer from information gaps that limit their ability to invest in clusters. Highly trained cluster disruptors may be able to overcome the information gaps (Donahue, Parilla & McDearman, 2018).

Cluster group analysis is a tool used to understand performance to economic development. Cluster analysis benchmarks clusters on the relative growth or decline of employment (National Governors Center, 2009). While employment metrics may not be an accurate assessment, a basic tenet of good economic development practice is that interventions should be organized around addressing the shared needs of groups of firms. This mindset enables regions to approach economic development not as a succession of reactive and opportunistic business attraction efforts, but rather as a series of strategic investments designed to spur self-reinforcing cycles of growth and development.

Small clusters such as the arts often lack industry classification and are hard to analyze. Traditional analyses often do not account for self-employment or nonprofit organizations. By not accounting for small clusters, not only is the impact of the creative sector underestimated, but also communities and states

Figure 1. Understanding Cluster Groups

miss the opportunity to help ignite the competitiveness of this significant industry. Cluster groups operating in the same community or a regional innovative and creative environment can effectively influence the growth of the economy. However, some are successful, others are not. Some do harm. The evolution of variables may influence the outcome. The variables may change and evolve leading to behavioral changes. Innovation and creativity are needed to create the dynamism that influences successful development of cluster groups. The absence or loss of this dynamism influences productivity, employment, sales, and exports. Cluster groups are affected by the business environment they operate in, the life cycle of the industry they belong to, and by worldwide competition, all of which have an influence on cluster group dynamics (Molina, Molina, & Garrigos, 2010).

The existence of cluster groups is important to regional development, but fundamentality it is their dynamics that contribute to a steady rise in regional income and in developing the creative economy. The dynamics of cluster groups is based on the evolution of cluster groups to the forces that drive the evolution. Many scholars see this as the life cycle going from birth, through growth and maturity, until their decline (Molina, Molina, & Garrigos, 2010). However, other scholars resort to the same variables used to analyze the evolution of an industrial sector, including the number of employees and companies, production, exports, and productivity (Russo, 2004). This may be limiting to a disruptive business. Most relevant factors for determining cluster group dynamism are the following: business creation, the number of workers, production, turnover, productivity, and exports. The variables with the strongest influence on cluster dynamics are those, which affect both the competitiveness of regions and the clusters themselves. The most important measurement are those businesses that continually measure inputs/outputs and invest in research and patents, thus contributing to the overall creative economy (Russo, 2004).

Marino, Marino and Garrigos (2010), determined that literature on cluster groups connects knowledge, creativity, and innovation to the variables that rise because of their dynamism. In addition, literature on knowledge, innovation, and intellectual capital connects the variables produced by cluster dynamics to a rise in regional income. Cluster groups have been the focus of a large body of research that defines a *cluster* as a "geographical proximate group of interconnected companies and associated institutions in a particular field, linked by commonalities and externalities" (Molina, Molina, & Garrigos, 2010). Scholars have documented many benefits of the firms that are part of the regions where they operate. The cluster concept is easy for economic development organizations to embrace. Built upon strategic ideas and illustrated with well-known examples, cluster development offers an enticing path to engage stakeholders with creditable science (Molina, Molina, & Garrigos, 2010).

Role of Cluster Groups

The widespread adoption of clusters as an organizing principle for economic development is a positive development. Clusters are simply the reality of how regional economies are organized. The concept can help local and regional economic development organizations build expertise that enables them to deliver relevant services to firms, and to strategically attract investments. Disruptive leaders need the investment opportunities to develop their ideas into reality and create a framework for understanding and organizing their concepts. Through cluster development, the more disruptive entrepreneurs that come together the more funding is available. The popularity of clusters stems from the idea that cluster initiatives bring about major investments aimed at eliminating the constraints for competitive advantage.

For all the compelling and widely accepted attention given to the concept of clusters over the past three decades, cluster initiatives in U.S. regions have, for the most part, failed to live up to their expected potential. Many regions market their clusters to attract businesses, rather than building robust local ecosystems to support the needs of existing firms in the cluster. In addition, many regions lack the fiscal and institutional capacity to sustain even well designed efforts for more than a few years. But most, believing that there are no alternatives to organizing an economic development strategy, diligently return to the drawing board every five years to try again (Molina, Molina, & Garrigos, 2010).

With an increase in global competition and outsourcing, the life cycle of cluster groups and their competitive advantage is a concern. Focus may be needed on working sub-groups that focus on who is joining and leaving the cluster group. Cluster groups have a four-stage life cycle: incubation, takeoff, maturity, and decline (Menzel & Forahal, 2009). Survival may depend on the ability to improve the knowledge base by establishing a permanent creativity and innovation incubator to improve the knowledge base (Spencer, at el, 2010).Consequently, the role of universities, research centers, and a forward-thinking disruptive leader act as beacons to attract others and key players in a creative and innovation incubator. Furthermore, the proximity of companies, non-profits and universities influences the introduction of creativity and innovation.

Research has determined there is evidence that a growing cluster group is characterized by higher rates of workforce mobility within the area designated for the cluster group (Power & Lundmark, 2009). Cluster groups can attract investment and talent, export goods, services and knowledge, encourage the creation of enterprises, attract risk capital, and increase industrial production and related activities. In addition, they help knowledge and labor to circulate around the local environment. By promoting competitiveness, they stimulate new enterprises and innovation capacity that brings about long-term sustainability of growth and prosperity.

Creativity and innovation can be stronger within an environment of cluster groups, because the workforce will be more motivated and passionate with other sectors. However, strengthening communities or region's creativity and innovative environment may not be enough for improving the dynamism of its cluster groups. Some clusters will be stronger than others naturally; therefore strengthening the environment may not matter. Cluster groups evolve overtime and this evolution goes through various stages. Many factors determine the strength of the cluster groups. However, by boasting the creativity and innovation of the community or region, it may enable the development of emerging sectors, but it is not a guarantee to the long-term stability of the cluster groups already in existence (Marino, Marino and Garrigos, 2010).

Local and regional economic development are beginning to demand effective specialization that is driven by innovation, entrepreneurship, and strong institutions. Small and niche industries are more specialized by function and less specialized by industry. However, mergers and acquisitions have concentrated headquarter functions of large-scale industry into a few global cities, which have left mid-size cities and small local areas in need to develop a different kind of economy based on niche and specialized industries.

The development of ideas, products, and processes that improve productivity are considered innovation. Ten years ago, many felt that innovation and entrepreneurship was in decline, and did not match previous decades (Marino, Marino and Garrigos, 2010). However, the national view is that new entrepreneurship is becoming increasingly concentrated in regional areas (micropolitan), allowing them to replenish their economies with smaller cities and rural towns making them more dynamic (DeVol and Wisecarver, 2018). Local institutions are moldable, creating quality institutions with uniquely capable disruptive leaders leading this effort. These disruptive leaders can lead a local or regional group to shared economic growth.

Knowledge-Based Cluster Groups

Knowledge is defined as a base of an economic capacity to create new ideas, thoughts, processes, products; and by converting these new ideas, thoughts, processes and products to economic value; it improves the local or regional economy and generates wealth (Huggins et al, 2008). The idea that knowledge is a requirement for creativity and innovation is based on the theories of geographical business groupings and intellectual capital. The success of a community or region is based on the skill of its workforce and the ability to expand and create knowledge. The capacity to create intellectual capital is necessary for competitiveness. Research has always stressed that human capital is the most important component for the intellectual wealth of a nation. The renewal of structural capital assets come from citizens who codify their knowledge in the country's systems and processes. When this knowledge is combined with research and development, the climate is ripe for cluster development. Therefore, knowledge is the key asset for community and regional economic growth. Moreover, knowledge accumulated is transferred from one person to another while the knowledge of a specific sector becomes common knowledge in the cluster (Power & Lundmark, 2004).

Giving a cluster group definition is not a simple task. Often success is determined not on external knowledge, but on specific, internal knowledge that is not to be shared with others. (This is the importance of patents and copyrights, to protect intellectual capital.) The collective establishment of cluster-specific institutions are also responsible for successful cluster emergence. Moreover, firms located in cluster groups seem to be more competitive and innovative. Performance and success come from the benefits of proximity to other related organizations that open access to knowledge, collective resources, and opportunities of co-operation (Enright, 2003).

Local and regional governments have promoted economic development by increasing the productivity and competitiveness of firms in an area. Some have upgraded or developed clusters artificially to ignite economic development. These coordinated measures strategically support the development of regional industrial sectors. In addition, measures support research and development along with educational organizations with an international perspective (Feldman et al, 2005). Local and regional politicians evaluate their coordinated efforts to upgrade and development cluster groups by how many knowledge-based organizations have been established in the area during their efforts.

Organizations may be located simply because of an increase in supply and business space, or it might just be a trend in the overall region. The proper evaluation is the proportion of knowledge-based organizations settling in the district based on a control group. In order to assess whether the policy and upgrade of development was successful in creating a cluster group, we may have to compare the increase in the proportion of knowledge-based firms in the area by analyzing specific control groups. However, using a control group can only be feasible if the treated group and the control groups were similar before.

Common Mistakes

Growing a cluster group is not a goal. It is best when cluster groups grow organically. Clusters are a way to understand what matters to specific environments with a goal of creating programs that achieve broader economic development goals, which might relate to overall job growth, innovation capacity, or economic inclusion. The appropriate method to identify and prioritize clusters is organic and morphs according to what a region is trying to accomplish by developing a cluster group. If a region's goal involves overall job growth, it might identify clusters based on supply chains in order to understand gaps and create a more targeted entrepreneurship or business attraction effort. If that same region instead adopted a goal related to inclusive growth, it might instead identify clusters based on occupational similarities in order to create a better workforce development system (Donahue, Parilla & McDearman, 2018). A clear understanding of the end goal is also a prerequisite for deciding which clusters to prioritize. Many regions contain a variety of clusters.

There is no scientific answer as to whether it is better to focus on growing an emerging, high-wage industry or reviving an older, larger, and relatively low-wage industry. The answer is entirely contingent on the region's broader goals. When regional and state leaders do not have a clear purpose for why they are investing in clusters, they tend to fall victim to the tendency to create a new strategy based on different "trendy" clusters that change every five years. Based on this philosophy, there is an inconsistency when making investments or gaining the deep industry knowledge that make cluster efforts effective (Donahue, Parilla & McDearman, 2018).

As stated before, most regions assume that the "right" clusters can be identified through analysis of employment and output data. Cluster identification is more art than science. One key problem is that clusters involve complex cross-discipline relationships that extend both vertically and horizontally, many regions fail to escape the confines of hierarchical groups. For understanding the complex linkages between firms and sectors, there is no substitute for on-the-ground business intelligence and academic research (Donahue, Parilla & McDearman, 2018).

Most regions have a difficult time prioritizing potential clusters, because they want a diversified economy. However, political pressure is the biggest issue. This can take the form of "bottom-up" pressure from major employers or industry groups exerting influence on the selection process (out of concern that being left out will deprive them of public resources or attention), or "top-down" pressure from political leaders that may fear the reaction of those firms, or may have ulterior motives for including certain clusters. The outcome is that most regions claim six to eight industries in which they have some specialization as priorities or targets. These targets are often understood to be clusters, though usually most of them are not. The target industries are either too small to truly exhibit cluster dynamics or are so broad as to be meaningless to the firms that are purportedly part of them. Specialized manufacturing is a great example.

CONCLUSION

In theory, there is little downside to having many targets. Economic development organizations should have a broad understanding of the local economy, and the marginal cost of doing marketing for one additional industry is small. The danger is that, after publicly committing to targeting six to eight industries, economic development organizations often are limited in how they distribute funding. This theory drains resources needed to more effectively develop cluster groups. Furthermore, resource constraints prevent practitioners from gaining an adequate understanding of any one-cluster group or making investments large enough to change the strategic initiative of an existing cluster group. Identifying clusters that can form the basis of an effective strategy requires moving beyond targets and picking one or two specific priorities.

As stated throughout this chapter, cluster groups cannot be created by force of will, they must evolve organically. Virtually every successful cluster has emerged from creative and entrepreneurial activity that relates to some strength in the region. Mistaken assumptions that economic development strategy must revolve around clusters could give measurement errors and a false sense of strength that can lead local and regional leaders to chase fads in which they have no real specialization or asset base. The concept of clusters is flexible enough that nearly any region that begins with clusters as the predetermined foundation of a strategy can easily stretch the definition until several plausible examples emerge. Nevertheless, not every group of similar firms is a cluster. By failing to distinguish between the two, regions end up pursuing unrealistic and expensive cluster initiatives without considering more efficient and effective non-cluster interventions.

CASE STUDIES

The following case studies are examples of one cluster group that failed. The textile industry in Maine virtually was lost due to a lack of innovation, bowing to union demands, and lack of adaptation to a new era of business, which is a sign of no disruptiveness. This could have been a long-term creative economy initiative, but died in the inability to change. The second cluster group, the ag-tech business, started in St. Louis in 1859 around 40 years after the textile industry started in Maine. Through disruptive leadership, it has continued to grow, and with the organic development of a cluster group, this industry is more vibrant today than in any period of its history.

Case Study 1: The Textile Industry, Maine

The state of Maine has a rich history in the textile industry. In its heyday, Maine was the primary powerhouse behind textile industrialization in the United States. At the start of the 1820s, cotton textile mills made their way from Massachusetts to Maine. The largest site for cotton manufacturing was Lewiston, home to the original Bates Mill Manufacturing Company, which was located on the Androscoggin River. However, due to the rising popularity of textile production overseas and unionization, Maine's textile industry over a period it was decimated.

Lewiston was one of the first factory towns created on the Waltham-Lowell system - a labor and production model used frequently in the early years of America's textile industry. Under this popular model, all aspects of mass production could be completed in a single plant, allowing for complete control. Mill complexes were frequently established on rivers and waterfalls, which served as a main source of power. Lewiston Falls provided Bates Mill most of its energy. Although Lewiston was the largest cluster, it was not the only one. Cluster groups of cities on major rivers were also main players of the textile industry. The towns of Biddeford, Saco, Augusta, Waterville, and Brunswick were all part of the textile cluster group. The group in Biddeford, Saco and Brunswick supplied cloth that was well known for its unique plaids and colored material, while the Waterville group supplied military uniforms. Each had a niche market within the cluster group.

Preceding the Civil War, Maine textile mills primarily relied on farm girls from the surrounding area for labor. Upon the start of the Civil War, most New England mills started selling their cotton stock, thinking the civil war would only last only 90 days. Instead, Benjamin Bates bought as much cotton as he could find (despite the skyrocketing prices) and became the main supplier of Union textiles during the 4-year war. Maine was the primary supplier to the Union Army, supplying uniforms and blankets. Throughout the Civil War and both World Wars, the Bates Manufacturing Company continued to weave fine quality products with bedspreads being the focus for the past 50 years.

In the years following the Civil War, the industry grew, and more workers were needed. During this time immigrants flocked to the mills, providing them with a steady stream of employees. A high percentage of these later workers were French Canadians, who migrated down from Quebec and New Brunswick specifically to work in the mills. Immigration was so common that by the mid-20th century, 30% of Maine's population was made up of

Franco-Americans. The towns of Lewiston, Biddeford and Saco still hold a large Franco-American population. Many of the current Bates workers are of Franco-American heritage, having ancestors who started their American lives as mill workers.

Maine's textile industry remained vibrant for over 100 years. As late as 1948, Maine mills employed over 28,000 people. As unions gained popularity, many of the mills moved to southern right-to-work states. Maine's textile industry began to look bleak. Textile production moved overseas, sadly forcing many American manufacturers to close their doors, unable to survive the economic pressures. The original Bates Mill was no exception, shutting down in 2001, leaving thousands of workers without jobs, and many abandoned buildings that eventually went into decay. After the Bates Mill shut down, the others soon followed (Maine History, 2017).

Gone was the Maine textile cluster group. However, thanks to the passionate efforts of the Maine Heritage Weavers, the Bates name was able to survive, and currently Bates bedspreads, blankets, and accessories are being made today by 18 employees. The current crew is in Monmouth, Maine (about 20 minutes north of Lewiston). Maine Heritage Weavers proudly carries on the traditions of weaving the high-quality standards of the original bedspreads. Today the Bates Mill Store is a family-owned retailer located alongside the Maine Heritage Weavers (Bates Mill Store, 2017).

Most of the mill buildings are in decay, some are being demolished, and some are being renovated for office space and apartments. Today there are 117 textile companies listed in Maine, but most of these sell yarn, canvas bags, and boating materials.

What turned a textile cluster group employing over 28,000 people into a group of 18 people? Many feel that with the advent of unionization, and labor demands and cost drove the business an unstainable level. With the need for equipment upgrades plus material and transportation costs, companies could lower their cost and realize greater profits by going overseas. Others sensing that the mills would always be there, an apathy that change was not needed, caused the collapse. Perhaps it was the life cycle of this cluster group simply just ended. Many people left the state to find work elsewhere. The industry has never recovered.

Cluster initiatives need not be abandoned, but they do need a rethinking. With rigorous planning, large investments, and significant industry engagement cluster-based economic development can be transformed, as this case study indicates. Local, regional, and state leaders need to be focused on the level of commitment—both institutional and financial—that transformative cluster initiatives require and weigh that approach against many other evidence-based, industry-relevant interventions that can support economic growth and development.

This next case study can help provide insights in the importance of disruptive leaders creating a new cluster that drives economic development in an urban core. By developing the toolkits for business development, civic and university support, and championed by government leaders they revitalized a dying city.

Case Study 2: AgTech Cluster Group in St. Louis, Missouri

Agriculture technology has been a key industry in St. Louis since 1859, when the Missouri Botanical Gardens was established. St. Louis is still a global center of plant research today, even though it took a series of economic disruptions. Today it is now a recognized agtech cluster, related to life sciences, and has been instrumental in the area's economic development. The history of the region presents many economic struggles: defense cutbacks at McDonnell Douglas, a lost TWA hub, the acquisition of Anheuser-Busch, closure of the Ford and Chrysler manufacturing plants, and the layoff of Pfizer employees. The losses created a major shift in economic development strategy. Through disruptive leadership and innovation ideals a cluster group was formed.

Today St. Louis fosters local innovation-based startups that have led to the development of a bioscience cluster group. Through this cluster group, St. Louis has experienced a regional economic renewal. Recently from this bioscience cluster group, an agtech cluster group has emerged as an equally important economic development opportunity in the region. The region's agtech strategy borrows from its proven approach to the life sciences, by customizing the specific needs of the cluster group. This cluster was created from capital investment, facilities, talent, and networks for innovative firms, coupled with robust and targeted efforts to attract foreign investment (Donahue, 2018).

The St. Louis agtech cluster group has been principally defined by the handful of key entities at its core: multinational firms such as Monsanto and Bunge, as well as institutions like the Danforth Center, the Missouri Botanical Garden, and Washington University (along with other regional universities, including the University of Missouri in Columbia). When the cluster was originally conceived, these organizations defined the cluster group, which made it dominated by large industry and lacking in an entrepreneurial culture. Today, the cluster has evolved from this original core in terms of both size and composition.

While its exact size is somewhat debatable, what is clear is that the cluster group has shifted in terms of its structure and industry mix. Small organizations are now the base of the cluster group. There are close to 300 startups in the biosciences overall, and in the five years from 2010 to 2014, approximately 11 new agtech companies were founded in the region each year. Researchers believe that industry trends will continue to make the cluster increasingly entrepreneurial. Today's bioscience industry is "almost unrecognizable" because technological shifts have opened new paths to markets, such as gene editing. Technology examples include growing opportunities for non-biology tech applications, such as "precision ag" that use sensors in fields and technology related to traceability in the food chain (Donahue, 2018).

The agtech cluster group is becoming defined as a knowledge-based cluster group, which takes the form of 800-plant science Ph.D.'s (anecdotally, the highest concentration in the world). This academic concentration reflects a structural shift in the industry. In 2000, the cluster was dominated by manufacturing operations, and about 10% of jobs (2,300 jobs) were in research laboratories. In 2015, it was estimated that the region had nearly twice as many jobs in research labs (4,500 jobs). The emphasis on the cluster's knowledge base also reflects the fact that the local industry is increasingly characterized by labor market fluidity, spinoffs from research labs, and cross-sector research (Donahue, 2018).

The cluster group continually branches out from its innovative and creative core in several important ways. The first is incorporating farmers (the end users of agtech products) and the grower associations that represent the farmers. This builds an understanding of the state's strengths in agriculture (an $88 billion industry supporting over 350,000 jobs–are highly relevant to the cluster). The cluster group is working to connect organizations with the grower associations in order to create a network of farmers that would pilot local innovations. The cluster also incorporates finance, insurance, and law firms (Donahue, 2018).

Had the region relied on standard methodologies to identify its clusters, agtech may not have emerged. Further, agtech is not heavily represented among the region's largest firms–of the 20 largest, Monsanto (12th) is the only one in the bioscience sector. No other agtech firms, even headquarters operations, come close. However, several key firms in adjacent industries, such as InBev and Nestle, pay substantial attention to agriculture and food technologies. Even if the basic contours of the cluster had been identified, those contours may not have captured key characteristics of the cluster that have come to shape the region's interventions, such as its connections with the life sciences, the overlap with tech fields, and its rapidly evolving entrepreneurial base (Donahue, 2018).

The agtech cluster and biosciences overall has remained a regional economic development priority for nearly two decades despite the lack of obvious distinction or progress on measures such as size, growth, and specialization. With total biosciences employment of 15,000 of which agtech accounts for less than half and somewhere between 50 and 400 agtech firms, the industry is far smaller than other potential priorities. The innovative startups generated by the agtech industry are helping St. Louis address the concerns about its large industry economy (Donahue, 2018).

The Danforth Center was the physical hub of this innovation. Its researchers are given 20% of their time to commercialize their research and have created 60 patents. In addition, universities in Missouri are primarily focused on biosciences. They spent $845 million on related research in 2014 (of which 10% was for plant sciences), accounting for 83% of all academic research in the state (compared to a national average of 61%). However, an equally important driver of innovation is industry scientists and executives (many from Monsanto) that start their own firms (State of Missouri, 2018).

This is injecting dynamism into the regional economy. Given the R&D emphasis of the agtech industry and the presence of several large headquarters operations in the region, it is no surprise that jobs in the industry pay significantly more than the regional average. The Danforth Center, for instance, have an average salary of $80,000, compared to a regional average of about $52,000. (Statewide, bioscience wages overall are approximately $72,000 compared to state average of $45,000.) This is an important feature for any region, but is especially important in St. Louis, given that it ranks in the bottom third of the 100 largest metros for wage growth over the past decade (Donahue, 2018).

Two key characteristics differentiate the agtech cluster effort in St. Louis. The first is that much of the work is being done by organizations that have considerable industry expertise. It is important to approach cluster group development with industry expertise, technical expertise, business expertise and investor savvy. The second key characteristic is the region's persistent, patient, long-term commitment to building the cluster. The industry has, to varying degrees, been a focus in the region for nearly 20 years, even though the industry has not posted major job growth numbers that attract economic development organizations. In addition, the Danforth Foundation closed its doors in 2011, and the federal government's commitment to local and regional economic development is in question. This could be a key challenge for the region going forward, and the cluster group may have to investigate new sources of funding to reach its potential.

REFERENCES

Bates Mill Store. (2017). History of Bates Mill. *Bates Mill Store*. Retrieved from, https://www.batesmillstore.com/blogs/news/139104199-maines-rich-textile-history

DeVol, R., & Wisecarver, S.J. (2018). *Micropolitan Success Stories from the Heartland.* The Walton Family Foundation.

Donahue, Parilla, & McDearman. (2018). *Rethinking Cluster Initiatives.* Metropolitan Policy Program, Brooking Institute.

Enright, M. J. (2003). *Regional Clusters: What We Know and What We Should Know*. Springer.

Essig, L. (2014). Arts Incubators: A Typology. *The Journal of Arts Management, Law, and Society*, *44*(3), 169–180. doi:10.1080/10632921.2014.936076

Menzel, M. P., & Fornahal, D. (2009). Cluster life cycles-dimensions and rationales of cluster evolution. *Industrial and Corporate Change*, *19*(1), 205–238. doi:10.1093/icc/dtp036

Molina, B. (2018). Stephen Hawking Warns that AI, "Superhuman" Could Wipe Humanity in Posthumous Book. *USA Today*. Retrieved from, https://www.usatoday.com/story/news/nation-now/2018/10/15/stephen-hawking-warns-superhumans-ai-posthumous-book/1645963002/, web.

Power, D., & Lundmark, M. (2004). Working through Knowledge Pools: Labor Market Dynamics, the Transference of Knowledge and Ideas, and Industrial Clusters. Department of Social and Exonomic Geography, Uppsala University of Sweden.

Russo, M.V. (2003). The Emergence of Sustainable Industries: Building on Natural Capital,. *Strategic Management Journal, 24*, 317-331. Doi:10.1002mj.298

Spencer, G., Vinodrai, T., Gertler, M., & Wolfe, D. (2010, July). Do Clusters Make a Difference: Defining and Assessing their Economic Performance. *Regional Studies*, *44*(6), 697–715. doi:10.1080/00343400903107736

State of Maine. (2018). *The History of the Textile Industry in Maine*. State of Maine, Maine Memory. Retrieved from, https://www.mainememory.net/sitebuilder/site/905/page/1316/display?page=5

State of Missouri. (2019). *Global AgTech Leader*. Missouri Partnerships, State of Missouri. Retrieved from, https://www.missouripartnership.com/industry-strengths/global-agtech-leader/

Chapter 6
Toolkits, Framing, and Advisory Councils

ABSTRACT

The most successful groups that survived change over the long term have been able to constantly reposition themselves; rein inventing and staying economicallyfocused are those who have successfully developed and launched toolkits. These groups constantly "reframe" and have active advisory councils. A toolkit is a set of resources and skill development tools to be used together for a particular purpose. The goal is to provide access to information or knowledge needed to succeed in certain areas. To "frame and reframe "is a technique to make sense of how a group or organization works effectively. This chapter explores toolkits, framing, and advisory councils.

INTRODUCTION

The tools and technologies we've developed are really the first few drops of water in the vast ocean of what all I can do- Fei-Fei Li

Is important to understand how a group or organization is organized to work at optimum performance. If not at optimum performance, the organization needs change to reach its goals and achieve success. Often this is achieved with outside expert advice. Advisory councils often can point out glaring mistakes or see opportunities that those in the daily operations are too close to the group or organization to see.

DOI: 10.4018/978-1-7998-3416-8.ch006

In development and launching of toolkits, industry and community experts are needed for mentoring. Mentors advise and guide. The three C's of mentorship are consultant, counselor and cheerleader. Mentors share information about their own career paths or businesses. In addition, they provide guidance, motivation, emotional support and role modeling. Mentors often provide a rich learning experience for the mentee. To help entrepreneurs develop the skills sets to succeed the toolkits offer the basic skills but mentors provide first hand practical knowledge.

After interviewing state agencies who are, all on the forefront of developing their creative economies it became apparent that the most successful groups were all disruptive leaders who had very clear goals and strategies to be successful. They had high energy and heightened creativity. Each group had something in common. They were collaborating with other groups, and they had developed toolkits to teach the skills needed to succeed in entrepreneurial opportunities. In addition, groups all had mentors and advisory councils working hard to develop launch and teach the toolkits.

Toolkits

The term *toolkit* has various meanings. Most definitions state that toolkit is usually a set of documents, such as informational summaries and form letters that we use to inform others about a topic of interest. The tools are designed to be used together or for a particular purpose. Often the toolkit provides a fixed set of procedures, guidelines, and criteria to establish a desired outcome and prevent oversights (Harper Collins, 2014). Toolkits provide an open-ended flexible and low-cost approach to learning new skills.

When engaging the expertise of business, government and the non-profit community experts create a rich and meaningful learning environment. The ability to create interesting learning material designed by experts creates heightened creativity. Toolkits along with mentoring creates long-term success. The two case studies in the chapter are examples of two disruptive communities who have developed and re-developed toolkits that have been instrumental in their long-term success.

To develop a business plan, the toolkit gives a framework to explore an idea and create a model that will fulfill ones hopes, dreams and motivations. In the creative economy, the toolkit helps lead an organization in finding information and advice together with a series of activities that explore and develop the basic idea, build the story for the organization, and develop a business plan. The organization members will be able to fully understand what they must to do to make their idea work, how the customer will benefit from the organization's products or services, and most of all, how the organization can build a sustainable organization.

In a rapidly changing world, opportunities are many but so are the risks. To capture an opportunity it may mean taking a risks, therefore, creatively solving problems could lead to making ideas happen and alleviating that risks. Disruptive leadership with heightened creativity and clear focus, as well as passion and persistence are vital for success. Traditional methods of developing a business plan, engaging with bankers and bank managers, gathering support from business agencies, and having help from family and friends may not be enough. In a modern world of turbulence, an approach to draw out creative skills and decision-making help to design a vastly different approach in business planning. Workforce development and early-stage risk capital along with entrepreneurial support is a new and different approach (Oxford, 2018).

A toolkit designed for the creative economy may have a series of handbooks designed to lead the organization through a logical path, from scoping your idea through to practical considerations of marketing and finance. Creating a model or visual representation of reality helps to determine and explore various aspects of an organization and to better understand and predict the future. By modeling and performing activities, ideas can generate products or services that are wanted and needed. In addition, a deep understanding allows the creation of values and vision based on evidence modeling, customer wants and needs, relationship building, marketing, structure, human resource needs, political parameters (both internally and externally), and the development of critical needs. Disruptive leaders understand this, and will seek the help to be successful.

Framing

Framing is a disruptive process; it provides a detailed look at the overall environment and resources needed for sustainable results. Creating a successful story is fundamental and self-disruptive leaders can create an overall vision and look to predict the future of the organization. Disruptive leaders are constantly seeing what others are not. Disruptive leaders and organizations are constantly planning and executing those plans daily. Simply put, the best disruptive ideas are an organization's ability to implement them (Furth,

2018). The workflow processes will determine their own unique strategic accountability.

Defining the vision, beliefs, and values creates the story an organization needs to tell and builds the symbolic framework in which the entire organization is built. The symbolic frame creates what is most important and the meaning of every activity. If you do not build a solid symbolic frame, every event and action will have multiple interpretations, and the organization will lack unity. When facing uncertainty and ambiguity, people create symbols and stories to resolve confusion, find direction and hope to keep faith in their ideals. These symbols and stories weave a tapestry that defines the heroes, rituals and ceremonies that provide a stable force in times of turbulence. Culture then forms from the united efforts and the desire to reach goals. This rich tapestry from the symbolic framework defines the organization's culture (Bolman & Deal, 2008).

Stories and visions communicate the unconscious and help an organization strengthen and intensify. Values determine what an organization believes, what is worthy of esteem and commitment. Values determine the overall character and help employees and customers see what makes an organization special. "Vision turns an organization's core ideology or sense of purpose, into an image of the future", (Bolman & Deal, 2008, pp254-256).

An organization's culture is usually built over time when group members develop values, beliefs, practices, activities, and symbols that define the daily life of the organization. The heroes and heroines are the role models that determine the ceremonies and rituals that bring cohesiveness, spirit and passion. Peak performance emerges when an organization has a soul worth fighting for. Disruptive organizations do not have the luxury to build culture over time; the soul of the organization develops on a rapid scale.

Disruptive organizations may not have all the above attributes of most organizations; they have their own traits. They often start with high growth from the beginning; because of this growth, they need alternate funding, cash flow, and agility. For this reason, they need to quickly frame and define who they are. By performing activities, you are testing different scenarios to ensure a sustainable organization. In doing this, you are connecting to a wider environment, and your ideas may be changing rapidly and evolving. This change and evolution will allow the organization to continually check the viability of their ideas and changes in the marketplace.

Disruptive leaders know the importance of strategic planning. Developing toolkits through disruption keeps entrepreneurs from falling into two mindsets, (Furth, 2018). Furth calls the first one "creative visionaries". These leaders are forward thinking, analytical, and enjoy the creative mindset, but they bore easily by details. They tend to shift direction, which keeps them from implementing. They are the dreamers who need a good executer, a counterbalance to their planning and plotting. The second are the "doers". These leaders become so obsessed with the daily operations of their businesses that they cannot vision the future. This creates missed opportunities and can cause confusion (Furth, 2018).

A disruptive leader starts with a good strategic plan for turning their idea into a business idea, and they go through various stages:

- Fantasy
- Create Vision
- Testing/Research
- Developing Structure

The first stage *fantasy* is the moment of seeing a better way, how to improve something, and having an idea of creating something new. That moment of saying: "Wouldn't it be great if…", "I've got this idea…," or "Would it be better if…" This is the fantasy stage when we have an idea that we think is worth exploring and developing further.

Then you start to create a vision. At this stage, things become clearer, you start to think about what you want to achieve, what your organization will offer, what customers or clients you can attract, and how to go about forming the result of the vision. Further research might still be needed to develop the idea; including knowing if, there is a need or demand for it.

Next, you are testing your idea to see if it could be a sustainable business, by doing activities you are creating an animated vision for the future. You are considering all aspects of your vision, such as partners, finance, delivery, and marketplace (Bolman & Deal, 2008).

At this stage, developing the structure of the organization will create rationality. The development of the structural frame determines how to reach goals and objectives, monitor performance, workforce development, and creative problem solving. The first step of organizational structure is the development of coordination and control through vertical or lateral coordination. Vertical coordination exists when higher levels of an organization coordinate and control the work of the workplace through authority, rules, and policies. Lateral coordination is when behavior is untouched by commands, rules, and systems. Lateral coordination is less formal and more flexible meaning they are simpler and quicker. In designing a structure, leaders determine a set of options to apply resources and to allocate workload. The purpose of the structure is to design an environment with the talent of the workforce to achieve the desired outcomes (Bolman & Deal, 2008).

However, great disruptive leaders fully understand that often the difference between success and failure is the team they put together, and the ability to hire and keep talented individuals. Their ability to develop disruptive leaders is paramount to their success. By surrounding themselves with talented, likeminded individuals, a deep trust develops, that creates high performing teams. This was evident in the case study, "David Shaw and Idexx", Shaw being a disruptive leader, created a team of disruptive leaders, who all had a deep trust of each other and commitment to the organization. From this high performance, teams spun off and led to Idexx's success.

The organization's core functions build the structure. Strategic decisions are future oriented, concerned with long-term direction (Mintzberg, 1994). A variety of goals are considered as part of the short- and long-term strategic plan. This is referred to as the social architecture of work. If the structural frame is overlooked, an organization may misdirect resources and time. Structural flaws often create high turnover and wastes money and resources. "However, understanding the complexity and variety of design possibilities can help create prototypes that work for, rather than against, both people and collective purpose." (Bolman & Deal, 2008).

People are an organization's most important asset. People's skills, attitudes, energy, and commitment determine the success of an organization. Additionally, organizations exist to serve human needs and people. Organizations need ideas, energy, and talent. People need careers, salaries, and opportunity. When the structure or systems are weak, both the people and organization will suffer. A good structure and system promotes satisfying and meaningful work.

With global competition, turbulence, and rapid change, the need is greater than any time before for heightened creativity. An organization may need to have specific training to compete and thrive. Evidence exists that in investing in professional development, hiring a talented, motivated, and highly skilled workforce gives an organization a competitive advantage in the modern world (Boland & Deal, 2008).

It is important to include in the toolkit a guide on developing a human resource philosophy that outlines the organizations core beliefs on leading people. First step is developing a shared philosophy for leading people. Second, is a commitment to hire the right people, understand the needs, be selective, build a good compensation package, promote within, invest in life-long learning, and share the wealth. Third, adopt diversity and inclusion.

Fourth, provide support, encourage autonomy, foster teams, and encourage participation.

When people find meaningful work and enjoy what they are doing, their work is enhanced, they are satisfied. Organizational effectiveness equates to the quality of interpersonal and intrapersonal relationships. "By developing a human resource psychology, organizations can create a fully engaged workforce that supports working as a fundamental human act that is the birthright of each person," (Blustein, 2006, p. 291).

All organizations in conception, and as they grow, have internal and external political issues that need to be framed and a strategy put in place to handle the political issues effectively. To handle the political issue effectively, you must consider all stakeholders. Organizations of all sizes are coalitions of diverse individuals with specific interests. Coalition members have long-standing different values, beliefs, interests, and perceptions of reality. Members will look at resource allocation differently, which may cause conflict or a jockeying for power.

All stakeholders will form specific alliances with common interests. Recognizing individual and group needs is important, but at the same time having a deep understanding of the overall need to ensure that resource allocation is based on reaching goals and not political power grabs. Power is not bad, it is a way of life, but it is important to know how to mobilize power to reach goals and build alliances. An over-bounded system of power is highly concentrated, and everything is highly regulated. Whereas, an under-bounded system has less power and it is loosely controlled, where open conflict is encouraged. The challenge is to recognize and manage conflict and build successful relationships (Bolman & Deal, 2008).

In establishing traditional organizations, legitimate power is controlled by those in authority who set goals, design, and structure. In the modern world, the political frame creates organizations that are coalitions composed of individuals with diverse interests who share resources in an environment of turbulence. This diversity creates an environment that puts power and conflict central in decision-making. When power and conflict is central in decision making, then leaders must have to determine how communication is distributed within this environment; informal or formal. Furthermore, it is important to develop a communication plan to handle issues both externally and internally and develop strategies for likely and unlikely issues that may occur.

Many new organizations let other entities (consultants) build their external relationships, or they are effective at building relationships in the beginning but fail to continue to nurse those relationships. To build political influence, organizations must identify the relevant relationships, assess who might be difficult to get along with, and develop links and communication plans. Organizations need allies or friends to effectively get things done and goals met.

Advisory Council

You may establish an advisory council to obtain input, direction, and buy-in from the creative industry businesses in your region. An advisory council provides strategic advice to the organization, in an informal nature. The council provides support and guidance to leaders and an organization's board of directors. A new entrepreneur can use an advisory council to network, weather challenges, build resources, and find opportunities. The advisory council's role is to coach, have alignment with the organization, have industry knowledge, have passion about the goals and purpose of the organization, and be action focused in helping the organization reach their goals. Communities working to develop their creative economy will benefit in having a diverse skill group of individuals who are committed to helping new organizations find their way. They should be able to join advisory councils, work with toolkits to develop organizational frames, and use case studies for examples of learning. These are key people who drive short- and long-term results.

CONCLUSION

Disruptive leaders are ambitious but they are not blind to what is needed to be successful. They have high egos, but are able to put egos aside to be strategic and successful. They are all highly intelligent and understand the importance of have talented and skilled individuals helping them to succeed. They create with training, education and frame disruptive organizations. Communities are able to do the same, the communities that are able to continually re-frame, have long-term success. When communities become disruptive, they create a vibrant creative economy.

CASE STUDIES

A case study is a research technique used to study an individual, group, or organization to provide detailed analysis. Case studies feature real entrepreneurs who have used the worksheets and exercises contained in the toolkit to successfully shape their business. They include commercial companies as well as social businesses working in a range of creative fields such as fashion, jewelry, technology, product design, festivals, and creative hubs. When developing toolkits and organizational frames, it is important to develop case studies.

Case study is a detailed analysis of relevant information or issues. When developing a case study, you should identify at least five facts or issues. Highlight the important work, facts, or issues that have been overcome or need to be worked on. The case study should be an example or illustration of a theory or concept. They can be explanatory and focus on questions or a phenomenon.

The following case studies are excellent examples of disruptive leaders who have develop disruptive organizations operating within the creative economy and have influenced two communities from the beginning of their inception to today. Each of these communities dared to change and rethink their environments; and they did so over time. Both Huntsville, Alabama and Greensville, South Carolina have had active community advisors, disruptive local government, that have created toolkits, and constantly were able to frame and reframe their communities. Entrepreneurial disruptors understand the need for collaboration, advice, and the tools available for their success.

Case Study 1: Huntsville, Alabama

In 1805, a Revolutionary War veteran by the name of John Hunt moved from Tennessee to what is now known as Huntsville, Alabama, when Alabama was still a portion of the Mississippi Territory that the Indians called Ah-la-bama. John Hunt built a log cabin in the beautiful wooded valley just above the “Big Spring” thus founding the town that would bear his name. Other pioneers, attracted by the rich bottomlands, also settled around the “Big Spring” making it a thriving community. On December 13, 1808, a proclamation of Governor Robert Williams of the Mississippi Territory created Madison County. In 1819, Alabama was made a state, and Huntsville was chosen as the first Capital (NASA, 2018).

The Civil War and Reconstruction period brought hard times to the people of the area. By the turn of the twentieth century, industry was emphasized, and the scars of the Civil War began to heal. Huntsville set the pace by opening the first textile mill in Alabama. In all, ten textile mills were in Madison County. Sometime after WW, I, Huntsville expanded, but industry declined during the depression in the 1930s. During this period, Huntsville became known as the "Watercress Capital of the World," and Madison County was Alabama's leader in cotton production (City of Huntsville, 2018).

When the United States entered World War II, Huntsville Arsenal was constructed to manufacture chemical artillery shells. A few months later, another plant was constructed to assemble explosives for the shells. During the peak of World War II production, the two arsenals—Huntsville and Redstone—employed about 20,000 people. During the immediate post-war period, arsenal activities were sharply curtailed. However, in 1950, the Army transferred its small group of missile experts to Huntsville from Fort Bliss, Texas. The group included the famous Dr. Werner von Braun and his team. As a result, the complete U. S. Army missile development and training program and the space vehicle center for the National Aeronautics and Space Administration were firmly established in Huntsville (NASA, 2018).

The U.S. Space and Rocket Center is the legacy of the space and rocket program. Guests can experience astronaut-training activities, feel simulated weightlessness, and view large-screen movies filmed by astronauts in space. The Center's U.S. Space Camp attracts young people from throughout the world who spend a week experiencing space flight training and participate in mock space missions. Guided bus tours of the NASA Marshall Space Flight Center take visitors through large hangar-sized buildings such as where engineers built the nation's first permanent space station (NASA, 2018).

Despite becoming the space capital of America, Huntsville maintains close contact with its past. The literal birthplace, "the big spring," still flows from a rock bluff underneath the 1835 Regions Bank. The flow winds through a lushly landscaped park into a lake surrounded by scores of trees. A new three-story building to house the Huntsville Museum of Art and the Huntsville Botanical Garden has been built in Big Spring Park. Facing the park is the city's civic and convention center named for the legendary German-born rocket scientist. The Von Braun Center contains an arena, exhibit hall, banquet hall, and theater and meeting rooms. A variety of special events, ranging from tours of historic homes in the spring to brilliantly lighted Christmas festivals in December; fill the annual calendar of events. Air travelers arrive at the

Huntsville International Airport just 12 miles west of Huntsville. Some 70-jet flights depart daily in addition to several weekly non-stop cargo flights to Europe (NASA, 2018).

NAIDA

The North Alabama Industrial Development Association (NAIDA) is the oldest regional economic development association in the U.S. Established in 1949 to serve thirteen counties in northern Alabama. As of 2016, more than 1,200 manufacturing facilities from an array of industries thrive in the area. Through the cohesive collaboration of the leaders in North Alabama for more than 50 years, NAIDA has matured into a multifaceted development association that has the experience to successfully assist companies and site location consultants with projects of varying sizes (NAIDA, 2018). This long-standing tradition of economic development has engendered the economic development of today. Nowhere is this seen better than in the local commitment of a group of highly skilled professionals working as an advisory council.

Committee of 100

The mission statement of the Committee of 100 is to: "Serve as a catalyst in stimulating Huntsville area economic development by working with community partners to develop cooperative solutions." Committee members are local CEOs, business professionals, and community leaders who are invested and are active in the community. The Committee of 100 supports entrepreneurial players and change makers who continue to invest and nurture entrepreneurship in the area. From the Committee's work, economic development provides important perspectives for policy makers, educational institutions, business owners, change agents, and non-profits. The Committee believes that nurturing entrepreneurship can only result in a positive impact for the future of our economy and society (Committee of 100, 2018).

The Committee of 100 focuses on several long-term strategies. The founding members established the organization to develop a vibrant and active downtown. The Committee of 100 worked for four years to form and get non-profit IRS status for Big Spring Partners, a privately funded organization to stimulate downtown development. It was modeled after a successful organization in Chattanooga and launched in October 2004. The Committee of 100 also played a key role in forming Downtown Huntsville,

Inc. in 2012 as a private membership organization focused on economic growth and vitality and hired an experienced full-time CEO. The Committee of 100 continues to support both organizations financially and politically in their missions to bring new retail, residential, and commercial activity to stimulate the downtown economy and attract and retain a young professional workforce (Committee of 100, 2018).

The Committee of 100 continues to help strengthen young professional networking organizations and helps stimulate new groups within large employers. The Committee has encouraged elected leaders to invest more in downtown development and the development of public parks, hiking trails, the riverfront and greenways, and quality of life features that are especially attractive to young professionals. They are working with other organizations to involve college students and young professionals in the community and provide additional co-op and intern opportunities. The Committee of 100 has collaborated with the Chamber of Commerce of Huntsville-Madison County and The Arts Council on a research effort to evaluate the success of each organizations' overall strategic plans and develop new strategies. This collaboration has been key to the many successes of each organization (Committee of 100, 2018).

The Committee of 100 does not stop with business development but also sees public education as a key component in the overall strategy of the area. Part of the attraction of the area to young professionals is the quality of the public-school system. Members actively engage in the public schools, attend school board meetings, and work with community and civic groups to help identify solutions and alleviate academic issues. One of these being a tax renewal that had overwhelming community support. The projects are endless, and the Committee of 100 is vital to the community in terms of supporting the creative economy, supplying toolkit material and being a tremendous help as an advisory council.

Huntsville/Madison County Chamber of Commerce

The Mayor of Huntsville and the Chamber of Commerce see the priority of pushing for a Science, Technology, Engineering and Math (STEM) Economy. The mayor determined that the whole American economy today is built on STEM. He launched several initiatives one being the Gig City Initiative, a partnership with Google that provides fiber internet access in homes throughout the city. The mayor attributes Huntsville's rise as a tech city to the high quality of life and attractive amenities. Pay scale recently ranked Huntsville at the top of the list for year-over-year job growth in the technology industry. Top employers of the area are the U.S. Army, NASA, Boeing, and the city's hospital system. Huntsville is home to the first genomic medical clinic. In addition, Blue Origin announced that they would be manufacturing the BE-4 engines in Huntsville, and Aerojet Rocketdyne plans to consolidate several facilities and relocate operations to Huntsville (Huntsville Madison County Chamber of Commerce, 2019).

To further quality of life, a master plan was created and maintained to develop a healthy and economically viable core for downtown Huntsville. This strategic initiative is based on the philosophy that downtowns serve as activity centers, employment hubs, and public gathering spaces and represents the civic identity of the community. Across America, cities are recognizing the importance of downtowns in improving the quality of life, workforce recruitment, economic development, and creating civic pride. In the nation's history, downtown was the public gathering places that built good social norms (Huntsville Madison County Chamber of Commerce, 2019).

The Future

In the 1950s, a team of rocket scientists transformed what was then known as the watercress capital of the world into a technology hub that today is home to the country's second-largest research park and the U.S. Space & Rocket Center. The people of Huntsville are working hard to continue this tradition and going beyond by developing a STEM economy and a vibrant downtown. Their success has been based on the long history of economic development, meaning it has become the norm.

Case Study 2: Greenville, South Carolina

The city of Greenville is situated on land that was once Cherokee Native American hunting ground and closed to settlement. Around 1770, Richard Pearis, an Indian trader from Virginia who was living with a chief's daughter, received about 100,000 acres of lands from the Cherokees. Pearis set up a plantation on the banks of the Reedy River in what is now downtown Greenville. His Great Plains Plantation included a sawmill, gristmill, and stables together with a trading post. When the Revolutionary War came, the struggle in the South Carolina backcountry between Tories and Patriots was fierce. Pearis threw support to the Tories and their Cherokee allies, and together they terrorized upstate Patriots. In retaliation, a Patriot troop raided his plantation, burned his mill and home, and briefly jailed him in Charleston. He never returned to Greenville (City of Greenville, 2018).

After the Revolution, the new state of South Carolina claimed the Cherokees' territory and began distributing it to Patriot soldiers as payment for their wartime services. In 1786, the state legislature formed Greenville (originally spelled Greeneville) County, naming it for Gen. Nathanael Greene, the hero of the American southern campaign. The first owner of the land that became the city of Greenville was Thomas Brandon of Union, who purchased 400 acres that had once been Pearis's in 1784. Several years later, Lemuel Alston purchased Brandon's holdings plus additional acreage, amassing over 11,000 acres around the Reedy River (City of Greenville, 2018).

The General Assembly put the county's courthouse on Alston's property in 1794. In 1815, attracted by the rich soil of Alabama, Alston sold his acreage for $27,557 to Vardry McBee of Lincolnton, North Carolina, a 40-year old tanner and merchant. Although McBee was an absentee proprietor, he understood community building, and he encouraged Greenville growth. Through McBee's efforts, the little town of Greenville became a trading center for surrounding counties. Greenville also became known as a health resort for the low country people escaping the malaria and humidity of the coastal regions.

During the early nineteenth century, Greenville grew slowly, steadily, and by the 1850s, Greenville had become an established town. In 1850, Greenville's population was three times its 1834 count of 500. These bustling times brought Fuhrman to Greenville. In 1853, the town received its first railroad, the Greenville and Columbia Railroad. The Greenville Female College was established in Greenville in 1855, along with the Southern Baptist Theological Seminary in 1859. By the late 1850s, Greenville had the South's largest carriage and wagon plant employing about eighty workers (City of Greenville, 2018).

The post-Civil War period brought Greenville new challenges and a change in social and economic prosperity. The city received its second railroad in 1872, the Richmond & Danville Railroad, and the 1870s saw the birth of Greenville's major business, the cotton textile industry. In 1874 and 1875, the Camperdown Mill was built in Greenville for weaving cotton. The mills proved that Greenville could produce quality cloth with its good water supply and cheap labor. Other companies followed suit, and by 1894, eight cotton mills were operating in Greenville County, the earliest being established in 1820 on the Enoree River. By 1902, this number had increased to fourteen mills. The mills brought prosperity and stability to Greenville. Greenville evolved into a small city as new businesses were established in the downtown area.

After World War II, the city continued its industrial growth. With the expansion of textile and allied industries, the city became known as the Textile Center of the World. The increase in wealth and the establishment of a streetcar system formed new residential neighborhoods (City of Greenville, 2018).

The Great Depression began in the South about 1926. It hit the rest of the nation in 1929. When the boll weevil decimated crops, farmers had less cash to purchase goods, and the value of their land fell. Mills, losing money, "stretched out" work and fired older workers. The Bank of Commerce failed in 1926; three more, including Woodside National Bank, closed their doors by 1931. Both Furman University and the Greenville Women's College struggled to survive. Conditions were so bad in the early 1930s that telephones were removed from city hall, and salaries of police, fireman, and schoolteachers, already reduced 20 percent, were paid five months late. Furman and the Women's College were forced to merge.

The General Textile Strike of 1934 brought martial law to the city and National Guardsmen to the mill villages. The threat of war became a reality in December 1941. The town strongly supported the building of the Greenville Army Air Base (later Donaldson Air Force Base) near Conestee and worked to support national goals, raising money, entertaining soldiers, and accepting wartime austerity and rationing (City of Greenville, 2018).

In 1958, Furman College moved to 1100 acres location on the Poinsett Highway, leaving behind their campus in the shabby West End. In 1961 the college started enrolling women, with the influence of the women, the arts center was renamed Heritage Green. In the early 1960s, Greenville Tech opened, and soon afterwards, the Greenville-Spartanburg Jetport began providing enhanced air services. However, local business leaders as well as city officials were increasingly dismayed by Main Street vacancies (City of Greenville, 2018).

Greenville was facing what other American cities were faced with, a dying downtown even though the region was growing. Greenville leaders decided to create an atmosphere that would bring about a downtown renaissance. This has been a concerted effort for the last thirty years. Greenville leaders focused on a master plan that outlined a strategy for implementation that has been modified and adapted over the years to meet the need of changing market conditions. The willingness to try new approaches, take risks, make mistakes, and learn from the successes and the failures has led to tremendous success (Save Our Gateways, 2019).

Main Street Greenville was remade to create a pedestrian orientation without sacrificing vehicular traffic. Greenville was not blessed with an attractive streetscape; instead, quite the opposite. A major thoroughfare, Main Street had overhead power lines, four lanes of moving traffic, parallel parking, and little landscaping. When the department stores and shops lined the streets, the lack of physical amenities did not seem to matter—Greenville had people and activity. When the stores left, so did the people. The streets and sidewalks suddenly turned into vast wastelands. It was often said that you could shoot off a cannon on Main Street at night and not hit a soul. This was not an image that Greenville wanted to have. A streetscape plan was born that condensed the existing Main Street from four lanes down to two lanes of vehicular traffic with free, angled parking. The vast expanse of bare pavement made way for trees. The trees, which are now the signature element of Main Street, made it appealing to pedestrians and covered up some of the unattractive and vacant buildings. Sidewalks were made extra-wide to provide a festive atmosphere and to encourage outside dining and other sidewalk activity. Greenville now had an identity as a tree-lined street with a welcoming canopy of lush green trees that provided cool shady spots for outdoor dining during the warm weather, an ideal that is characteristic of South Carolina (Save Our Gateways, 2019).

Greenville had to work to uncover is uniqueness. Investments focused on plazas, public spaces, with concentration on Falls Park. Falls Park featured a suspension bridge overlooking a sixty-foot waterfall. Long ago, the waterfall had been covered with a state-owned bridge. This ruined the environment and ambiance. A decision was made in 2001 to remove the bridge and free the falls. Currently the park now has twenty acres of gardens plus amphitheaters for concerts and theater performances. The area is now a signature public space providing a gathering for people of all ages and has enormous public pride (Save Our Gateways, 2019).

Greenville Commons was one of the first public/private partnerships that incorporated a Hyatt Regency Hotel. A dedicated group of Greenville businesses put their investment at risk to ensure the Greenville Commons project happened. The city purchased the land, built a convention center with parking, and then leased the space. The hotel atrium was considered a city park. The project was a financial success and fueled new development (Save Our Gateways, 2019).

The Peace Center for Performing Arts linked downtown to the river, waterfall, and park. The center included the addition of major facilities, renovated several historic structures into productive space, and gave people a reason to come downtown at night and on weekends. The Peace Center is another example of a public/private partnership, with a lead gift given by a prominent local family, and the entire community lending support. The city acquired the property (primarily through tax increment financing) and provided the landscaping and amenities. Eminent domain, typically used sparingly in Greenville, was necessary to secure some of the property (Save Our Gateways, 2019).

Greenville's next major project required a different approach. The historic west end of downtown was blighted, yet strategically connected. Even after completing streetscape improvements and providing low interest loans, the private sector was reluctant to invest. With a private donation of neglected historic buildings, the city took the risk of developing the West End Market, a major 45,000 square foot destination for residents and visitors. Recognizing that private investments would not be taking the lead in developing in this location, the city assumed the developer role, along with the attendant financial and market risk, to create a facility with office, retail, restaurants, artisans, and a traditional farmer's market, all in a festive and park-like setting (Save Our Gateways, 2019).

The financing structure required the pooling of several sources: tax increment financing, a HUD Section 108 loan, grants, city general fund dollars, and even the sale of personalized bricks. The city took on a significant risk but learned firsthand the private side of a deal. The West End Market was sold in 2005, yielding a net profit to the city to invest in other projects. The establishment of the Market led to an arts and entertainment district of restaurants, theaters, and the Governors School for the Arts, a year-round residential school for the arts and humanities attracting high school students from across the state.

More public/private investment brought the Westin Poinsett Hotel, the West End Baseball Stadium, and River Place, which is a collection of buildings along the Reedy River with office buildings, residential condominiums, restaurants, artist studio spaces, and an interactive water feature. The revitalization of the adjacent Falls Park provided the vision for the riverfront project. This provided underground parking, public walkways, and plazas that link the Riverfront project with the park (Save Our Gateways, 2019).

Greenville has focused on creating a place that is authentic, sustainable, and foremost for its citizens. The city invested in public spaces, parking facilities, and critical infrastructure required for quality private development. The city's mantra has been public/private partnerships, but it has not shied away from solely taking on a development project in a blighted area if necessary, to draw private developers out of their comfort zone. The desire to create an award-winning city is not just about pride; it is also about creating jobs. The success of downtown is a selling tool for recruiting and keeping quality employers, whether in downtown or within the region.

The success of Main Street and downtown Greenville is a result of nearly 30 years of hard work and strong partnerships between the public and private sectors. Greenville's next focus is to build beyond Main Street. The city must create gateways into downtown that are aesthetically appealing and consistent with the area. As the city undertakes these new challenges, they may have to change their strategic plan. Toolkits and framing may need upgrading to change directions. A stronger advisory council is needed to bring about more help for entrepreneurs and strategic development.

REFERENCES

Blustein, D. L. (2006). The Psychology of Working. Lawrence Erlbaum Associates.

Bolman, L. G., & Deal, T. E. (2008). *Reframing Organizations: Artistry, Choice, and Leadership. Jossey-Bass, A Wiley Imprint.*

City of Huntsville, Alabama. (2018). *History, City of Huntsville, Alabama.* Retrieved from, https://www.huntsvilleal.gov/business/city-of-huntsville/the-history-of-huntsville/

Furth, J.F. (2018). *Owning Tomorrow: The Unstoppable Force of Disruptive Leadership.* Indie Books.

Greenville, S. C. (2018). *History of Greenville, City of Greenville, S.C.* Retrieved from, https://www.greenvillesc.gov/DocumentCenter/View/1317/History-of-Greenville-PDF?bidId=

Mintzberg, H. (1994, Jan.). The Fall and Rise of Strategic Planning. *Harvard Business Review.*

NAIDA. (2018). History. *Northwest Alabama Industrial Development Association (NAIDA).* Retrieved from https://www.naida.com/about/history/

NASA. (2018). The History of Huntsville, Alabama. *NASA*. Retrieved from, https://history.msfc.nasa.gov/huntsville/hsv_history.html

Chapter 7
Education

ABSTRACT

Our educational system is in need of disruptive leadership, and it will take disruptive leaders who are able to lead change and influence a collaborative mindset. The shortage of talent in the workplace is a sign that education is not fulfilling this basic need. In countries rated the highest in education, businesses are complaining that candidates have the basic skills but lack critical thinking skills, communication skills, creativity, and the ability to handle ambiguity. Educators lecture on the importance of disruptive leadership and creativity, but fall short in providing the graduates ready for the current modern workforce. However, disruptive educators are starting to change the old norms of academia and disrupting the educational systems. Systems of silos are being replaced with collaboration based on disruptiveness, heightened creativity, divergent and critical thought, and decision-making. A new disruptive education is on the forefront. This chapter explores this.

INTRODUCTION

Learn to see a problem from a higher level of understanding. Then, it dissolves before your eyes - Vernon Howard

Foundations of leadership studies include higher-order thinking, decision-making, and divergent learning. Higher-order thinking skills (HOTS) is a concept popular in American education and its roots lie in Blooms Taxonomy. Benjamin Bloom created Bloom's Taxonomy in 1956, as a classification of

DOI: 10.4018/978-1-7998-3416-8.ch007

learning outcomes and objectives. Since 1956, these classifications have been used for everything from framing digital tasks and evaluating applications to writing questions and assessments. The classification was based on a sequence of cognitive skills: knowledge, comprehension, application, analysis, synthesis, and evaluation. Lorin Anderson and David Krathwohl removed the synthesis, and added the creation to produce the highest-level of Bloom's Taxonomy (2001). The highest level being the most complex or demanding cognitive skill, or at least the representation of a pinnacle for cognitive tasks (Krathwohl, 2002).

Good pedagogy leads to informed ways to generate ideas that is divergent thinking, and we analyze these ideas with convergent thinking. When we learn divergently, we use brainstorming, spontaneity, and increase our ability to randomly associate information, which develops our cognitive and metacognitive abilities. Divergent learning and decision-making are a thought process or method used to generate creative ideas by exploring many possible solutions.

The divergent creative process is the act of making new connections between old ideas. While convergent thinking is straightforward and simple, divergent thinking is complex. Personality traits that promote divergent thinking are important, more important than IQ. Research has determined that a high IQ alone does not guarantee creativity. Divergent thinking is found among people with personality traits such as non-conformity, curiosity, willingness to take risks, and persistence (Dyson, et al, 2016).

Divergent thinkers and decision makers become self-disruptive leaders. Self-disruptive leaders are the drivers of change. They can accelerate the flow of information to reach business goals. They can build trust, and influence others to share their vision. They foresee what needs to be done, before problems occur. Our education system needs to develop self-disruptive leaders quickly, because they are currently in short supply. For our socio-economic health, our workplaces need the self-disruptive leaders to thrive (Korn Ferry, 2019).

HIGHER ORDER THINKING AND PEDAGOGY

In education, the framework is used to create assessments, evaluate the complexity of assignments, increase the rigor of a lesson, and simplify an activity to help personalize learning, design a summative assessment, plan project-based learning, frame a group discussion, and more. Because it simply provides an order for cognitive behaviors, it can be applied to almost anything. There are six levels of Bloom's Taxonomy:

- Remember
- Understand
- Apply
- Analyze
- Evaluate
- Create

Putting the elements together to form a coherent or functional whole, reorganizing elements into a new pattern or structure through generating, planning, or producing are all important. Creating requires users to put parts together in a new way or synthesize parts into something new and different that creates a new form or product. This process is the most difficult mental function in the new taxonomy. Bloom was very aware that there was an acute difference between knowledge and the mental and intellectual ability to use knowledge. He identified specific types of knowledge as:

- Terminology
- Specific facts
- Conventions
- Trends
- Categories
- Criteria
- Methodology
- Generalizations
- Structures

Additionally, the revised taxonomy included metacognition:

- Factual Knowledge (basic knowledge to solve problems)
- Conceptual Knowledge (how things in a structure interrelate)
- Procedural Knowledge (inquiry)
- Metacognitive Knowledge (awareness of one's own cognition) (Krathwohl, 2002)

In addition, pedagogy refers to the interactions of teachers with students and the creation and success of the learning environment. The knowledge and skills imparted in the learning environment. Disruptive teachers can create a learning environment that engages student learning and create a heightened creativity where students use their own creativity to solve problems. This heightened learning environment stimulates divergent and critical thought and decision-making. This is done through a range of techniques, class participation in activities, structured group work, guided learning, and individual activities.

DIVERGENT THINKING AND DECISION MAKING

Good pedagogy leads to informed ways to generate ideas that is divergent thinking, and we analyze these ideas with convergent thinking. When we learn divergently, we use brainstorming, spontaneity, and increase our ability to randomly associate information, which develops our cognitive and metacognitive abilities. Divergent learning and decision-making are a thought process or method used to generate creative ideas by exploring many possible solutions.

The divergent creative process is the act of making new connections between old ideas. While convergent thinking is straightforward and simple, divergent thinking is complex. Personality traits that promote divergent thinking are important, more important than IQ. Research has determined that a high IQ alone does not guarantee creativity. Divergent thinking is found among people with personality traits such as non-conformity, curiosity, willingness to take risks, and persistence (Dyson, et al, 2016).

Divergent thinkers and decision makers become self-disruptive leaders. Self-disruptive leaders are the drivers of change. They can accelerate the flow of information to reach business goals. They can build trust, and influence others to share their vision. They foresee what needs to be done, before problems occur. Our education system needs to develop self-disruptive leaders quickly, because they are currently in short supply. For our socio-economic health, our workplaces need the self-disruptive leaders to thrive (Korn Ferry, 2019).

According to the Global Skills Shortage Report (HR Today, 2019), 83% of human resource managers say they have trouble recruiting talented candidates because, they lack communication skills, the ability to deal with ambiguity, lack critical thinking skills, and have no heightened creativity. According the Global Skills Shortage Report, education needs to foster partnerships from within and with business.

The four proposed stages of creativity are preparation, incubation, illumination, and verification. Stage One: Preparation involves trying to learn many things, rather than searching for understanding, your brain is using attention, reasoning, and planning to gather information. Stage 2: Incubation is where you let it go, whether you go meditate, go for a walk, take a bath, and stop consciously thinking about the problem. Let your mind wander. Stage 3: Illumination is where it finally comes together. When subconscious connections come together to solve the problem, you have a great idea. Stage 4: Verification is when you use your creativity to craft your message or idea. Using critical thinking skills to think about how to deliver your creative ideas (Dyson, et al, 2016).

Creative thinking creates something new, while critical thinking seeks to assess worth or validity of something that already exists. Creative thinking is generative, while critical thinking is analytical. Creative thinking is focused on possibilities, while critical thinking is focused on probability. Understanding the difference helps you look at problems and situations from a fresh perspective. Creating thinking is a way to develop novel or unorthodox solutions that do not depend on past or current solutions. Creative thinking moves us beyond barriers.

When someone can use imagination, it dramatically changes how he or she respond in the modern world where the environment is volatile and constantly changing. There are two kinds of change, one that exists naturally and is ongoing; the other is when changes are done by the action of people either by reacting to their environment or on purpose. If done on purpose, it requires certain skills and thought processes. Creativity is about changing or bringing something new into being. Making refers to the creativity of bringing something into being or a transformation. Creative thinking is ongoing, and change occurs when a better idea is developed.

Leadership scholars now consider creativity as a core leadership skill. In the book, *Creative Leadership: Skills That Drive Change*, Puccio, Mance and Murdock (2011) give a great example of leadership potential and closed thinking:

Upon a history professor passing, he entered heaven. Having a strong interest in military history, the professor asked to meet the person who had the greatest military mind of all time. The professor was brought to someone, and he was shocked to find a local tailor in his hometown. The professor was informed that the tailor had the greatest military mind of all time, and if he had found himself in the right circumstances, he would become one of the greatest military leaders of all time (Puccio, Mance and Murdock, 2011, pp. 6-7).

We meet people every day and have no way of knowing what their creative potential is and the collection of skills they have acquired. Higher order skills, divergent thinking and decision making develop critical leadership skills and heightened creativity. Therefore, creativity is not just about the arts; it is considered a crucial workplace skillset that is needed in every organization if the organization is going to thrive. Creative leadership's effectiveness hinges on the ability to resolve ill-defined complex problems and issues; therefore, the need to teach higher order thinking skills (HOTS), and development of divergent thinking and decision-making skills.

You can develop the skills for the mind, but for creativity to blossom, you also need the heart. Creativity, or the production of change, is a result of both thinking and emotion. Developing the creative insight is a cognitive act, but realizing its value, nurturing it and following through means to have emotional intelligence such as self-confidence, intuition, persistence, and the ability to influence and motivate others. Attitude comes from emotional intelligence and this gives us an openness for novelty, a tolerance for ambiguity, and a tolerance of complexity. An openness for novelty is being able to entertain ideas that at first seem outlandish and risky. A tolerance of ambiguity is when you can avoid coming to the wrong conclusions and are able to deal with uncertainty. The tolerance for complexity is the ability to stay open and not be overwhelmed so that you can persevere.

When facing complex problems, it is important to practice mindfulness. Mindfulness is taking time to be quiet and attending to your thoughts, feelings, and the sensations relative to the present. When critical decisions occur, they occur within our critical decision vortex, which features three poles, rational decision-making, intuitive decisions, and emotion. To make the right decision, it is important to stay centered within the critical decision vortex, allowing rational decision making, intuitive decision making, and emotion to inform, balance, and complement each other. If the balance does not occur, then it could cause a mistake (Puccio, Mance and Murdock, 2011). Mindfulness can give us that balance and helps us develop our visionary thinking.

Visionary thinking is when we articulate a vivid image of a product or service we desire to create. Visionary thinking helps you imagine future possibilities, picture them, and create a direction to make it happen. Kouzes and Posner (1995) stated, "All enterprises or projects, big or small, begin in the mind's eye; they begin with imagination and with the belief that what's merely an image can one day be made real" (Kouzes and Posner, 1995, p. 93). It may take years to achieve this goal, but it is how you see or perceive the result, that will determine you reaching the goal. Visionary thinking is visionary dreaming, which is the ability to imagine your dreams and desires coming to fruition. This results in expanding your possibilities and widens your view of reality beyond what you normally might consider. This does not mean we do not apply strategic thinking.

Strategic thinking is identifying the critical issues that need to be addressed to achieve the result of our dreams. It helps us understand what is needed to reach our goal and what barriers could impede reaching our goal. Strategic thinking is how you receive and process tacit information. By sensing gaps or becoming aware of discrepancies between what currently exist and what is desired or required, you become more aware of listening to your intuition, your hunches, and what is often described as your "gut" feelings. When one is not sensitive to gaps, they may find themselves in the mist of problems and barriers as they try to reach their goals (Puccio, Mance and Murdock, 2011).

Another important part of developing creativity and removing barriers is idealized thinking and playfulness. This is the ability to produce original mental images and thoughts that respond to important challenges and to freely toy with ideas. This releases our inhibition and allows freedom to explore. A person adept at idealized thinking generates many original ideas and has a playful attitude that releases inhibitions and allows them the freedom to explore new or different ideas or angles. Dreaming leads to storyboarding. Storyboarding is a visual look to explore vision and create a future story. This concept is useful in developing personal goals, business plans, or processes. To develop a storyboard:

- Identify the topic or specific issue.
- Decide how many panels you want to have in your storyboard. It should be laid out in sequence.
- Define your current situation; this should be done in the first panel.
- Project yourself into the future, be playful and imaginative, and put the future on the panel.
- Complete the story put the steps to move forward to your goal.
- Elaborate on the images on the panels; put words that address key issues or insights associated with each panel.

Identify elements from each storyboard to form the final storyboard. Then evaluate what the storyboard tells you. What is the answer? What is next?

Evaluative thinking is to take time to consider the reasonableness and quality of your ideas in order to develop workable solutions. This is the time when you consider how to proceed (Puccio, Mance and Murdock, 2011).

While formulating solutions, it is important to stay disruptive and creative and still nurture the crazy options. Still keep the vision of what you can do, and do not rush to closure. As a disruptive creative leader, it will not be enough to rely solely on your own creativity, it will take a team that is dependent on each other, who uplift the creative capacity of individuals and bring them into the group. When this happens, the application of creative thinking to resolve complex problems creates growth and potential. Given the times of turbulence we live in, the need is great for disruptive creative leaders working to build the creative economy in their communities and across the world. Disruptive leaders will draw out the talents of people. They will find the unique and emerging actions that will change the landscapes and community social structures needed to propel their communities forward into the creative economy, and thrive in the future (Puccio, Mance and Murdock, 2011).

It is up to us to light our own small fires in the darkness, Charles Handy (1993)

The following case study is an example of collaborations within universities, and with universities globally. Typically, universities have silos, different school or colleges within the university tend to stay to themselves, creating their own curriculum and maintaining pedagogies. This silo mentality often limits the education of students and keeps scholars in a small world not exploring what others are researching, let alone developing heightened creativity. Education is starting to change, and it is disruptive scholars who are leading change and developing disruptive universities.

The second case study is an example of the development of a HOTS activity added to a curriculum. Modern curriculum development is starting to go beyond bloom taxonomy to creating activities to help students think and make real world decisions of complex issues facing many countries globally. This example is covering the complex issues of migration and immigration. Central American people are migrating due to failed nation states, embroiled in high crime, gangs and lack of opportunities. They desire to immigrate to the U.S. This scenario is like migrations happening with people escaping war torn countries and trying to immigrate into European nations.

Disruptive leadership in both government and private sector is the only way to solve this complex problem facing the global society. The leadership of the past is not working. In addition, when granted immigration status, these people from different and diverse cultures are struggling to fit in, and the natives struggles with the newcomer's values and culture. Through education, a greater understanding of complex issues will give rise to greater collaboration, empathy, and will solve these issues. To accomplish this, education needs to change how they teach and collaborate.

The first case study is an overview of a collaborate class that has been going on since fall of 2019. This was a faculty led initiative to bring four colleges together from a major state university. Not only did students learn from each other's disciplines, so did faculty. This created a rich learning environment, in which student drove their own work, and the level of work produced was outstanding.

COLLABORATIVE CAPSTONE

According to Pew Research (2018), most Americans perceive higher education as going the wrong direction. Among adults, 61% believe higher education is going in the wrong direction, and 38% thinks it is going in the right direction. Society is losing faith in higher education. Many feel that faculty are teaching ideology not facts. Furthermore, different disciplines often perceive theirs as elite; dividing colleges or universities, and adding to the perception that you can only rise to greatness if you attend an Ivy League university. As college education is getting more expensive and student loan interest is compounded, many cannot even hope to pay off their student loans under these conditions.

The issue is the outcome for a student when graduating. Are they prepared, do they understand other disciplines, can they work as a team, can they think divergently, and do they have excellent interpersonal and intrapersonal skills? Most importantly, does the culture of the institution represent the best model for the student's future? Do colleges collaborate with different disciplines getting along, model the way, encourage the heart, and inspire creativity. On the other hand, do they divide with elitism toward disciplines and block creativity.

This case study is part of my own research. After several overall university surveys and listening to other faculty and administrators, I determined that the colleges did not fully understand other disciplines, and students were not informed of other disciplines. Hard feelings had developed between some programs. The need to listen, have reasoned debates, share leadership, and most importantly eliminate outdated procedures and policies were the overall concern of everyone. The university had no defining culture, and a creative movement was needed to begin changing the culture of the colleges.

After researching disruptive leadership and the creative economy for four years, a plan was put together to develop an incubator called the Disruptive Sphere the Center for Divergent and Creative Thought? A diverse group of faculties from each college was invited to attend, and the first phase of the incubator was kicked off with a collaborative capstone course. Students enrolled in a special topic or independent study class with their college. A partner came forward, a non-profit who is renovating a historical building that houses a theater and developing a state of art "Community Theater and community center".

PROJECT SCOPE: INTRODUCTION

Currently, creative economies are described in a variety of ways, depending on the composition and character of businesses, nonprofits, individuals, and venues that exist in any given area. The creative economy may include human, organizational, and physical assets with many types of cultural institutions, artistic disciplines, and business pursuits. Industries that comprise the arts and culture sector may include advertising, architecture, the art and antiques market, crafts, design, fashion, film, digital media, television, radio, music, software and computer games, the performing arts, publishing, graphic arts, and cultural tourism.

At the heart of the creative economy are the cultural and creative industries that lie at the crossroads of arts, culture, business and technology - (National Governors Association, 1999)

Creative leadership and the creative economy have the potential to offer numerous benefits to the socio-economic health of the community and build a sense of place that enhances a thriving community. Through the creative industries, states have an opportunity to create jobs, attract investments, generate tax revenues, and stimulate local economies through tourism and consumer purchases. In addition, creative industries are contributing to the contemporary workforce, making creative contributions to industries' products and services, and infusing culture into community development.

Theoretically, there are ten core characteristics needed for lasting long-term success in developing the creative economy:

- Self-worth
- Self-efficacy
- Interpersonal intelligence
- Emotional intelligence
- Personal mastery
- Vision
- Ethical inclusion
- Business knowledge
- Creative leadership
- Global citizenship

In addition to the core characteristic, the modes of developing the creative economy are through collaborative platforms with cluster development such as micro business development, incubators, toolkits, cyber laboratories, new technology development, and creative maker spaces.

The discipline of Leadership Studies and Organizational Leadership and Behaviors will have to adjust and change in this new modern world. Modern theories of leadership have not separated creativity into its' own category; however, it is time to embrace creativity as a new theory of leadership. Creative leadership has been defined as:

The ability to deliberately engage one's imagination to define and guide a group toward a novel (goal direction) that is new for the group. By guiding the group to a novel goal or direction, this creativity has made a profound impact of the overall success of the group (Puccio, Mance, Murdock, 2011).

Linking students with entrepreneurial opportunities both inside and beyond their disciplines offers many economic development possibilities. The importance and role of universities in igniting the creative economy and creating the environment of divergent learning and decision-making cannot be underestimated and must be looked at and explored. Professor of media studies and author Catherine Liu argues that universities have stopped educating people and are just training them to get jobs (Williams, 2014). In his article, "Anti-Intellectualism and the Dumbing Down of America," Ray Williams's points to the reason for rising anti-intellectualism can be found in the declining state of U.S. education compared to other developed countries (2014).

Mark Bauerlein's book, *The Dumbest Generation*, reveals the addiction to social media may lead to aversion to reading anything of substance (Williams, 2014), let alone learn skills such as mindfulness, reflection, and increasing cognitive and metacognitive ability to learn. Thus, the ability to apply oneself to create, innovate, and thrive in a turbulent diverse world may be more important in these modern times than ever before.

PROJECT PURPOSE AND JUSTIFICATION

The purpose of this project is to bring together students form cross disciplines to work together on a semester long project. In addition, these students will work with students from India, Chile, and Canada to complete the project. This project teaches students to collaborate with other disciplines like a multinational real-world workplace. By understanding the unique skills, other students offer to the project, students will gain a deeper understanding and increase their emotional and cultural intelligences.

Scope Description

Phase I

Phase I is the developing and launching of a Fall 2019 Collaborate Incubator class from all five colleges at the University of Arkansas Fort Smith (UAFS). This is a faculty-initiated project from many different disciplines. Students will work with students from India, Chile, and Canada via Skype on a semester long project.

Each college will determine the class and how to manage the class and their students. The lead for the overall project is Dr. Kristin Tardif and Mr. John McIntosh of 64.6 Downtown. The development team made up of faculty from each college will work together to oversee the project and report to each other on a monthly basis.

A formal program will be developed before fall 2019 as a handbook and guide for Students and faculty. A finished report will be turned in to the faculty development committee and stakeholders of the project. Students will have evaluated each other, and the primary stakeholder of the overall project will evaluate the students. Grades will be determined from the evaluations and the finished report.

Resources

Phase I

The Dean of the College of Applied Science and Technology has given the incubator 24 laptops for student use. Space has been given to the incubator by Mr. Steve Clark for the first year, to be used one day a week. Future space will be determined during the school year of fall of 2020.

Phase II

The project leads will be submitting grants for funding the incubator and future toolkits. The toolkits will be used for economic development. Grants will be submitted to large foundations, state and federal governmental agencies.

Project Deliverables

Phase I

- Pilot the first cross discipline incubator and determine future steps and re-development measures needed.
- Look for businesses and NGOs who may want to collaborate with the incubator in the future.
- Develop relationships with other state universities and foreign universities to collaborate with the incubator.

Phase II

As the project moves into Phase II, the College of Applied Science and Technology will offer a non-credit Global Leadership and Creative Leadership proficiency certificate. In addition to these two certificates, the five colleges will add more certificates and non-credit classes. Classes will be developed and implemented in Phase II for toolkit education use.

Scope Description

As the project moves forward in its lifecycle, more areas of interest will be added, more students and organizations will join the incubator. Figure I,

(Tardif, 2017) describes future projects and the overall concept for a Disruptive Sphere the Center for Divergent and Creative Thought. This would include a micro business development center for new entrepreneurs, a computer lab connecting too many areas globally, and a collaboration platform area specifically for brainstorming, new technology center and a maker's space.

Furthermore, the long-term vision is to be a globally recognized center for disruptiveness, increased enrollment, new technology, new business development, and economic development. By developing partnerships, the Five High Native American Nations, local, state and national agencies and organizations become a hub for the creative economy.

Below are the outlines for the course, class schedule and class rubric:

Collaborative Capstone Class Course Outline

- Weekly team meeting with the sponsor
    - Contract signed by each student stating their commitment to UAFS and the project
    - Team Charter developed the first day of class
    - Each student updates the faculty assigned to them from the Collaborate Capstone Team (Faculty will determine times and dates)
    - Social styles completed by each team member the first day (Dr. Tardif)
    - Learning styles completed by each team member the first day (Dr. Tardif)
- Course Subject
    - What the student can expect to learn from the class
    - What the outcome is for UAFS
    - What the outcome is for 64.6 Downtown (separate outline)
- Course Set-up
    - Each week a faculty member will join students at Propak for assistance
    - Student will follow up the rule and roles of the team and 64.6 Downtown
    - Students will be given an outline of the project to follow, but creativity is very important so students must be confident to speak up if they want to go another direction
    - Student must meet the timeline on the outline for the project by the end of the semester

- Learned Skills and Goals
  - Understand team behavior and team development
  - Understand the nature of cross discipline team development
  - Enhance self-confidence
  - Heighten creativity
  - Development of a higher level of the intelligences
  - Constructive feedback skills
  - Accountability when faced with adversity
  - The reward for accomplishment
- Assessment and Measurement
  - Teams will evaluate each other
  - Teams will be assessed by the business partner 64.6 Downtown
  - A written report will be given to the Collaborative Capstone Team
  - A formal presentation will be given to 64.6 Downtown and the Collaborative Capstone Team

Collaborative Class Schedule

- Week One – August 19th
  - Overview of class and project
  - Weekly team meetings at the sponsor
  - Contract signed by each student stating their commitment to UAFS and the project
  - Team Charter developed the first day of class
  - Each student updates the faculty assigned to them from the Collaborate Capstone Team (Faculty will determine times and dates)
  - Social styles done on each team member the first day (Dr. Tardif)
  - Learning styles done on each team member the first day (Dr. Tardif)
  - Overview of project (John McIntosh)
- Week Two – August 26th
  - Brainstorming session
  - Development of project timeline
  - Assign sub-teams and duties
- Week Three – September 3rd (Labor Day September 2nd)
  - Sub-team report on each of their specific duties
  - Each team does a SMART of their sub-team goals

    - The entire class does a Force Field Analysis for the project
- Week Four – September 9th
    - Calibrate work to timeline
    - Sub-teams report on progress
- Week Five – September 16th
    - Calibrate work to timeline
    - Sub-teams report on progress
- Week Six – September 23rd
    - Calibrate work to timeline
    - Sub-teams report on progress
- Week Seven – September 30th
    - Calibrate work to timeline
    - Adjust timeline if needed
    - Sub-teams report on progress
- Week Eight- October 7th
    - Calibrate work to timeline
    - Brainstorming on finishing project work
    - Brainstorm on finishing report and presentation
- Week Nine – October 14th (Mid-term week)
    - Calibrate work to timeline
    - Sub-teams report on progress
- Week Ten – October 21st
    - Calibrate work to timeline
    - Sub-team report
    - What needs to be finished
- Week Eleven – October 28th
    - Calibrate work to timeline
    - Sub-teams report
    - What needs to be finished
- Week Twelve – November 4th
    - Finishing project
    - Delegating work on report and presentation
- Week Thirteen – November 11th
    - Finalizing report and presentation
- Week Fourteen – November 18th
    - Peer evaluations completed and turned in to project lead from UAFS
- Week Fifteen- November 25th
    - Peer evaluations due

- Business partner evaluations due
- Report due
- Final team presentation due

- Week Sixteen - December 2nd Last week of school and team celebration

Collaborative Class Rubric

Table 1. Project Management

Novice	Apprentice	Proficient	Distinguished
Fails to analyze the problem and/or simply restates the facts of the situation without using appropriate concepts or theories. Jumps immediately to solutions without analyzing the current situation;	Identifies and describes some of the salient problems in the current situation but misses several critical points. Does not analyze the problem in depth or articulate their interrelatedness and complexity. Problem statements are not presented in a clear, concise fashion;	Identifies and describes many of the salient problems in the current situation but misses a few minor points. Analyzes the problem but does not clearly articulate their interrelatedness and complexity.	Identifies and describes a reasonable complete set of problems present in the current situation. Articulates a degree of interrelatedness and complexity in describing elements of the problem. Carries out problem analysis before recommending solutions;

Table 2. Literature Review: Existing Research

Novice	Apprentice	Proficient	Distinguished
No evidence of search, selection or source evaluation skills Repeats information provided without question or dismisses evidence without adequate justification Data/evidence or sources are simplistic, inappropriate, or not related to the topic	Below average demonstration of skill in searching, selecting and evaluating sources to meet the information need Limited discernment of fact from opinion; has difficulty recognizing bias in evidence. Somewhat improper data/evidence or sources provided; exploration appears to be less than adequate.	Above average demonstration of skill in searching, selecting and evaluating sources to meet the information need. Reasonably discerns fact from opinion and may recognize bias in evidence Appropriate data/evidence or sources provided, although exploration appears to have been routine.	Evidence of search, selection and source evaluation skills; notable identification of uniquely salient resources Demonstrates understanding of how facts shape but may not confirm opinion. Recognizes bias, including selection bias Correlations are distinct from causal relationships between and among ideas Information need is clearly defined and integrated to meet and exceed assignment, course or personal interests

Table 3. Hypotheses or Position

Novice	Apprentice	Proficient	Distinguished
Position or hypothesis is clearly inherited or adopted with little original consideration; Does not attempt to or fails to identify and summarize accurately; Position or hypothesis is unclear or simplistic	Position includes some original thinking that acknowledges, refutes, synthesizes or extends other assertions, although many aspects may have been adopted; Less than adequately presents own position or hypothesis, inconsistently throughout. Position or hypothesis is somewhat clear, although many gaps exist.	Position includes adequate original thinking that acknowledges, refutes, synthesizes or extends other assertions, although some aspects may have been adopted; Satisfactorily presents own position or hypothesis, though somewhat inconsistently Position or hypothesis is generally clear, although a few gaps exist	Clearly presents and justifies own view or hypothesis while qualifying or integrating contrary views or interpretations. Position or hypothesis demonstrates sophisticated, integrative thought and is developed clearly throughout.

Table 4. Methodology

Novice	Apprentice	Proficient	Distinguished
Unable to articulate methodology clearly; Essentially no link between the research question, hypotheses and methodology.	Sets methodology that is vague, unattainable, or irrelevant; Limited connection between the research question, hypotheses and methodology.	Satisfactory methodology. .Some connection between the objectives which aim to connect research question, hypotheses and methodology	Superior description of methodology; Clear connection between research question, hypotheses and methodology.

Table 5. Research Results

Novice	Apprentice	Proficient	Distinguished
Lack enough reporting of data. Incorrect data analysis is provided	Somewhat unclear organization and reporting of data Below average level of correct data analysis	Data reported and organized at an above average level. Mostly complete and correct analysis of the data	All data is reported and organized in a clear and coherent manner; Complete and correct analysis of the data is provided.

Table 6. Project Results

Novice	Apprentice	Proficient	Distinguished
Conclusions are little more than restatements of information or not adequately supported by evidence. Fails to identify conclusions, implications and consequences or conclusion is simplistic in summary	Conclusions could be supported by stronger evidence. Level of analysis is superficial. Conclusions somewhat considers or provides evidence of consequences beyond the current issue. Less than adequate implications are considered.	Good effort in analyzing the evidence collected. Conclusions consider or provide evidence of consequences extending beyond a single discipline or issue. Presents implications that may influence other people or issues.	Careful analyze of the information collected and draws appropriate and inventive conclusions supported by evidence; Identifies, discusses and extends conclusions, implications and consequences. Considers context, assumptions, data and evidence. Qualifies assertions with balance. Implications are clearly developed and consider balance.

Table 7. APA Style

Novice	Apprentice	Proficient	Distinguished
Few sources are cited or used correctly. Manuscript and APA format not followed	Limited number of sources cited and used correctly. Manuscript and APA format not strictly followed	Most sources are cited and used correctly. Solid manuscript and APA format	All sources are cited and used correctly, demonstrating an understanding of issues involved with the use of information. Nearly flawless manuscript and APA format

Table 8. Essay Structure

Novice	Apprentice	Proficient	Distinguished
No clear plan of organization—hard to follow; Little or no use of transitions; Paragraphs are weak—incoherent, undeveloped, and/or not unified; Topic sentences absent or inappropriate; Weak or absent title, introduction, and/or conclusion	Inconsistent organization—sometimes hard to follow; Awkward use of transitions; Paragraphs not always coherent, developed, and unified—sometimes off-topic; Topic sentences absent or inappropriate; Weak title, introduction, and/or conclusion	Clear plan of organization—logical order—easy to follow; Clear use of transitions; Coherent developed, and unified paragraphs; Appropriate use of topic sentences; Effective title, introduction, and conclusion	Clear plan of organization—logical order—exceptionally easy to follow; Superior use of transitions; Coherent, developed, and unified paragraphs; Appropriate use of topic sentences; effective title, introduction and conclusion

Table 9. Grammar and Usage

Novice	Apprentice	Proficient	Distinguished
Many grammatical errors, often distracting or confusing; Frequent errors in sentence structure and style; Little or no sentence variety (length and style)—overuse of simple form	Some grammatical errors, occasionally distracting or confusing; Occasional errors in sentence structure and style; Little sentences variety (length and style)	Few grammatical errors—no distracting or confusing; Generally accurate and sophisticated sentence structure; Good sentence variety (length and style)	Nearly flawless grammatical structure; Accurate and sophisticated sentence structure; Exceptional sentence variety (length and style)

Table 10. Mechanics

Novice	Apprentice	Proficient	Distinguished
Errors in punctuation, capitalization, and spelling often distract or confuse;	Errors in punctuation, capitalization, and spelling distract or confuse;	Solid use of conventional punctuation, capitalization and spelling—some errors, but no distracting or confusing;	Nearly flawless use of conventional punctuation, capitalization, and spelling;

Table 11. Totals

Criteria	Possible Pts	Your Pts
Research Question, Problem or Issue		
Literature Review: Existing Research		
Literature Review: Hypotheses or Position		
Methodology		
Research Results		
Conclusions and Implications for Practice and/or Future Research		
APA Style		
Essay Structure		
Grammar and Usage		
Mechanics		
Total	100	

After agreeing on the scope, outline for the course, class schedule and rubric, we started developing how to bring students into the process. We asked our university foundation if we could offer free tuition for the pilot class and give-a-ways. Then we put together an on-boarding process for the students, and a letter went out over the summer and a formal invitation two weeks before school inviting them to the first class.

Student Onboarding Process

Table 12.

PRIOR TO START	FIRST DAY	FIRST WEEK	SECOND WEEK	FIRST MONTH	MID-TERM	FOLLOW UP	ASSESS CLASS
Send Invitation	Kick off at site	Feedback	Brain-storming	Feedback with group	Assess Performance	Two weeks before semester ends	Final Report and Presentation
Discuss location	Welcome	Social styles	Sub-teams	Feedback by sub teams	Force Field analysis	Status	
Dress code	Owner of site	Class Culture	Assignment	Feedback		Plan for next semester	
Overview							
Expectation							Evaluation by peers
Q & A		Going forward			Reward	SMART plan for next group	Evaluation by site manager
							Rewards

The following activity is an example of higher order teaching. The students were put in the most diverse group possible. The students were given instructions on the importance of reasoned debates, to respect each other and value each other's opinions.

Higher Order Thinking and Decision-Making Activity

Thirteen Thousand People Coming to the United States

You are a group of United Nations peacekeepers. Your mandate is to prevent epidemics, and threats to the general well-being of the public. Your current concern is thirteen thousand people are walking from Central American countries to gain asylum in the United States. Below are issues that you are investigating: *(Providing focus to draw student into the activity)*

- Why are they coming?
- Who is leading this effort and why?
- Are the leaders tied to organized crime or are they criminal?
- How many non-profits are funding the trip, who are they, and why are they funding the trip?
- Where are supplies coming from?
- Who are passing out the supplies?
- How many countries are represented?
- How many families with children?
- Are drug cartels, terrorist and criminals trying to get in the country?
- What are the sanitation requirements, and are they being met?
- What are the water and food requirements, and are they being met?
- How did they get new vehicles and boats needed for the trip?
- How are medical needs being met or not?
- Why have they chosen the particular path they are on and not one closer?
- What do they do when it storms?
- What is happening when they reach the United States?

Students are put in diverse groups according to political preference, race, and ethnicity. Students are instructed that all are to maintain respect for each other and practice reasoned debates. They can use their laptops and cell phones. The media site www.newsprism.com was given as a reference, they have to use equal sources of each color: Red is conservative, blue is liberal, and purple is moderate. They can use additional sources. *(As they work on the activity, the instructor is going around the room to prompt questions, and ensure equal collaboration)*

Students are required to answer each issue, they will research each issue and develop an understanding of each issue, they will analyze and evaluate all information to formulate and create a plan to handle this complex issue. *(Independent work and collaboration to conclude)*

CONCLUSION

As we went through planning spring semester, more lead faculty wanted to join our group, and the group is genuinely engaged and excited to be part of the pilot and phase one of the overall project. When we got down to getting students, only half had their students enrolled and ready for the fall semester.

By fall, we were ready to start the project, and students were genuinely excited to start. Students were divided into groups crossing disciplines. The groups consisted of the following disciplines: Organizational Leadership, Business, Education, Art, Theater, Psychology, English, Information Technology and STEM. Students represented were from age 18 to 46, traditional and non-traditional students. This created a unique learning environment where an art student might think a business plan is too restrictive, an education student sees the benefit incorporating facets of educating the public and children to increase ticket sales and better use the facility.

The higher order thinking activity was one of many that we gave the students. Student's remarked that the activities gave them a new perspective, and of the future. Going forward, they would research issues of a complex nature to make informed decisions. In their class evaluations of faculty and peers, all the students remarked that at first they were scared when we informed them class was going to organic and were surprised how well the class came together. Each felt the class prepared them for graduation and the workplace.

REFERENCES

Dyson, S. B., Chang, Y.-L., Chen, H.-C., Hsiung, H.-Y., Tseng, C.-C., & Chang, J.-H. (2016). The effect of tabletop role-playing games on the creative potential and emotional creativity of Taiwanese college students. *Thinking Skills and Creativity*, *19*, 88–96. doi:10.1016/j.tsc.2015.10.004

Ferry, K. (2019). Self-Disrupt Or Be Disrupted. *Korn Ferry.* Retrieved from, https://www.kornferry.com/self-disrupt

Krathwohl, D. R. (2002, Autumn). A Revision of Bloom's Taxonomy. *Theory into Practice*, *41*(4), 212–218. doi:10.120715430421tip4104_2

National Governors Association. (2009). *Arts and the Economy: Using Art and Culture to stimulate the economy.* National Governors Center. Retrieved from, http://www.nga.org/cms/center/publications?begin7736bde9-79fd-493d-be2b-0f62416085cd=180&end7736bde9-79fd-493d-be2b-0f62416085cd=189&pagesize7736bde9-79fd-493d-be2b-0f62416085cd=10&

National Governors Association. (2019). *Rural Prosperity Through The Arts & Creative Sector: A Rural Action Guide for Governors and States.* National Governors Association.

University of Arkansas Fort Smith. (2019). *Collaborative Capstone Class.* UAFS.

Chapter 8
Emerging State Programs

ABSTRACT

When performing research for this book it was hard to pick the states to focus on. The following states opened the door to talk about their successes and failures. This chapter is about highlighting several states and position in the creative economy, what projects they are focusing on and their plans for the future. The author hopes that disruptive leaders will see the need and step up to fulfill the role of championing the creative economy in their states.

INTRODUCTION

At the heart of the creative economy are the cultural and creative industries that lie at the crossroads of arts, culture, business and technology - (National Governors Association, 1999)

In a recent study, fifteen agencies in various states were interviewed and studied. The states are a mixture of rural, semi-urban and urban, all quite different in culture and diversity. Some states have been successful in developing and implementing the creative economy, some are still working toward that goal, but all have dedicated professionals leading the charge and no doubt will be successful. Their tireless energy and passion to build state programs, with some on limited funding, is amazing, and their accomplishments are great. Talking to state agencies and looking at existing research, the economic environment gives a clearer picture of where the states stand, and if the creative economy is existing or flourishing. This amazing group of disruptive

DOI: 10.4018/978-1-7998-3416-8.ch008

leaders, who are collaborating with others, are developing their economies to attract business, entrepreneurs, and young talented professionals to their states, and it is working.

According to the U.S. Census Bureau (2018), Vermont, Iowa, Kentucky, Mississippi, Wyoming, South Dakota, and Arkansas are considered 50% rural. Kansas, Tennessee, and New Mexico 28.8% rural. Utah, Nevada, and Colorado are 10 to 28.8% rural. Louisiana and Washington are considered 10% rural. Let us look at their accomplishments by state.

Vermont

Vermont's creative economy is based on a broad collective of organizations, businesses, and individuals. This collective welcomes a diverse creative industry that benefits many people in the visual arts, crafts, performing arts, film, media design, artisan foods, literary arts, and publishing. These organizations are based on the state's unique culture and heritage. A quote by MacGregor sums up the overlaying creative culture of Vermont:

Vermont is a unique place. Here you have a cheese maker with a PhD. A farmer who studied at Vermont Law School, an engineer who sculpts. Such pockets of novelty! It is a place where the mind can flourish. (Forrest MacGregor, 2019)

The universities and STEM are not an active part of the creative economy in Vermont. However, Vermont is a success story with an organic homegrown creative economy, which fits the overall culture of Vermont. On the Vermont Arts Council website is a statement that declares it all: "We are working to build a Vermont where everyone has access to the arts and creativity in their lives, education, and communities," (Vermont Arts Council, 2019). The Arts Council's mission is to: *Cultivate and advance the arts and creativity throughout Vermont.*

Since 1965, the Vermont Art's Council is unique, because it is the only designated state arts agency in the U.S. that is an independent non-profit, and has been the state's primary provider of funding, advocacy, and information for the arts in Vermont. Currently there are three major objectives: Expanding arts opportunities, cultivate creative place making, and energize Vermont's creative economy. To do this they provide several grants, available for artists, schools, organizations, and to enhance culture.

In May of 2016, the Vermont Legislature established the Vermont's Creative Network as an initiative of the Vermont Art's Council. An in-depth study of the state's creative economy was determined to be a large part of what the Vermont Creative Network would develop. The goal was to develop a project that was a comprehensive, research-based action plan for moving Vermont's creative economy forward. The study would take several years of studying prior research, partnership building, community inquiry, and include national research. The overall goal was to cultivate economic growth across Vermont by developing a vibrant, resilient creative sector to analyzing the economic potential of Vermont's creative sector. By documenting workers employed in creative industries as well as creative occupations in other sectors employment growth over time, and the convergence of creative businesses with other key sectors (such as health, agriculture, and manufacturing), a plan of action could be developed to build the creative economy in Vermont (Vermont Arts Council, 2019).With a team of experts and grant money to fund the project, the work is currently underway.

Key findings from a 2018 report found that Vermont's share of creative economy jobs (9. 3% of all employment) is higher than the average across the U.S. Most of these jobs are design, specialty foods, crafts, and visual arts. In addition, the creative sector has always had a high proportion of entrepreneurs who own small businesses. In Vermont 50% of creative businesses are either freelance or self-employed companies, which is higher than the national average. Vermont is focusing on marketing, investing in new creative industries, education and training, and leveraging partnerships. Vermont has a high number of disruptive leaders forging the path in the creation of the creative economy.

Iowa

Iowa's creative economy has two important dimensions. The first is Iowa's creative workforce. The second is its creative industrial composition. The creative workforce is further segmented into two groups. The first, borrowing from Florida's work (2002), is the super creative core, which is composed of computer and mathematical professionals, architects and engineers, life, physical, and social scientists, education, training, and library professionals and arts, design, entertainment, sports, and media occupations (Swenson & Eathington, 2003).

The second subgroup is composed of the occupations termed "creative professionals". Creative professionals include managers and administrators, business and financial professionals, legal professionals and health care practitioners, high-end sales professionals, and community and social service workers. Creative industries are those that employ large factions of the creative workforce, invest heavily in research and development, or create and distribute technologically, and sophisticated artistic goods and services. These industries include specific kinds of manufacturing, broadcasting and communications industries, professional services; scientific and technical services and activities, membership organizations for business, labor, and other groups, all education providers, applied arts, visual arts, and performing arts, commercial sports, heritage institutions, and independent artists, performers, and writers (Swenson & Eathington, 2003).

Jobs in Iowa's creative industries account for 22.5% of all non-farm jobs, compared to a U.S. average of 25%. Nationally, there was a 24% gain in creative industry jobs between 1990 and 2000. The corresponding growth amount for Iowa was 14%. Most Iowa creative industries grew at a slower rate than their national counterparts did. However, jobs in performing arts and the visual arts grew more rapidly than the national rate (Swenson & Eathington, 2003).

Earnings per job in creative industries are dismal in many instances when compared to the national average. In all, Iowa's creative industries pays only 73.4% of the national average. Growth in average earnings between 1990 and 2000 was slower in Iowa than in the U.S. Iowa's creative industry jobholder earnings grew faster than the U.S. average in post-secondary education, performing arts, and in heritage institutions (Swenson & Eathington, 2003).

Iowa is doing better in creative occupation growth than in creative industry growth. Location quotients by occupation suggest the state has close to its expected number of creative occupations in many categories. Earnings by occupation are more competitive with national averages than they are at the industrial level. Few places in Iowa will likely realize most of the economic and social growth over the next decade. Still, the overall livability in those places and the rest of the state depends on far more than merely the number of jobs they create. There is great opportunity for growth and enhancement in nontraditional areas of Iowa's economy – its artistic, cultural, and recreational institutions. These opportunities can only be enhanced when state and community leaders recognize that the sum of a community is greater than the sum of its jobs (Swenson & Eathington, 2003). Iowa is lacking in disruptive leadership. By focusing on their unique micropolitan areas, Iowa could grow their creative economy.

Kentucky

The creative industry plays an active role in enhancing and growing Kentucky's economy. As a viable sector of the state's economy, it generates new wealth as measured by jobs, income, and investments. However, the creative industry also has other important economic functions and impacts. Many CEOs agree it increases productivity and competitiveness among companies. Through its contributions to creative place making and identity, it attracts and retains talented people, businesses, and tourists. Research shows, that for young people, amenities are more important to locational decisions than the job is (Kentucky Arts Council, 2017).

Furthermore, in developing a creative social environment, Kentucky can stimulate innovation across all sectors of the economy. Research has shown that when introduced effectively into the educational system; arts and design improve learning outcomes and are highly valued by employers.

The businesses in Kentucky's creative industry provide more than 108,498 jobs directly and indirectly. It accounted for almost $1.9 billion in total earnings in 2013. Kentucky's creative enterprises are a major contributor to employment and economic activity in the state. About 2.5% of total employment in the state represents creative enterprises. To put the number in perspective, it compares favorably with other key state industries. For example, by the numbers, employment in bioscience was 14,275, auto/aircraft manufacturing 47,209, IT and communication 48,792, and transportation, distribution and logistics 75,223. Earnings in the creative industries totaled more than $1.9 billion in 2013, with average earnings per job of $34,299. Kentucky's recent report determined there are key findings in going forward (Kentucky Arts Council, 2017):

- The total employed in all creative segments represented about 2.5% of all employment in the state in 2013. This was comparable to the transportation, distribution and logistics sector or the IT and communications sector.
- The total employment in the creative industry in 2013 was 108,498. This includes direct and indirect jobs in the creative sector and 11,708 in creative occupations in other sectors. The industry also can claim 36,286 in indirect jobs.

- About 38% of the establishments in Kentucky's creative segments were self-employed artists and designers. This number is many times larger than the proportion of self-employed establishments across all other industries in Kentucky.
- The full impact of creative enterprises on the state's economy was 108,498. This includes the estimated multiplier effect of earnings and business expenditures on other businesses within the state as well as the creative talent working in other industries.
- Among sectors, design and media have the largest share of employment. The larger share is because these segments include the greatest numbers of large employers.
- Design and visual arts have the highest concentrations of employment relative to national concentrations. These numbers are particularly significant considering the size of Kentucky's rural population, which is generally associated with lower concentrations of employment.

Much like other states, Kentucky has no major research university in the state involved in helping ignite the creative economy. Kentucky Arts Commission plays a traditional role in the art creative economy. STEM and technology fields are not involved. With disruptive leadership and focusing on metropolitan areas this could change.

Mississippi

Mississippi's creative industries represent 30,374 workers, including self-employed. The following table (Table 1) displays the number employed in each category, compensation, and annual revenue (Mississippi Arts Council, 2017).

Table 1. Annual Revenue

Industry	Number Employed	Compensation	AnnualRevenue
Film and media	10,972	$218 million	$857 million
Writing and publishing	8,889	$220 million	$694 million
Design	4,210	$147 million	$337 million
Visual arts and crafts	3,806	$51 million	$101 million
Performing arts	2,297		
Heritage and museums	230	$1.2 million	$6 million
	Total	$679 million	$2 billion

Mississippi and its state director, Joseph Donavan, who heads up The Entrepreneur Center, focuses not only on the arts as part of their creative economy, but technology as well. Technology is considered part of the innovation and entrepreneurism initiatives. The economic development in the state has grown in the last few years, and a paradigm shift has happened in the state. A well thought out plan and collaboration with small, medium and large business are what have made this initiative so successful. In addition, they collaborate with the military on high technology and getting this technology to market.

Several niche technology businesses have developed; one is Apple Apps, which is part of the K-12 program being administered by community colleges. The other is virtual reality. Libraries and communities are increasing gig speed to accommodate this technology. A paradigm shift is occurring where these niche technology businesses are taking the place of large industries who have tax incentives, such as automakers.

The state program excels with toolkits, business development, and planning. Funding is withheld until new start-ups go through the business development program. The start-ups that did not go through the process did not do well. However, those that did succeeded. In addition, incubators have been highly successful. Large corporations privately own some. County governments control most, and two are housed with the University of Mississippi and Mississippi State Universities.

There are three tiers to business development in the state, the first being lifestyle and small businesses, such as auto shops and boutiques. The second, middle size businesses that focus on creative industries. The third is large business focusing on technology. The non-profits in the state are licensed and audited through the Secretary of State.

Wyoming

The state of Wyoming has an arts council that is active in providing grant money for the arts. In addition, the University of Wyoming is actively involved with the creative economy and has done extensive research its economic impact to the state. The University also has a strategy to develop, support, and launch initiatives to stimulate and ignite the creative economy of Wyoming (University of Wyoming, 2019).

Desiree Brothe is leading the charge in Wyoming. One of her major initiatives is working with the Main Street America Association. Along with the Universities of Wyoming and Montana, Main Street leadership and other stakeholders are working to develop short- and long-term strategies. At the top is marketing.

The low population of Wyoming and long winters create problems not seen in other states. There are seventeen designated cultural districts with nine certified cultural districts. The next step is to help people grow, develop strategic plans for local art groups, leverage municipal public art, and develop an economic map as well as cultural mapping.

The University of Wyoming has created an innovation incubator. There is a Wyoming Technical Business Center working to build toolkits. Best practices are currently being developed. One issue is building a gig network in a state with low population and tight funding issues. In addition, fighting burnout when the season is short for tourism, festivals and community projects. Brothe and her collaborators are working on ways to develop winter programs and keep people motivated.

The Native American tribes need to develop resources not based internally but externally. Once this is done, funding opportunities for them will open. The creative economy is waiting to happen for these tribes and is a pathway for a better quality of life. With Native American involvement, branding, marketing and the efforts of people like Desiree Brothe, the future looks positive for Wyoming.

South Dakota

Andrew Reinartz, and Jim Speirs of the Arts South Dakota, along with Patrick Baker of the South Dakota State Economic Development office embody the collaboration needed to build a successful creative economy. The South Dakota Arts Agency is celebrating fifty-four years of existence. A quote taken from a brochure reads:

Arts are the soul of South Dakota. From Mount Rushmore's massive presence and the intricate regalia and movement of Wacipi dancers, to hometown band concerts and craft fall creations, the arts and those who support them positively impact our state and the lives of all South Dakotans (Arts South Dakota).

South Dakota Arts Council is the main initiative for the creative economy. In 2018, $19.48 million in grants were awarded for local projects and programs. Cultural Tourism is a major initiative as well as promoting Native American art. The Arts South Dakota estimate that 30% of Native people are practicing or emerging artists. In addition, 79% of home-based enterprises on the Pine Ridge Reservation consist of some form of traditional arts.

The creative production of art and artistic expression are, today, among the most promising ways to expand the market economy in rural and urban Native communities -Arts South Dakota, 2019)

Currently, South Dakota is home to 1,353 arts-related businesses that employ 6,489 people. 91% of South Dakotans believe that arts are necessary for a balanced education. The school art programs took artists to 80 sites across the state in 2018, which provided 201 total weeks of arts education residency. 71.4% of South Dakotans attended a least one arts event per year, while 51.4% actively performed or created art in the same period. The South Dakota Arts Council sponsored activities reached 86% of the counties in the state (Arts South Dakota, 2019). This is a tremendous amount of work and effort, and it is paying off.

The state introduces a new strategic plan every three years. South Dakota's focus is on equity. During the next three years, the state will strive to be equitable more through policy, process, and practice. The state will seek to develop a sustainable equity practice through access, inclusion, diversity, and equality.

To develop this practice, the state plans to organize the power structure between the state agency, partnered organizations, and constituencies to work in a way that more fully democratizes voices and to engage in more collective processes. The overarching goal, striving for equity, takes South Dakota in a new direction. The current political environment is fracturing communities, and the arts can help people persevere through the difficult times, understanding each other when no other method works.

Three driving forces guide the state through their plan for equity: learning, connecting and progressing.

1. Learning
    - Workforce Development: Promote youth participation in the arts to develop skills and careers. Motivate and support artists and arts businesses to flourish in our state.

2. Connecting
   - Professional Development: Provide and support continuing professional development opportunities to artists and arts leaders throughout South Dakota.
   - Resources and Information: Develop regular, ongoing methods for artists, organizations, and communities to access information and resources to support their needs in the arts.
   - Outreach and Technical Assistance: Increase efforts to include the voices of all South Dakotans and access to staff or other professionals to assist in individual and community efforts to advance the arts.
   - Cooperation: Advance shared goals through partnerships with other state agencies, private entities, and the business community.
3. Progressing
   - Community Development: Foster strong communities locally and statewide with a sense of place that is creative and beneficial to all.
   - The Essential Arts: Clearly and effectively, communicate the importance of the arts in education, community livability, and the economy to policy-makers and stakeholders throughout South Dakota. Each of these goals has major objectives that the state strives to meet throughout the three-year plan (South Dakota Arts Council, 2015).
   - In Sioux Falls, a new business incubator has started along with an Arts Council Incubator.

In addition, a Land Grant Extension program is awarding grants to help with building costs. Also, reaching out to Native American tribes to convince them to apply for funding, and finding creative solutions to make the process easy to understand and acquire the much needed funding to develop their economy.

The work of the collaboration of Reinartz, Speirs and Baker is reaping great rewards, their efforts are tireless. The amount of momentum and the passion they have is a great asset to South Dakota. It is paying off; the brain drain that has threatened South Dakota in the past may be ending. In 2019, South Dakota has had small increases in population that is not related to any one industry. The increases are young professionals from California wanting a future with a quality life.

One of the most exciting things happening in South Dakota is in the city of Brookings. . According to The Walton Family Foundation Report, "Micropolitan Success Stories from the Heartland," by Ross DeVol and Shelly Wisecarver, Brookings is a success story. It is home to well-informed entrepreneurs who are highly educated, are establishing tech companies, access to early-stage risk capital, bioscience firms, and advanced manufacturing. Once classified as quasi-rural, it is now classified as a micropolitan area. Current inward migration is creating economic growth. Brookings has created an environment of low taxes, great education, and healthcare. The arts and culture thrive there. This combination attracts young professionals who want to raise children in a safe place.

Kansas

Kansas, like Missouri, is 28.8% rural; they not submitted a current report to the American Arts Council. However, they have developed the Kansas Creative Arts Industries Commission, which is focused on the creative industries sector of the Kansas economy. The commission is dedicated to measuring, promoting, supporting, and expanding the creative industries to grow the state's economy and create industry jobs. There are two main initiatives:

- Strategic Investment Program
- Arts Integration Program

The Strategic Investment Program recognizes the important role individual artists and creative industries play in building and sustaining the cultural and economic vibrancy in Kansas. By funding a variety of professional and organizational development opportunities that impact cultural programming, these grants support initiatives that use the arts to enhance community vitality, revitalize neighborhoods, generate local business, create and preserve job opportunities, and impact tourism. Applicants must make a compelling case as to why this self-identified activity or opportunity was selected, how it will have a substantial impact on their work and community, and how it will enhance the national reputation of Kansas. Grants are given to fund projects such as:

- Organizational Development – to provide opportunities for an organization to strengthen business practices and sustainability.
- Hiring consultants to build administrative and business skills.

- Develop or upgrade marketing and promotional materials such as brochures, DVDs, print ads, and websites that fulfill strategies to expand audiences, outreach to underserved populations, and promote regional identity.
- New and expanded works – This is support for the arts and culture. The purpose is to create or preserve jobs by funding new or expanded programs that use arts and culture to enrich the quality of life for participants, promote economic development in Kansas, generate business development and promote neighborhood revitalization.
- Capital Investment
    - New and expanded works – which includes support of new arts and culture productions, exhibitions, programs or events by individual artists or non-profit organization, that takes place in Kansas.
    - Grants to improve and expand cultural assets:
    - Purchase equipment, materials, and/or technology upgrades to expand or improve an applicant's organization.

Grants from the Arts Integration Program support the role of the arts in education, community service, and workforce development. Additionally, this program provides funding for educational institutions, arts organizations, and community service non-profits to use the arts to increase student success, foster creative thinking, develop critical job skills, and enhance community development. There are two categories for this program:

- Visiting Artists – This program encourages the integration of Kansas' artists into a variety of settings. Grants may be used to fund residencies and professional development collaborations that feature partnership among artists, schools, and arts organizations.
- Integrated Arts Education and Innovative Partnerships – This program supports innovative educational curriculum development and emerging technologies. In addition, this program supports strategic partnerships of collaboration (State of KS, 2017).

There is no major involvement of the universities in Kansas; however, several professors sit on various boards. As a side note, Kansas University has taken an interest for research, building incubators, and expanding the creative economy. There is no economic research or report generated by a major university on the economic impacts of the creative economy in Kansas.

Oklahoma

The arts, non-profits, and cultural sectors provide significant economic development in the state of Oklahoma, generating $872.8 million in total economic activity. The non-profits generate $331.2 million, with cultural organizations providing an additional $541.6 million. In addition, the state's non-profits, arts, and cultural organizations provide employment for a wide variety of jobs. These sectors drive tourism in the state, in which 57% of tourists said their purpose for visiting the state was to attend an art or cultural event.

Ardmore, Oklahoma, is the home of Sylvan N. Goldman who owned a grocery store chain. He noticed how women would stop shopping when their arm-carried baskets were too full and heavy to carry. Mr. Goldman solved this issue by inventing the shopping cart in which women could load a cart with merchandise and push it easily. It is virtually the same cart we use today. Goldman, along with several other entrepreneurs, have placed Ardmore in a successful micropolitan ranking. Opportunities exist for employment growth in a culture of hard-working rural labor toughness, (DeVol and Wisecarver, 2018).

The city of Ardmore recognizes the need for an enlightened philosophy, where small businesses are considered vital to the long-term vibrancy of the community. The Ardmore Development Authority is recognized nationally for its *thought leadership*, which focuses on attracting and retaining businesses in the southern Oklahoma region (DeVol & Wisecarver, 2018). The strategy to diversify the region's economy and increase the knowledge base is attracting new startups. By collaborating with Oklahoma State University, new technology in agricultural biosciences is providing worldwide conferencing and distant educational opportunities. With the geographic location of Ardmore along major interstate highways, business tax incentives, stable workforce, economic development, and strategic efforts, the region is attracting young professionals and retaining young professionals.

The Native American nations provide additional economic development. Nations such as the Cherokee and Choctaw are thriving. By driving economic development based on their own unique culture, they are creating new entrepreneurial businesses and igniting their own unique economies. This economy is no longer being driven by casinos, but by a variety of businesses. The most successful are the ones built on their culture and art. According to Joel Gavin, Oklahoma has thirty recognized tribes.

New Mexico

With the assistance of the University of New Mexico and the Kellogg Center, a strategic plan was developed and implemented for New Mexico. Their findings were to start with cultures and cultural entrepreneurs. Economic development practitioners and policy leaders have largely ignored cultural/creative entrepreneurs. . The research data suggests that investing in cultural/creative entrepreneurs supplies the building blocks to ignite a regional economy that addresses poverty, embraces cultural diversity, and creates broad-based economic opportunities (Kellogg Center, 2010).

Cultural/creative entrepreneurs participate in unique markets and need resources designed for their unique needs: resources and programs that have deep expertise in cultural enterprise development. Investing in cultural/creative entrepreneurs and building bridges into communities where cultural talent is deep and enterprise resources are scarce is the key levering point for creating holistic community and economic development in diverse communities (Kellogg Center, 2010).

Utah

Utah is home to 7,006 arts-related businesses that employ 27,210 people. The creative industries account for 4.5%of the total number of businesses located in Utah, and 2.2% of the people they employ. The State of Utah has taken a research-based approach to understanding the scope and economic importance of the arts in Utah. The creative industries are composed of nonprofits, museums, symphonies, theaters, architecture, design, and art organizations. However, Utah does not list the STEM or technology fields within the creative economy of Utah, nor is there a research university associated with the creative economy efforts.

The organization Utah Genius recognizes the creative people and companies behind Utah's economy. The organization gives awards that are based on objective data collected from the US Patent and Trademark Office. Utah Genius 2019 will recognize and honor the inventors and innovators based on the 2018 US Patent and Trademark Office results (Utah Genius, 2018).

Nevada

During fiscal year 2017, spending by both the State of Nevada's nonprofit arts and cultural organizations and their audiences totaled $471.7 million. Nonprofit arts and culture organizations are active contributors to their business communities. They are employers, producers, and consumers. They are members of the Chamber of Commerce as well as key partners in the marketing and promotion of their cities, regions, and states. Spending by nonprofit arts and cultural organizations totaled $227.3 million in the State of Nevada during fiscal year 2017. This spending is far-reaching: organizations pay employees, purchase supplies, contract for services, and acquire assets within their community. These actions, in turn, support jobs, generate household income, and generate revenue to local and state governments (American Council of the Arts, 2017).

The State of Nevada's nonprofit arts and cultural organizations provide rewarding employment for more than just administrators, artists, curators, choreographers, and musicians. They also employ financial staff, facility managers, and salespeople. In addition, the spending by these organizations directly supports a wide array of other occupations spanning many industries that provide their goods and services (e.g., accounting, construction, event planning, legal, logistics, printing, and technology).

Data was collected from 164 eligible nonprofit arts and cultural organizations that are in Nevada. Each provided detailed budget information for fiscal year 2015 (e.g., labor, payments to local and nonlocal artists, operations, administration, programming, facilities, and capital expenditures/ asset acquisition). However, there is no STEM or technology fields associated with Nevada's creative economy and no research university associated with Nevada's creative economy (American Council of the Arts, 2017).

Colorado

The state of Colorado has put together creative districts that are based solely on the arts. They are listed as part of the Colorado creative economy. Research universities are involved only with the arts. There are no STEM or technology segments within the creative districts listed. However, they are there and can easily be added.

Employment in the creative enterprises in Colorado are 46,902 in creative occupations, 75,385 in non-creative occupations. Employment is currently 3.2

million total jobs in the creative sector of the state. The largest occupation was that of photographers with 21,890 jobs, followed by graphic designers with 10,409 jobs in 2016. Self-defined artists, which would include the SOC Codes 27-1012, 271013, 27-1014, and 27-1019 (craft artists; fine artists, including painters, sculptors, and illustrators; multimedia artists and animators; and artists and related workers, all others) totaled 9,648 jobs (Western Colorado University, 2016).

The industries of the Art Market can be measured in terms of both earnings and sales. Earnings are calculated by aggregating the compensation paid for the labor of all workers in a given industry. This includes wages, salaries, supplements, and proprietor earnings. The Colorado Art Market achieved $917,835,636 in earnings in art market industries in 2016 (Western Colorado University, 2016).

Louisiana

The creative industries of Louisiana represent 4,271 businesses, employing 60,357 people. Wages total $1.6 billion and more than $5.5 billion in revenue. The non-profit arts, culture, and humanities are the core of the state's creative industries. Leading industries are film and media, writing and publishing, independent performers, retail, sports, and architectural services. For every 10,000 residents there are 140.6 that are employed in the creative economy (American Council for the Arts, 2017).

Research universities support the traditional arts in Louisiana; however, there are no STEM or technology initiatives. Moreover, research universities have not taken the lead to support creative initiatives. Louisiana has struggled to rebuild their economy after Hurricane Katrina. Gradually the economy is coming back; the creative economy is an important segment for their overall success.

Washington

Washington State considers the big win of the creative economy is jobs. Since 2005, the Washington Arts Council has collaborated with the Western States Arts Federation to track data annually on Washington's creative economy. They measure their accomplishments by the Creative Vitality Index, or CVI. The most recent CVI data paints a compelling picture of job growth in the state, indicating that the creative industry has been resilient in tough economic times. In 2017, there were 117, 816 creative jobs Revenues for nonprofit and for-profit creative business totaled $1.84 billion (State of Washington, 2017)

The CVI results also indicate potential areas for growth in the arts sector. Although art galleries and individual artists added more than $622 million to the state's economy in 2011, Washington falls 25% below the national baseline in this category. Revenue from performing arts organizations also trailed the national baseline by 11%. Although Washington generated more arts-based revenue than did Oregon, they lagged on a per capita basis. Overall, creative vitality in Washington exceeded the national baseline in 2011 by 2%. This represents a slight dip from 2010, but an upward trend, nonetheless, since 2005. Unfortunately, there is no involvement of STEM or a research university in the creative economic strategic plan (State of Washington, 2017).

Arkansas

Arkansas has a formal Arkansas Arts Council and efforts have been made to develop the creative economy in Arkansas. A report published in April of 2007, "Creativity in the Natural State," highlighted the creative roots and culture and how to turn Arkansas's rich history into economic advantage. A follow-up report published 2008 titled, "Ducks, Documentaries, & Design: Tales from Arkansas' Creative Economy," highlighted the many initiatives happening around the state that support the creative economy (Arkansas Arts Council, 2008).

A follow-up report in 2019 titled "Deep Roots, High Hopes," highlighted the development of creative assets such as associations, education and training, events and performances, places and space, design talent, and resources. This was the beginning of the development of clusters. From here, regional focus groups and creative assets that identified the competitive strengths and challenges to growing the creative economy. Each of the clusters was broken down into sub-clusters such as visual, literary, performing arts, entertainment, new media, product and environmental design, cultural heritage and preservation (Arkansas Arts Council, 2019).

In 2009, a final report titled, "Unveiling the Creative Economy in Arkansas: Strategies to Increase Creative Capacity and Competitive Advantage," summarized some of the most important findings. It also included on-the-ground interactions with Arkansans working with organizations through a series of grants. Arkansas-based organizations received grants to pursue innovative strategies to build their communities. Rather than simply looking at where Arkansas's creative economy stood, the report offered a wide range of recommendations on how it could be enhanced. Recommendations were developed through input from an advisory board of leaders in economic, workforce, and cultural development as well as through discussions with key individuals throughout the state. The goal was for the final report to help Arkansas reach its full potential as a center of creative activity, thereby contributing to its economic growth. Goals put forth by the final report (Arkansas Arts Council, 2008) are:

- Goal 1 – Strengthen recognition of and support of Arkansas's creative economy within the state's economic development community
- Goal 2 – Nurture the development of creative talent and the pipeline of creative workers
- Goal 3 – Promote the growth and profitability of creative enterprises
- Goal 4 – Utilize creative talent and assets to increase the competitiveness of other key clusters in Arkansas
- Goal 5 – Support and expand the creative infrastructure

The Arkansas Arts Council offers many programs. Get Smart is a series of workshops that cover art-related topics for individual artists and arts organizations. The program was established in 2014 and is designed to provide networking opportunities and training. The Arkansas Living Treasure Award recognizes an Arkansas artist who excels in the creation of traditional craft, and who actively preserves and advances their craft for community outreach and education. The Governor's Arts Award was established in 1991 and recognizes individuals and corporations for their outstanding contributions to the arts in Arkansas. The recipients are nominated by the public and selected by an independent panel of art professionals from around the state. Each recipient receives an original work of art created by an Arkansas artist. Poetry Out Loud is a free high school program that encourages the nation's youth to learn about poetry through memorization and recitation. The goal of the program is to develop self-confidence, public speaking skills, learn history and compete for more than $20,000 in awards at the national level. In addition, many grants are available through the Arkansas Arts Council (Arkansas Arts Council, 2008).

One of the unique places in Arkansas is the non-profit Innovation Hub in Little Rock, Arkansas. The Innovation Hub opened in 2014, with a goal of improving the lives of Arkansans by inspiring innovation and expanding opportunities. The facility is state-of-the-art and provides tools and training to entrepreneurs, students, and others, to prepare them to join and grow in the economic environment of Arkansas.

The Hub was created to help meet the challenges of the modern world by providing a collaborative community that exposes everyone to creative possibilities, offering information, instruction, and resources to engage and create. It is an open environment full of tools, technology, equipment, and support. It is most likely one of the best assets to the creative economy in Arkansas.

CONCLUSION

It is important to understand the struggle to develop a vibrant creative economy for many states. They struggle with finding disruptive leaders to lead the creative movement. They struggle with funding. As we have learned in prior chapters, a disruptive leader is needed to develop other disruptive leaders, and implement the programs needed for success. State government is not permanent. A new governor can change the trajectory. It is very important that leaders are informed and educated about the present and future. No one can be assured of thriving if they are not collaborative, open-minded, and functioning at a higher level. Those that have heightened creativity and are self-disruptive will be the ones who thrive.

REFERENCES

Alliance for the Arts. (2006). *The Arts as an Industry: Their Economic Impact on New York State and New York City.* Alliance for the Arts.

American for the Arts. (2019) Funding Resources. *American for the Arts.* Retrieved from, https://www.americansforthearts.org/by-topic/funding-resources

Americans for the Arts. (2017). Creative Industries Reports and Dunn and Bradstreet. *American for the Arts.* Retrieved from, http://www.americansforthearts.org/by-program/reports-and-data/research-studies-publications/creative-industries

Arkansas Arts Council. (2019). The Arkansas Arts Council. *Arkansas Arts Council.* Retrieved from, http://www.arkansasarts.org/

Arts of South Dakota. (2019). *South Dakota Arts Council, State of South Dakota*. Retrieved from, https://artssouthdakota.org/

DeVol, R., & Wisecarver, S.J. (2018). *Micropolitan Success Stories from the Heartland.* The Walton Family Foundation.

Iowa Economic Development. (2019). *This is what opportunity looks like*. State of Iowa. Retrieved from, https://www.iowaeconomicdevelopment.com/

KEDA. (2019). *Kansas Economic Development Council, State of Kansas*. Retrieved from, http://www.kansaseda.com/Pages/default.aspx

Kentucky Arts Council. (1998). Arts and the Kentucky Economy. *Kentucky Arts Council*. Retrieved form, http://artscouncil.ky.gov/whtsnew/artsecon/artsecon.pdf

MEDC. (2019). *Mississippi Economic Development Council, State of Mississippi*. Retrieved from, https://medc.ms/

National Assembly of State Arts Agencies. (n.d.). State Arts Agency Creative Economy Initiatives. *National Assembly of State Arts Agencies*. Retrieved from, http://www.nasaa-arts.org/artworks/creativeeconomy_initiatives.html#ar

National Governors Association. (2009). Arts and the Economy: Using Art and Culture to stimulate the economy. *National Governors Center.* Retrieved from, http://www.nga.org/cms/center/publications?begin7736bde9-79fd-493d-be2b-0f62416085cd=180&end7736bde9-79fd-493d-be2b-0f62416085cd=189&pagesize7736bde9-79fd-493d-be2b-0f62416085cd=10&

New Mexico. (2019). *New Mexico Arts, State of New Mexico*. Retrieved from, http://www.nmarts.org/

OEDC. (2019). *Oklahoma Economic Development Council, State of Oklahoma*. Retrieved from, https://oedc.net/

Vermont Art's Council. (2019). About, History and programs of the Vermont Art's Council. *Vermont Art's Council*. Retrieved from, https://www.vermontartscouncil.org/

Wyoming Arts Council. (2019). *Wyoming Arts, State of Wyoming*. Retrieved from, https://wyoarts.state.wy.us/

Wyoming Economic Development Association. (2019). *WEDA, State of Wyoming*. Retrieved from, http://www.wyomingeda.org/

Chapter 9
Branding and Funding

ABSTRACT

Branding is important in building the creative economy. Branding is the story of your history, values, beliefs, and vision. Branding is not based on whims, but on careful well thought out ideas, and the most powerful branding comes from disruptive thinking. The power of changing the thought process to using new methodologies and modern ideas cannot be underestimated. Creative cultural branding centers on branding that ignites the creative economy in your specific unique area. It is important to not only get early stage capital when building the creative economy, but all the help you can receive through grants. Government agencies and foundations can give disruptive leaders a start in developing the creative businesses to thrive in our modern times. Federal funding for the creative economy initiative can complement local and foundation funding. Typically, federal funding is for capital investment, not for planning or ideation. Understanding funding options and requirements is important. This chapter explores branding and funding.

INTRODUCTION

Your premium brand had better be delivering something special, or it is not going to get business. - Warren Buffett

Large foundations have taken an active role in community re-development and support the creative economy initiatives. Foundations can act quickly, take risks, seeding innovations, and challenge tradition. Often foundation

DOI: 10.4018/978-1-7998-3416-8.ch009

grants serve as first-in patient capital, independent from political and market forces. Research has consistently recognized the relationships between government funding and private philanthropy is a significant force in U.S. society (Wardip, Lambe and Zeeuw, 2016). Both government and private philanthropy intersect, and understanding the distribution of grant funding could help shape policy (Coutts Institute, 2015).

Branding builds from the culture of a community or organization by depicting the heart of the culture. In essence, what are the overlaying beliefs, values, traditions and stories of the community or organization? A majority must agree that the brand reflects these overlaying beliefs and values. When the community can stand together on their culture, they can build their brand. This is not a marketing ploy or for advertisement. This is the lifeblood of the community, organization, region or state. Many states have re-branded for tourism, and tourism is part of the creative economy. Arkansas used the tag line *the Natural State,* which reflects the beautiful lakes, forests, and rivers that are enjoyed by many tourists. Maine uses the tag line *It Must Be Maine.* Kentucky's tag line is *Unbridled Spirit;* New Mexico's tag line is *Land of Enchantment.* New York's famous tag line *I Love New York* is known by the distinct logo with love being replaced by the heart. For the creative economy to be strong and sustainable, it is necessary to build a strong brand. The strong brand attracts people to your community, region, or state.

CREATIVE CULTURAL BRANDING

If it is branded well, cultural tourism is one of the mainstays of the creative economy. Cultural tourism has developed rapidly and is considered an important sector to global tourism. Cultural tourism is an experience of everyday life. Tourists prefer to avoid the formal cultural settings, such as museums and galleries, for a cultural experience that includes going to cafés, bars, shops, and everyday common places (Patrascu, 2013). Cultural tourism may be designated as food, wine, and experience.

Creativity branding is a joint effort of a large group of community leaders, businesses, teachers, artists, and stakeholders. In other words, the rich accumulation of knowledge with individuals working together to enhance the creative potential of a community, region or state for the greater good of all. This collaboration based on cultural identity and creativity produces a unique and special brand.

To begin the process nictitates requiring lots of input. This process is the most boring part of branding, but it is the most crucial and represents eighty percent of the process. Surveys and roundtable discussions with all stakeholder groups, business focus groups, government agencies and community groups, plus research on demographic, psychographics, and market analysis are all necessary to define the brand. From this input, the culture (i.e., brand) develops from the stories, values, and beliefs that every one of these groups share. When this is done, all stakeholders feel involved. They may not all agree, but the stakeholders had the chance to give input and fully define their cultural and their brand.

FUNDING

Federal funding for the creative economy initiative can complement local and foundation funding. Typically, federal funding is for capital investment, not for planning or ideation. Understanding funding options and requirements is important.

The Community Development Block Grant program was established in 1974 and is one of the oldest programs administered by HUD. According to the National Governors Association (2019), HUD Community Development Block Grant programs included artist housing, which is associated with low-income housing tax credits. Initially launched in Berkshire County, Massachusetts, Assets for Artists broadened its scope in 2011 to provide opportunities to artists throughout Massachusetts with further expansion to Portland, Maine in 2013. In Maine, the community grant program funded a project for the Creative Portland Cooperation: Assets for Artists. Assets for Artists has piloted an innovative matched savings grant program and financial and business training opportunities for low to moderate-income artist.

In Rhode Island, New Urban Arts, Providence, purchased a 4,200 square foot commercial space in excellent structural condition. The structure is accessible to youth from diverse neighborhoods and allows for a safe, gang-neutral space. New Urban Arts intends to transform the vacant space into a vibrant facility serving at-risk youth and local artists. The goal of the center is to provide economic development and public participation in the arts (Americans for the Arts, 2014).

Additional Federal Programs that Support Arts and Cultural Projects

U. S. Department of Commerce

The U.S. Department of Commerce, Economic Development Administration offers funding for innovative regional incubators, space for entrepreneurs in the creative economy, and commercialization strategies through the office of Innovation and Entrepreneurship Regional Innovation Strategies program.

The University of Missouri's Center of Innovation is an example of the grant opportunity. The center provides technical assistance with a focus on services such as business management counseling that improves entrepreneur's probability of success by assessing resources, marketing, and technology. The Center received a $162,500 grant.

In response to the Choctaw Native American Nation to implement an economic development program in Southeast Oklahoma, a $750,000 grant was awarded to support the exploration of business development, industrial parks, ports, and other economic development activities to diversify and strengthen the regional economy.

U.S. Treasury

The U.S. Treasury awards more than $200 million in grant money to spur economic development in low-income urban, rural, and native communities. In 2015, highlights of awards listed recipients by geographic market including 56 major urban awards, 34 minor urban awards, and 33 rural awards. Out of 23 states, 11 were awarded grants for the Healthy Food Financing Initiative, and 148 organizations received funding.

National Endowment for the Arts

The U.S. Congress established the National Endowment for the Arts (NEA) in 1965. The NEA is the independent federal agency who's funding and support gives Americans the opportunity to participate in the arts, exercise their imaginations, and develop their creative capacities. Through partnerships with state arts agencies, local leaders, other federal agencies, and the philanthropic sector, the NEA supports arts learning, affirms and celebrates America's rich and diverse cultural heritage, and extends its work to promote equal access to the arts in every community across America. The National Endowment of Arts has funding for planning, design, and recently has granted funding for competitive grants for organizations, individuals, and partnership agreements. Each category has separate guidelines. Examples of organizational grants are:

1. Art Works II. 977 awards totaling $23,983,500. Examples of Art Works-supported projects:
   - A $10,000 award to Shreveport Opera in Louisiana to support the Shreveport Opera Xpress educational touring program, which offers performances and activities for public school students in central and south Louisiana.
   - A $15,000 award to the Pioneer School of Drama in Danville, Kentucky, to support Voices Inside: The Northpoint Prison Writing and Performance Project, where theater professionals conduct workshops for inmates at the Northpoint Training Center.
2. Our Town. 57 awards totaling $4,115,000. Examples of Our Town-supported projects are:
   - A $50,000 award to the City of Granite Falls in Minnesota to establish an artist residency program within local government. The program is the first of its kind in a small, rural setting and has the potential to serve as a national model for other small communities.
   - An $85,000 grant to the Santa Fe Art Institute to re-enliven the shuttered campus of the former Santa Fe College of Art and Design by inventorying the campus's cultural assets and creating community arts events to build enthusiasm around the campus's development potential and to advance community goals.
3. State and Regional Partnership Agreements. 64 awards totaling $51,456,500. Examples of state and regional programming funded by partnership agreements are:
   - The Delaware Division of the Arts and Delaware State Parks have been working together since 2008 to offer arts-in-the-park programming that has increased the number and diversity of visitors to state parks.
   - Through its Arts and Military Initiative, the Oklahoma Arts Council works with the state's Department of Veterans Affairs and a local partner to provide arts activities to residents at the Oklahoma Veterans Center in Norman.

4. Research Art Works. 15 awards totaling $724,000. Examples of this year's awardees are:
    - A $20,000 award to MINDPOP in Austin, Texas, supports a study led by researchers from the Austin Independent School District and the University of Texas at Austin that examines relationships between schools and arts partners participating in a collective impact arts education project.
    - An $88,000 award to the Cleveland Clinic Foundation in Cleveland, Ohio, supports a randomized controlled trial examining the arts' ability to improve health, resilience, and well-being in individuals with chronic health conditions.

Appalachian Regional Commission

The Appalachian Regional Commission is a regional economic development agency that collaborates with federal, state, and local governments. Thirteen Appalachian states are in this region. The commission funds investment in entrepreneurial and business development strategies that strengthen the Appalachian economy. Projects funded are cultural, environmental, leadership, community, and structural assets.

National Governors Association

The National Governors Association (2019) suggests that strategies should focus on traditional arts, culture and heritage, local entrepreneurism, and tourism. In January 2019, the commission awarded $1.3 million in grants for economic development to support projects in West Virginia. In 2018, the commission approved $150 million in grants for 600 economic development projects across all of Appalachia.

USDA Rural Development Grants

The USDA Rural Development program has funded several projects that were featured in the National Governors Association Rural Action Guide (2019). Several different grants and loans are available. One is the Business & Industry Loan Guarantees. The program is to bolster the availability of private credit by guaranteeing loans for rural businesses. This loan is for non-profits, for profits, cooperatives, federally recognized tribes, public organizations, and individuals. Funds can be used for business conversion, enlargement, repair, modernization, development, to purchase and develop land, easements, right-of-ways, to purchase equipment and inventory and acquisitions. Funds cannot be used for lines of credit, occupied housing, golf courses, racetracks, gambling facilities, churches, fraternal organizations, lending, agricultural production, or payment to a beneficiary.

Rural Business Development grants are designed to support targeted technical assistance, training, and other activities leading to the development or expansion of small and emerging private businesses in rural areas that employ 50 or fewer employees and has less than $1 million in gross revenue. Towns, communities, state agencies, authorities, non-profits, higher education institutions, federally recognized tribes, and rural cooperatives can apply for the loans. These funds can be used for training, acquisitions of buildings and equipment, pollution control and abatement, distant adult learning, community economic development, leadership and entrepreneur training, incubators and long-term business strategy.

Value Added Producer Grants help agricultural producers enter the value-added activities for processing and marketing new products. The goal of this program is to generate new products, create and expand marketing opportunities, and increase producer income. Funds can be used to meet matching grants, working capital expenses such as processing, marketing and advertising cost, and inventory and salaries expenses.

National Governors Association

The National Governors Association (2019) encourages governors to align the effort with federal funding programs. Often states can counter federal efforts, and this can be easily changed. States can serve as facilitators for regional development, local communities and small businesses particularly on funding. Manufacturing associations, technology centers, maker spaces all can be funded by private donors and businesses. In addition, this fosters networks for creative entrepreneurs and stakeholders, and develops targeted funding for small communities and small business. To support these networks along with state and local funding efforts, working with local, regional and state elected officials is important. These efforts are most successful to fund seed capital for the creative economy. In local, regional and state economies, funding is limited; convincing elected officials that these programs can actually strengthen the overall economy is perceived as money well spent. In addition, states have found that tax incentives support the creative economy. Four main tax incentives that spur the creative economy are:

- Property tax incentives that encourages developers and landowners to look at ways to create new possibilities from current holdings.
- Incentives for artists selling their work and paying income tax or state sales tax.
- An abatement of the admissions or ticket sales tax. Some states have an entertainment tax.
- Historic tax credits for museums or cultural place making areas.

With many challenges, evaluating policies and statutes can prevent adverse impacts on creative economic development. A dedicated group of people, all collaborating with passion and vision, can change the world.

ENGAGEMENT

Getting people engaged in community activities is challenging. By bringing together the appropriate agencies, local and statewide foundations, and community leaders, resources are allocated for the better use. Foundations can build capacity. A perfect example is the Kresge Foundation. The Kresge Foundation worked with more than 300 stakeholders to advance a collective agenda to increase public and private investments in African American communities in Detroit. This initiative, *The Detroit Story, Detroit is Rival,* has brought this group together to solve the many issues plaguing Detroit. In February 2019, Kresge's Human Service Program announced they would participate in its Detroit Next Generation Initiative with grants totaling $1.25 million. Grantees were award $250,000 each and received additional support from a learning and collaborative network. In addition to the Human Service Program, Kresge's Social Investments team provides funding to support the framework to design best practices for Opportunity Zones. This framework is a voluntary guideline designed to define best practices for investors and fund managers looking to invest in Opportunity Zones. An incubator was developed to assist with the Opportunity Zones.

Kresge was able to attract other foundations to be involved with the Opportunity Zones. One being Calvert Impact Capital who invested $390,000 in grant money to support the Opportunity Zone Incubator. This grant provides a technical assistance program for social impact entities that are interested in exploring an Opportunity Fund to market. In addition, Kresge selected five mission-aligned organizations that are exploring funding to support the Opportunity Zones Incubator. In partnership with the Rockefeller Foundation, a call to action in the summer of 2018 sent letters to which 141 organizations responded. From these, Kresge selected a dozen to move forward with technical assistance for the incubator program and to develop a due diligence process for impact investments. The five original organizations that are exploring starting the Opportunity Zone Fund Incubator are:

- Craft3, a regional nonprofit that makes loans in Oregon and Washington to strengthen the resilience of businesses, families, and nonprofits.
- New Orleans Startup Fund, a nonprofit venture fund established by Greater New Orleans business and community leaders that provides seed capital and technical assistance to early-stage firms that demonstrate significant growth potential.
- Gulf Coast Housing Partnership that works in the Gulf Coast region to promote community and economic development through various programs implemented to deliver effective and meaningful results.
- Renaissance HBCU Opportunity Fund, a partnership between Renaissance Equity Partners and an affiliate of the HBCU Community Development Corporation to invest in value-added and opportunistic real estate on or near the campuses of Historically Black Colleges and Universities.
- Fifth Ward Community Redevelopment Corporation, which seeks to enhance quality of life for individuals and families living in Houston's fifth ward, eliminate blight, attract investment and resources, encourage commercial and business development, coordinate government and public service, and offer a sense of destination and creative place making.
    - (Kresge, 2018)

The Opportunity Zone Incubator is a free-market approach unmatched by any federal spending guarantees. The designation as an Opportunity Zone does not mean that a community receives money for school, health care, or other public services, or even that they will receive money at all. Most importantly, these five organizations truly understand the needs and what it takes to invest in low-income communities.

FOUNDATIONS

In their Foundation Review, Wardip, Lambe and Zeeuw (2016) tell us to follow the money for economic development and grant making. They challenge many beliefs about grant making. One, that small socioeconomically distressed metro areas do not attract a proportional share of grant capital from the nation's largest foundations. Two, they analyzed foundation grants made from 2008-2013 and determined certain characteristics that are associated with higher levels of grant receipt. Three, the density of non-profits and the presence of large local foundations are shown to be consistently significant predictors of grant receipt. Their analysis determined that areas of high poverty received significant grants.

When seeking to develop higher paying jobs, infrastructure, affordable housing, better education, health care improvements and revitalization, additional foundational funding is relied upon for success. Not to say that the government grants are not important, but they may not be enough. In 2018, philanthropic contributions in the U.S. totaled $427.71 billion. Corporation donations totaled $20.05 billion, and foundation giving totaled $75.86 billion. Grants from foundations are generally small, but significant. Foundations can act quickly, take risks, seeding innovations, and challenge tradition. Often foundation grants serve as first-in patient capital, independent from political and market forces (Wardip, Lambe and Zeeuw, 2016). Research has consistently recognized the relationships between government funding and private philanthropy is a significant force in U.S. society (Wardip, Lambe and Zeeuw, 2016). Both government and private philanthropy intersect, and understanding the distribution of grant funding could help shape policy (Coutts Institute, 2015).

Many sources are available to help an organization find foundation grant opportunities. Some states and cities have regional foundation directories. Maine State Philanthropy Association has a good up to date directory, and a great on-line toolkit. The Foundation Center at www.foundationcenter.org is very helpful with an on-line directory. The Fundraising Authority at www.thefundraisingauthority.com has a newsletter, articles, and webinars to help navigate the world of foundations.

GRANT WRITING

The American Grant Writers' Association (AGWA) is the national association of professional grant writers, grant researchers, and grant managers. Among their members are grant consultants, employees at government agencies, school districts, higher education institutions, corporations, foundations, native tribes, and non-profit organizations throughout the U.S. and abroad. Their mission statement follows: (AGWA, 2019).

The mission of American Grant Writers' Association is to enhance the professional standards and ethical practices of grant seekers and grant managers through education, certification, networking, and professional growth.

AGWA has a list of services and strategies on the web site. For funding purposes, professional grant writing leads to bigger and more successful grants.

CONCLUSION

This chapter is a tool to examine the many funding avenues to develop the creative economy. Nothing should under-estimate the disruptive leaders' ability to acquire early stage capital and seed money. Disruptor will not wait on grants and that caught up in funding that may take several months to finalize the financial outcome. For disruptors the funding mentioned in this chapter is operating funding to ensure a good financial base. This funding can provide security for established creative industries who are already well established. I one is looking for seed money foundations or venture capitalists is the right pathway.

Case Studies

The two case studies below are great examples of two communities using every resource they could find to successfully ignite the creative economy in their community. Disruptive leaders led the initiatives. In South Fork, Colorado a group of disruptive leaders saw what was lacking (community programs). By asking community members and businesses to support their initiatives, they have been successful in launching many events and programs. Their next step was to research and get deeply involved in grant writing. The second case study, Eastport, Maine is an example of branding and heightened creativity. A group of disruptive leaders decided to create a unique wacky brand, and to launch this they created the yearly Pirate Festival. From there more events were started, with a goal of finding more businesses. The endeavor was successful and now Eastport is a thriving community, with the help of the creative economy.

Case Study 1: South Fork, Colorado

In the fall of 2017, a group of citizens got together and realized the town did not have the budget to add much needed holiday cheer to the town visitor center that contained bare Aspen trees. The group was named the Yuletide Committee and was comprised of concerned individuals and business owners. This group had a vision to see South Fork, Colorado, come alive in the cold winter months. Their goal was to light the Aspen trees and create an annual celebration on the Friday after Thanksgiving. In addition, they wanted to create a warm inviting setting to kick off the holiday season with Christmas carolers, bonfires, hot cocoa and Santa Claus. Two months of fundraising resulted in $7,000 from private funding

Inspired, the Yuletide Committee envisioned future projects to enhance tourism and economic development in South Fork. The Yuletide Committee morphed into the Friends of South Fort, a legal non-profit association in the state. In 2018, the Friends of South Fork started to develop new projects. They added a dozen lighted Christmas trees around the historic South Fork water tower, hired an electrician to lay underground conduit to the Visitor Center and the historic tower trees, purchased softball and kickball equipment for weekly games at Graeser Field, sponsored a kids game table at the South Fork Halloween celebration, purchased ten window flower boxes to decorate the South Fork Community Center, and sponsored an annual town yard sale.

This group did not rest, in 2019 the Friends of South Fork partnered with the Rio Grande Golf Club and the South Fork Powder Busters to sponsor the first annual Woof Creek Classic Dog Sled and Skijor Races that included six-dog teams, four-dog teams, and ski racing pulled by one or two dog teams. Over $5,000 in prizes and donations were raised from individuals and merchants for the winners. Hundreds attended the first year; more are expected in 2020.

The mission of the Friends of South Fork: "Is to build community spirit and enhance South Fork's unique appeal."

Friends of South Fork see themselves as "The Little Engine That Could," from the classic tale of the little engine that, despite its size, triumphantly pulls a train full of toys to the waiting children on the other side of a mountain.

This childhood story, which teaches the values of hard work and optimism, bears similarity to another small, but no less determined nonprofit called the Friends of South Fork.

The Friends of South Fork models itself after an Ohio organization founded in 2006 called 100 Women Who Care. Their idea was born out of a desire to fund projects that benefit a charitable cause, and the structure was for each member to commit to giving $100 per quarter each year. In this case, South Fork is the cause, and membership in the organization is open to all who care to join. When the Friends membership grows to 100, $10,000 will be available each quarter to fund a project or event that benefits South Fork. Members meet quarterly, although attendance is not mandatory. Members learn about prospective projects or events to which funds could be applied and are welcome to submit their own ideas as well.

Having recently filed with the Colorado Secretary of State as an unincorporated, nonprofit association, which is a legal entity when at least two people agree to pursue a common lawful purpose that is not for profit, the Friends of South Fork is now officially off and running.

In the face of many obstacles, the Friends of South Fork learned the value in asking others to work alongside them to achieve a common good. In this case, the Friends of South Fork are eager to continue spearheading projects and economic development through the creative economy that positively sets South Fork apart and highlights its amazing natural beauty and unique history.

Case Study 2: Eastport, Maine

Eastport is the deepest natural harbor on the eastern seaboard of the USA. The harbor never freezes over and, for many decades, the main activity was catching and curing fish. The City of Eastport is a series of islands in Washington County, Maine. Its incorporation as a town took place in 1798, and then as a city, almost a century later in 1893. Settled initially by the French, it was known for smuggling early in the 19th century. The main island is called Moose Island and is connected by a causeway to the US mainland. The islands are located between Cobscook Bay and Passamaquoddy Bay, the latter known for its tides and strong currents. Many boats have been lost in the strong currents.

Eastport's population remained stagnant for many years. From 1990 to 2000, the population dropped 16%, and by 2010, 18% of the population had left. This led the town of Eastport to undergo an aggressive branding and revitalization program in 2013. Several ideas were put forth. One was to capture the rich history. The first European anglers and traders came to the coast in the 1600s and settled in 1772. The area was known for piracy as well as smuggling.

One idea of the branding and revitalization effort was to offer Eastport as the site for a proposed oil refinery, which would have involved navigation of supertankers in the surrounding waters. Citizen's concerns about oil spills and environmental threats defeated the proposal. Nevertheless, Eastport did not give up and decided they would fight for their community and would recover. Eastport knew that to recover, the citizens had to apply lessons of success, keep to a positive narrative, and tell their own success story. They decided on a 20-year plan with a branding effort to be modern, funky and a little wacky.

Reviving the once thriving port seemed the most logical. With mad cow disease in Europe and other parts of the world, companies are making profits by shipping pregnant cows. Sexing Technologies, a company based in Texas, has a business where they sperm-sort to ensure that nearly all calves are female, which is desired by dairy farmers. Sexing Technology saw Eastport as an ideal transit point. Since 2017, over 40,000 cattle have been shipped abroad. Those European beef and dairy herds, reduced by mad cow disease and other factors, are now being rebuilt, largely with American stock.

With the decline of the newspaper-publishing industry, a niche business has risen in Maine for wood pellets and other wood products. Torrefaction—its name taken from the Latin word *torrefacere*, meaning heating and drying (see *torrid*)—is a process designed to convert pulp and wood by-products, including stumps, into briquette-like pellets. When these are substituted for coal in electric-power plants, they can significantly reduce carbon emissions and are a cost-effective home heat source. With state and federal aid, the Port Authority invested $9 million in an enormous conveyer-belt system that makes Eastport the fastest, cheapest site for sending pellets and wood chips to Europe.

One of the most aggressive projects has been to capture tidal energy. For example, the Bay of Fundy has the world's most powerful tidal forces, with a volume of water that flows in and out each day that is the equivalent to all the world's rivers. A group of engineers, investors, and university professors from the University of Maine Orono decided to focus on Eastport to test, design, and develop tidal-power electricity. Private investors and research grants from the Department of Energy in roughly equal amounts fund Ocean Renewable Power Company, a Portland based company. In 2012, it ran an eight-month trial of one large turbine in Cobscook Bay off Eastport. The trial was a success: the system fed power into Maine's electric grid and survived the harsh undersea environment.

The fish-farming industry had a rough start in the Eastport area some 30 years ago. Diseases swept through overcrowded pens, and the large corporations then dominating the business pulled out of local operations. A family-owned Canadian firm, Cooke Aquaculture, set up salmon farms around Eastport and have been successful.

Lobstering is an important business to the economy in Maine and especially in Eastport. Harvesting sea urchins and sea cucumbers is also profitable. Local clammers have a thriving business. The typical North Atlantic scallop boat might spend two weeks at sea and return to port with a catch that has been on ice for many days. The waters in Cobscook Bay are the last good scallop grounds in Maine; where local anglers bring in their catch daily. In the past, the fresh scallops from Eastport have been marketed with other New England scallops that have been iced for days. Currently, dockside processing houses and distribution centers are under construction that will get Eastport scallops to market quicker. Which give Eastport scallops the advantage. Adding to this industry are the boatyards, boat repair and maintenance, and suppliers that support the fishing industry, and are significant to the local economy.

In addition to industry, Eastport has concentrated on downtown revitalization. A cartoonish super-life-size statue of a bearded angler holding a big fish dominates Eastport's four-block-long downtown. It was a gift to the town from Fox TV, in recognition of Eastport's allowing the summer filming for 2001's Fox reality television series, *Murder in Small Town X.* Eastport was cast as the mythical city of Sunrise. This entire project matched the funky branding of the city as well.

A group of friends called the *Women of the Commons* bought a crumbling downtown building with a view from Eastport across the water to Campobello. They carefully renovated the building with luxurious rental condominiums upstairs and a gallery featuring local artisan's work below. These six friends returned the former elegance of the buildings and gave new hope to Eastport by developing a symbol of hope for its re-emerging downtown. In addition, to this historic rebuilding, there are many more ventures that are unique to Eastport, such as the locavore farmers and the century-old Raye's Mustard Mill, which ships jars of specialty mustards all around the country. Other examples a new boat-manufacturing company, and a defense contractor that makes hazmat suits for military and police departments.

For the last 14 years, the town of Eastport has hosted the Pirate Festival. The Pirate Festival is three fun-filled days for people of all ages. It includes several events featuring people in pirate costumes, the Pirate Parade, and the Great Pirate Lobster Boat Race on Passamaquoddy Bay. The festival includes fireworks, bed races, kid events, live music, and much more. What started out, as a small local festival is now renowned with visitors coming from parts of the United States and Canada.

On New Year Eve, Eastport hosts the Great Sardine and Maple Leaf drop. From the third story of the Tides Institute & Museum of Art, a giant red maple leaf is lowered to commemorate the Canadian new year at midnight, Atlantic time (11 pm ET), while the New Year's Eve Brass Band plays a rousing "O Canada," (singing along is encouraged). At midnight Eastern Time, an 8-foot sardine takes the plunge as the band plays Auld Lang Syne. Live music plays from 9 pm until just before midnight, and people kiss the sardine for luck in the year ahead.

Eastport is an example of hard work, creativity, and passion. There is not a place more authentic *down east* than Eastport. The spirit of Maine and the Mariner is in Eastport leading the people to bring back the quaint but thriving port that was long lost, and in doing so, creating a unique brand that honors its past as pirates and smugglers.

REFERENCES

Alliance for the Arts. (2006). *The Arts as an Industry: Their Economic Impact on New York State and New York City.* Alliance for the Arts.

American for the Arts. (2019) Funding Resources. *American for the Arts.* Retrieved from, https://www.americansforthearts.org/by-topic/funding-resources

Americans for the Arts. (2017). Creative Industries Reports and Dunn and Bradstreet. *American for the Arts.* Retrieved from, http://www.americansforthearts.org/by-program/reports-and-data/research-studies-publications/creative-industries

Appalachian Regional Commission. (2019). Grants and Funding. *Appalachian Regional Commission.* Retrieved from, https://www.arc.gov/funding/GrantsandFunding.asp

Arian, E. W. (1992). The Unfulÿlled Promise of Public Arts Subsidy in a Multicultural Society. In *Culture and Democracy: Social and Ethical Issues in Public Support for the Arts and Humanities*. Boulder: Westview Press.

Coutts Institute. (2015). *Million-dollar donors report 2015*. London: Author.

Kresge. (2017). Expanding Opportunities in Americas' cities. *Kresge Foundation*. http://kresge.org/, web.

National Endowment of the Arts. (n.d.). Funding and Grants. *National Endowment of the Arts*. Retrieved from, https://www.arts.gov/

National Governors Association. (2009). *Arts and the Economy: Using Art and Culture to stimulate the economy*. National Governors Center. Retrieved from, http://www.nga.org/cms/center/publications?begin7736bde9-79fd-493d-be2b-0f62416085cd=180&end7736bde9-79fd-493d-be2b-0f62416085cd=189&pagesize7736bde9-79fd-493d-be2b-0f62416085cd=10&

National Governors Association. (2019). *Rural Prosperity Through The Arts & Creative Sector: A Rural Action Guide for Governors and States*. National Governors Association.

U.S. Department of Commerce. (2019). Grants and Funding. *U.S. Department of Commerce*. Retrieved from, https://www.grants.gov/learn-grants/grant-making-agencies/department-of-commerce.html

Wardrip, K., Lambe, W., & de Zeeuw, M. (2016). Following the Money: An Analysis of Foundation Grantmaking for Community and Economic Development. *The Foundation Review*, *8*(3), 7. doi:10.9707/1944-5660.1313

Chapter 10
International Programs and Possibilities

ABSTRACT

Leaders are responsible for allocating and managing resources for agility and absorption. The orange world may mean short-term careers, but short-term projects, with key leaders as the core of the organization who remain for long periods. In the blue world are global influencers. Capitalism is leading growth, and employees have everything they need to develop innovation, health insurance, and technology. In this blue world, leading and seeing people is the most important asset. The corporation will develop corporate cultures that empower the workforce and quality of life for employees. The green companies develop a powerful and influential social conscience and sense of responsibility. Often consumers will demand this by lobbying for a change in corporate behavior. Green companies develop strong controls over their supplier networks and demand ethical practice from all vendors in their supply chains. With the world becoming more complex and turbulent, now more than ever we must look at how we frame and reframe our organizations to fit the future. This chapter explores international programs and possibilities.

INTRODUCTION

Without culture, and the relative freedom it implies, society, even when perfect, is but a jungle. This is why any authentic creation is a gift to the future. - Albert Camus

DOI: 10.4018/978-1-7998-3416-8.ch010

Michael Rendell's team at Price Waterhouse (2007) along with the James Martin Institute for Science and Civilization at the Said Business School in Oxford, UK, looked at the future of work and identified three worlds of business. By examining the ways organizations might operate in the future related to societal changes, the environment, and what is needed in the workplace, they came up with three new themes. One being that business models will dramatically change. Two, leadership will be a skill needed and a great challenge. Third, the role of leaders and human resource professionals will be fundamentally changed.

As these changes occur, businesses are framing and re-framing all aspects of their organizations. These new models and frames mean there may be a thinner line between work and home life, and companies are recognizing the importance of the social welfare of their employees. The need to control, monitor and measure productivity and performance means success or failure. When combined with social capital, leaders must be proactive and focused on strategy while becoming the heart of the organization. Rendell's (2007), (Morgan, 2015) team identified two global forces that influence organizations. One being individualism versus collectivism, and the second corporate integration versus fragmentation. From their research, they determined a vision for business in the future. They divided the business world into three parts: the blue world where corporate is king, the green world where companies care, and the orange world where small business is beautiful.

In the blue world are global influencers. Capitalism is leading growth, and employees have everything they need to develop innovation, health insurance, and technology. In this blue world, leading and seeing people is the most important asset. The corporation will develop corporate cultures that empower the workforce and quality of life for employees. Leading in the new blue world means framing and re-framing to link all systems for business improvement, identify talent, and manage succession planning, training, defining rewards and workplace quality of life. The blue world focuses on long careers and succession planning for top performers to move up in the organization. The blue world is highly structured with a focus on corporate culture and behaviors.

The green world is a model of the Leaders-Member Exchange Theory of Leaders (Northouse, 2018), where managers and lead employees change places to force change. The green companies develop a powerful and influential social conscience and sense of responsibility. Often consumers will demand this by lobbying for a change in corporate behavior. Green companies develop strong controls over their supplier networks and demand ethical practice from all vendors in their supply chains. They measure the greenness, and demand fines and penalties from those who do not. Leading in this green world means recruiting employees who will uphold the values and beliefs for the organization. It may mean that many employees work at home to save energy costs. In the green world, successful organizations engage across a broad footprint, where communities, customer's employees, shareholders and vendors all become equal stakeholders. The essence of the green organizations is holistic with a broad spectrum of talent, passionate people who are engaged, working toward work-place balance, social accountability, and hoping for lifetime careers.

In the orange world the free markets system flourishes. Trade barriers no longer exist, and business is operating in a global network linked together with an efficient on-line buying, selling, and trading of services or products. Businesses are smaller than the blue world business and more agile. They have strong supply chains and organic business associations. They operate from market to market and region to region. In this orange world, people networks are needed that are tied to guilds and professional networks. Incentive and reward systems are crucial in recruitment. Employees are likely to see themselves as members of a unique specialized industry.

INTER-AMERICAN DEVELOPMENT BANK

The Inter-American Development Bank recently published their "The Orange Economy: An Infinite Opportunity" (2013) report and consider this a guideline to the road for new knowledge. The report was published as a guide for the development of the creative economy in Latin America and the Caribbean. In this publication, the authors refer to the creative economy as the *Orange Economy*. They refer to orange economy as such because it encompasses the immense wealth of talent, intellectual property, interconnectedness, and the cultural heritage of Latin America and the Caribbean region (Restrepo and Marquez, 2013). The publication is unique, with lots of white space for notes, and the placement of information is done in a way to spur creative thought. "One important point worth mentioning is that, almost a decade later, the creative economy still does not register on the radar of most economists"(Restrepo and Marquez, 2013, p.15). That is surprising considering the modern world we live in, especially since the creative economy is often referred to as the sector of our economy that is based on intellectual pursuits. Restrepo and Marquez (2013) suggest that the creative economy is two and a half times the world's military expenditure. Where the creative economy has soared is through international trade. The creative economy is less volatile and most likely to avoid the pitfalls of financial crisis, commodities like oil. Restrepo and Marquez present list facts that are more interesting:

- The entertainment industry is now contributing $2.2 trillion to the world's economy, which is 230% higher than the actual value of oil exports.
- Hollywood in the United States, Bollywood in India, and Nollywood in Nigeria jointly produce more than four thousand movies per year.
- Video games represent 70% of all tablet use.
- More than 25 billion songs have been downloaded from Apple iTunes.
- More than 50 billion apps have been downloaded from Apple AppStore.

Why then, does the creative economy get little attention by governments? Economics is a social science. Economists should be touting the benefits of the creative economy. As an example, in a speech in 2019, the Prime Minister of India, Narenda Modi, talked about the importance of the creative economy to India in completing his goal of building a $5 trillion economy.

THE WORLD BANK

The World Bank has set two goals: to end extreme poverty by decreasing the percentage of people living on less than $1.90 a day to no more than 3% and, second, to promote share prosperity by fostering the income growth of the bottom 40% of global population. The bank sees itself as a unique partnership to poverty and to support development. By providing low-interest loans, zero to low-interest credits, and grants to countries, the bank can support the creative economy. By offering innovative knowledge sharing, they can support economic development through policy advice, research and analysis, and technical assistance.

The World Bank sees the creative economy as a convergence of science and technology with industry, as well as the fusion of culture with industry. New research by the World Bank shows that young, growth-oriented companies contribute significantly to net employment growth and help enhance competitiveness and productivity by introducing new products, developing novel business models, and opening new markets. This unique creativity allows companies to specialize and upgrade quality. Start-ups are likely to succeed when having a healthy innovation ecosystem (World Bank, 2019).

At heart of the World Bank is education and learning for all. The banks' research indicates that cultivating a creative and innovative economy starts through education that develops the intelligences', cognitive skill development and changing behaviors. Personality traits are as important as cognitive ability for a person to thrive in a learning environment. Intelligence, personality traits, and socioeconomic background are all factors that determine performance. Creativity and innovation are promoted not only education, but also economic policies, which are influenced by culture. According to the World Bank (2018), a creative economy is built through education and economic policy. Personality traits are often defined as the enduring patterns of thoughts, feelings, and behaviors that differentiate us from one another. Research has determined that higher levels of intelligence or cognitive ability and personality are associated with better education outcomes. These abilities directly affect innovation and creativity (Roberts, 2009).

Socioeconomic backgrounds have been deterrents to educational performance. For this reason, scholarships, grants, and financial assistance are vital for long-term success and equality. Identifying families where grandparents and parents have poor literacy and math skills often predicts which children will struggle with those skills. As the World Bank works to control socioeconomic characteristics and environments, they invest in education for both children and adults (World Bank, 2019).

The World Bank has found the most important factor to the creative economy is an individual's ability to generate novel ideas. An individual's ability or tendency to be creative enough to generate novel ideas comes from cognitive and metacognitive skills, underlying intelligences, and personality. Studies on creativity as a process determine that stimulating creativity is not only about stimulating personal imagination, but also one's lifestyle, personality, and the environment. Most creative people show an interest in their field at an early age, and most have benefitted from a supportive mentor or coach in their area of interest. Building an expertise in a specific field requires many hours of study and applying what you have learned. This is further reiterated in Malcom Gladwell's book *Outliers (2008)*. Gladwell contends that you need to have practiced 10,000 hours in a discipline before you become an expert.

The World Bank (2019) determined that the dimensions of development need to be addressed along with cultural activities to find the solutions to complex problems and to foster social inclusion, climate research and action and commerce. World Bank contends that cultural products can help reduce extreme poverty in areas of the world where people are economically poor but endowed with a rich and diverse heritage. Cultural activities can foster nation building, bridge social differences and much more. Culture is not restricted to just money. The social contribution of culture deserves scrutiny in building foundations of human and sustainable development. Additionally, cultural activities are vehicles for a collective voice, gender equality, social capital, mental health, education, environmental issues, national identity, cultural heritage, and more.

One area for concern is intellectual property rights, such as the creation of the mind in commerce areas namely literacy, art, design, music, symbols, names, and images. Currently, intellectual property rights are viewed as a Western construct that is traced back in history to ancient Egypt. The ancient Egyptians respected trade secrets and artisans. Hieroglyphic tablets from 2000 BCE on display in the Louvre museum depict this. Egyptians branded cattle, Chinese marked their pottery, and Romans used logos and brand names for stores, lamps and other products. They were all marking ownership and owning ideas (World Bank, 2018).

Today, the World Trade Organization is coordinating intellectual property rights. Some say that the effort is good, but still does not address the needs of developing or under-developed countries. Western artists, writers, inventors, and others who create intellectual property enjoy monetary rewards and contribute to their country's creative economy. Developing and under-developed countries have immense natural resources, but their intellectual property protection is weak or non-existent. This area of law or basic rights is still controversial because some feel it makes it harder for the poor to access knowledge. With the complex problems facing the developing and under-developed worlds, it has become urgent that further educational, cultural and technical development can be disseminated (World Bank, 2019).

Currently, there are three global movie industries: Hollywood, Bollywood, and Nollywood. Hollywood is based in the United States and produces 400-600 films annually. In the U.S., this industry contributed $47 billion to the economy in 2017, but was down to $38 billion in 2019. The industry employees around 310,000 people. Bollywood is based in India and produces 1000 films annually. This industry contributed $3.4 billion (USD) to India's economy. According to the film statistics, the value of Bollywood is $138.2 billion (USD). Nollywood is based in Nigeria and produces 900 movies annually. This industry contributed $800 million (USD) to the Nigerian economy and employed 300,000 people. Typically, they have produced low budget films, but with a recent investment by Netflix, they are hoping to change this image (Vanguard, 2019).

The Times of India in 2008 reported a piracy cost for Bollywood at $959 Million (USD) and about 571,000 jobs. In the U.S., Hollywood claimed a piracy cost in the billions of dollars. Nollywood in 2009 believed they were losing up to 50% of their profits due to piracy. World Bank (2018) admits these numbers may vary and are often disputed. However, some economists' say that piracy is actually good for artists, their industries, and the public at large because their art promotes positive social messages that may be good for the public.

World Bank's development strategy going forward is to develop the creative economy globally in earnest. The two goals set by the World Bank, one to end extreme poverty and the other to promote shared prosperity in less than two decades are very ambitious. The United Nations Millennium Group had fifteen strategic goals to accomplish by 2015, and they are far from completing them. However, cultural advisors speak, engage, and influence, and they are increasingly becoming recognized as drivers of meaningful progress. However, they are now largely dormant in the creative economy globally. Now is the time for the World Bank to pay attention.

UNITED NATIONS

In the UNESCO (2013) report over the global creative economy, "Widening Local Development Pathways," it is stated that culture is a driver of development led by growth of the creative economy. Culture enables development and empowers people with capacities to take ownership of their own development processes (UNESCO, 2013). This powerful statement is people centered.

By taking local values, conditions, resources, and skills, it teaches that a person or community can transform and change beyond their expectations. Unlocking the potential of the creative economy promotes the overall creativity of societies by affirming their unique identity and using their strengths to promote economic development. UNESCO (2018) definition of culture reads:

"Culture is who we are; shapes our identity, is a means of fostering respect and tolerance among people; is a way to create jobs and improve people's lives; is a way to include others and understand them; helps preserve our heritage and make sense of our future; empowers people."

Currently the creative economy has been associated internationally with inequality and associated with large cities. Realizing that unrealistic expectations should not be placed on the creative economy is important. Diverse locations might provide products to world markets but should not be held by power brokers. Policy and governmental changes are needed to change these conditions. Moreover, a lack of intellectual property protection in the developing world is a barrier to the creative economy. There is increasing evidence that indicates the worldwide creative economy can be promoted and used as an engine for sustainable human development (UNESCO, 2013).

LEADERS THAT ARE PAVING THE WAY

The priority of leadership is to engage the right people, at the right time, to the creative work. That engagement starts when the leader inspires the vision. The greatest successes come from the creativity and innovation of the people. Frans Johansson, author of *The Medici Effect*, described his finding—based on interviews with people doing highly creative work in many fields—that innovation is more likely when people of different disciplines, backgrounds and areas of expertise share their thinking. The potential for passionate engagement is seen as a noble endeavor (Harvard Business Review, 2008). All over the world, leaders are seeing the potential for the creative economy. These disruptive leaders are paving the way for countries and helping developing countries find their way.

Dr. Shashi Tharoor, Minister of State for Human Resources Development for the government of India, believes the creative economy is a very complex ecosystem that is built on age-old culture and heritage. The traditions that come from this heritage are not only vital for the modern world to motivate the creative innovators for economic development, but also for the preservation of all humanity. Tharoor believes that the creative economy has definitely emerged as one of the most dynamic sectors of world commerce and has prevailed in times of economic downturn. The grassroots interventions that attract small to medium-size innovators are crucial for the growth of the overall economy. "I value the role of creative entrepreneurs, as well as civil society organizations, for making sustained efforts, even in troubled times, to retain the vital support system of millions at the bottom of the pyramid." Tharoor feels strongly that the creative economy is a pathway to wealth equality (UNESCO, 2013).

The Deputy Prime Minister of Finance of Thailand, Prayut Chan-o-cha, has a strong message on the creative economy. In his opinion, the development of a creative economy and society is considered essential to the achievement of the country's true development potential. Countries in East and Southeast Asia, where considerable quantities of manufactured goods are produced, have so far not generated much benefit and innovation. In Thailand, it is recognized that a creative economy is based on culture and heritage and is an integrated process that combines culture and design with innovation and technology. Thailand has realized that successfully blending all of these elements will lead to the production of unique products and services that will ultimately improve the well-being of its people. Indeed, the creative industries have already become drivers of sustainable economic growth, as shown by the rapid expansion of production and exports, which are both contributing to poverty reduction, broader-based economic development, and social transformations. For the South-East Asian region as a whole, the establishment of the Asian Economic Community helps facilitate the development of the creative economy. Social connectivity and economic linkages will further foster transfer of knowledge and development among member countries.

Reina Buijs, Vice-Minister for Foreign Trade and Development Cooperation, Kingdom of the Netherlands, in 2019 signed an agreement with the World Bank to support the developing countries of Africa and the Middle East with domestic resource mobilization. The agreement represents the commitment of the Kingdom of the Netherlands to help countries in crisis and develop new creative initiatives for economic change (UNESCO, 2018).

EUROPEAN UNION

Domenech and Koster's (2018) research quantified the direct and indirect impacts of the creative industry on employment, production, technological progress, and long-term economic development in the European Union. They found that the relationship between culture and developing the creative economy produces vision and values. Compared to transactional values, the values emerging from the creative economy are to produce and innovate. These values are not based on instrumental rationality, but on beneficial exchange.

Creative Europe is the European Commission's framework program to support the culture and the creative economy. Creative Europe as established by the European Union in 2014, brought together the current Culture, MEDIA and MEDIA Mundus programs under a common framework, and created an entirely new facility to improve access to financing. The European Parliamentary Research Service has said that the Creative Europe program consists of three distinct strands: a media sub-program, a culture sub-program, and a cross-collaboration program, which includes a self-standing financial instrument, the "Guarantee Facility". The Guarantee Facility was designed to help provide support for small and medium-sized enterprises working in the cultural and creative industries. Creative Europe's budget for the 2014/20 period is set at €1.46 billion with 31% pledged for the culture strand, 56% for media, and 13% for the cross-collaboration program.

If the United Kingdom leaves the European Union, more than 1,000 artists and cultural organizations may be affected. Several organizations will lose funding. However, leaving the European Union does not mean that cultural collaboration and trade would end. The United Kingdom may have more access to other trading partners and no longer fall under the European Union trade policies. The European Union is the United Kingdom's largest trading partner, which means new trade opportunities will need to be investigated. The outcome is yet to come, but one that should be monitored.

WORLD TRADE ORGANIZATION

The World Trade Organization (WTO) sees the creative industries as having unprecedented growth in recent years, and this is likely to continue. Even though developed countries have dominated this sector, WTO sees developing economies growing 143% in the last five years. This growth is in technology and tourism. Most importantly, the creative industries are a catalyst for positive change. A large majority of developing countries are not able to understand the capacities of their creative industries and use them for economic development. The WTO has put forth several policy recommendations for the creative economy. They help governments to develop strategies so their creative industries can use these policies. (WTO, 2019) Some recommendations include:

- Mapping inventories of cultural assets and creative industries
- Develop financing
- Develop intellectual property right laws
- Tourism promotion
- Education, training, and skill development
- Support for artists, technology, and culture conservation

GLOBAL LEADER COMPETENCE

As the creative economy grows, so does the potential of international trade and global assignments. The development of global citizens that are truly globally competent is important going forward. Research determined that becoming globally competent is more than being socially responsible and culturally intelligent. Global competence does not come easy and takes years of working in the global society to develop. Global competence means having an open mind and actively seeking to understand other cultural norms and expectations with an understanding that enables you to effectively communicate and work outside of your own environment, while demonstrating an interest and knowledge about world issues and events.

In my research, I conducted one-on-one interviews with top leadership with a global NGO, executives in business and professionals who have had ten or more year's engagement in global assignments or international trade. Questions were opened ended and based on social responsibility, cultural intelligence, global civic engagement, and global competence. Some of the responses are below:

I see cultural intelligence more as a specific high-level awareness that is based on cultures different from your own. In addition, global competence is the leadership you have attained, a high level of skill and experience, more than a general idea that you are aware of what is happening globally.

I think global competence is the second phase of cultural intelligence. You need to have cultural intelligence and constantly work on being aware and knowing the issues. Being sensitive and constantly working to improve your awareness and educating yourself so that you can be globally competent. To function successfully and fluently anywhere in the world.

I think the ability to do your practice or your service to the highest standards, such that if you are sampling water or sediments and trying to understand what caused that contamination, you want to be competent in doing the work, this is key. Nevertheless, without understanding, or without being able to flex to the culture or having somebody that is from that area, you are not necessarily going to get the same level of work that you would otherwise. You need the knowledge of the local history.

There are always forward-thinking companies, and they take the time to understand issues and how issues are interlinked at a greater level. In other words, across more disciplines and more understanding of the geopolitical connections and how they affect everything. I think people are successful if they understand and take the time to do the due diligence across a large spectrum of issues and subjects.

Several themes derived from the interviews were not specifically asked about in the research questions. Below are comments consistently mentioned by all participants. Some felt that competence could develop and grow from training and education given by their organizations, or trade center training, however, others saw this as deficient.

Cultural training is more behaviorally oriented, focusing on language and business practices. If one wants to succeed globally, knowing the language and understanding the history and value systems is very helpful. It puts the business practitioner at a higher level. Acceptance will be greater and trust will evolve faster. Most misunderstanding can be avoided. Therefore, some training it is better than none. However, if it is not comprehensive, it may not work.

This experienced and highly intelligent group of people all had another common theme, the need to be competent in their geopolitical, social and governmental issues. Two of the participants expressed the need for cyber security and personal security for company staff and facilities. Participants working for global non-profits expressed the need to be informed and educated when working for the greater good in other societies. They expressed that they often see projects done that are not needed or used. They expressed the need for better communications and have a philosophy of "teaching someone to fish is better than giving someone a fish." Four participants used this specific quote.

CONCLUSION

The phenomenon of the global citizen leader is the new disruptive leader, one who has personal mastery, with a high level of cultural intelligence, transcends to a high level of global competence. Through practical experience and cognitive and metacognitive abilities, they form an exceptional attitude toward others, develop relationships, able to solve difficult problems, make excellent decisions, influence, motivate and create clear visions. Their personal and professional behaviors align to high standards of integrity, honesty and straight forwardness. These new disruptors of world are globally competent citizen leaders who are needed to bring about the new rendition of the creative economy. Furthermore, as we focus on unique cultural areas, we bring about a new unique economy.

CASE STUDIES

The following case studies are examples of global citizen leaders developing programs to ignite the creative economies of their countries. Argentina is has develop a training program for you artists with the help of UNESCO's International Fund for Cultural Diversity. From this program, new programs all developing in several South American countries. The second case study is a collaboration of many groups in Nairobi, Kenya that are joining forces to bring the arts to Kenya. This scared place is a new art's center to advance the country's valuable art assets and its creative economy. These are disruptive leaders build their countries resources and training their most valuable assets, their people.

Case Study 1: Argentina

In Argentina, some 300,000 people represent 3.5% of the country's GDP. While market demand for skilled practitioners is also on the rise, many talented young people find it hard to break into this area. Aspiring stage designer, Diana Caraballo, explains, "It is very rare for artists to find affordable training and development opportunities that are practical." She was lucky enough to have recently completed a one-year course in stage design and tailoring at a new vocational school for the performing arts in La Plata, near Buenos Aires.

The school was set up in 2011 by the Fundación Teat Argentino de La Plata, a nongovernmental organization working to bring the performing arts to a broader audience, with support from UNESCO's International Fund for Cultural Diversity (IFCD). The school was established within the Argentine Theatre district to develop the skills of unemployed youth and adults by teaching them theatre and production techniques at a minimal cost. The project involved establishing student selection criteria, producing and designing intensive one-year courses, and helping to meet market demand for creative skills and expertise.

Modules include audio-visual, communication strategy, stage management, stage performance, and creative writing. The Cultural Institute of Buenos Aires was brought in to jointly develop four performing arts workshops taught by internationally renowned experts, notably from the Latin American Opera organization. Courses included carpentry, sculpture and props, scenic and space design, lighting design, and hair and make-up.

One student note, Diana Caraballo, “The highlight of the one-year training was the request I received from an events company to create their wardrobe,” adding that, “It’s great because we also got help to finding employment in the cultural sectors.” The school’s job training and placement program is helping students obtain internships, and many graduates have already found work in performing arts institutions upon leaving the course. Meanwhile, collaborating with the Ministry of Labor’s Independent Entrepreneurs Program (IEP), still more graduates have set up businesses, including an art gallery and a publishing business. With private sector support, students have also held exhibitions and taken part in job fairs. The school is also reaching out to countries across Latin America. Links have been established with similar institutions in the region and students from Colombia, Chile, and the plural-national state of Bolivia, Brazil, Ecuador, Peru, and Uruguay have participated in some of the trainings. A network has also been created to sell student artwork, with profits going to the artists and the school.

Case Study 2: Nairobi, Kenya

In Nairobi, the idea of thinking local as sacred development, is very important to the economic value of the creative industries and is critical in ensuring the restoration of justice, dignity, and respect. Ample evidence of the position of the creative industries within the development agenda has emerged over the past several years. For Nairobi, it is under- stood that they should never forget the place of the arts as a sacred space, and that these sacred spaces, both internal and external to individual or community, are as critical to development as bread, clean water, and shelter. They are the places from which present realities transform into imagined futures. The artists dream dreams and evoke in their work imaginable futures, no matter how well rooted these may be in present realities, thus creating a necessary tension between what is a rather lonely and individual experience and one that has a public face or interface. “This is the call of a young African scholar, Grace-Ahingula Musila:

We need to take seriously the power of fiction and the imagination, even more so in the face of realities that degenerate daily. However, we can acknowledge these harsh realities, and simultaneously create new possibilities. Art should stretch the horizons of possibility, not merely mark where the horizon currently is.

Her call broadens the frame in which we think about the arts and culture in the development agenda. If one journeys along the path to which it points, the creative industries also stimulate and lead change. When the arts invite communities and individuals to dream new futures, they transform our vision of development from the formulaic, systems-based solutions so often employed by development agencies into new and refreshing ones. They create an energy and vibrancy that engages deeply with existing as well as emerging challenges.

The first of its kind in East Africa, the GoDown Arts Centre is housed in a renovated warehouse located five minutes from the central business district of Nairobi, on the fringes of an industrial area. It was created by a pioneering set of individuals who had a critical outlook, took initiatives and sought new approaches and solutions, and who were all returnees from the diaspora, having made the choice to come back to Nairobi and invest in their urban home. After reviewing many such spaces in Europe, the group designed a two-year development phase plan for the center to consolidate organizational frameworks, establish center management and operation systems, try out programming for audiences, plan financial sustainability, and identify regional networking and collaboration opportunities.

Finding the right space for the center took close to two years and included three false starts. By 2003, however, GoDown was ready to launch itself as a performing and visual arts center, providing a unique multidisciplinary space for arts and host organizations representing a variety of art forms. It has become a focal point in East Africa for innovation, creativity and performance. The Centre comprises studios, rehearsal and performance spaces, and an exhibition gallery and promotes professional development through regular training workshops that encourage innovation and collaboration. These include the "East Africa Arts Summit," in which regional arts leaders meet every two years to discuss a range of issues related to its role and relevance. The recently launched project entitled, "Nairobi – Urban Cultural Anchors and Their Role in Urban Development," explores questions of identity and belonging in the city and implications for city planning. The project was organized in collaboration with writers, visual artists, photographers and performing artists. In addition, architects, city planners, anchor institutions (such as Kenya Polytechnic), and big city landowners one being (the Kenya Railways Corporation). The project engages with topical issues and reaches out to marginalized artistic communities.

Ownership of the venue represents an unencumbered source of income – the rent from resident organizations. Yet audience building is also crucial. Through a yearlong program of events, it not only bolsters the financial base, but also becomes more attractive to local corporate sponsors. Current funders of GoDown include: the Ford Message from Ms. Hoda I, Al Khamis-Kanoo Founder, and Abu Dhabi Music & Arts Foundation Creativity enshrines the soul of a nation. The Centre is the bedrock of its cultural, economic and social development.

The arts hold the keys to releasing the creative potential of the greatest resource of any country – its people. Artistic expression is not only a fundamental human right, it is also the fuel that feeds the hearts and minds of a society – spurring citizens to develop their creative potential, broaden their horizons and realize their ambitions.

REFERENCES

Johansson, F. (2004). *The Medici Effect*. Harvard Business School Publishing.

Morgan, J. (2015). The Scenarios of the Future of Work. *Forbes*. Retrieved from, https://www.forbes.com/sites/jacobmorgan/2015/04/13/three-scenarios-for-the-future-of-work/#6fb31de37b75

Northouse, P.G. (2019). *Leadership*. Sage Publications.

Rendell, M. (2007). *Managing tomorrow's People*. Price Waterhouse Coopers.

Restrepo, F.B., & Marquez, I.D. (2013). *The Orange Report*. Inter-American Development Bank.

The World Bank. (2019). Creative Economy and Innovation Policy. *The World Bank*. Retrieved from, https://www.worldbank.org/en/news/feature/2016/01/04/forum-explores-the-critical-roles-of-the-creative-economy-and-innovation-policy

UNESCO. (2013). *Creative Economy Report: Widening Local Development Pathways*. UNESCO.

Vanguard. (20). An Infusion of Cash. *Vanguard*. Retrieve from, vanguardngr.com/2019/07/nigerias-nollywood-film-industry-reels-in-foreign-investors/

World Trade Forum. (2009). Creative Economy: A Dynamic Sector in World Trade. *World Trade Organization*. Retrieved from, http://www.tradeforum.org/Creative-Economy-A-Dynamic-Sector-in-World-Trade/

Chapter 11
The Future

ABSTRACT

As we learned in Chapter 10, we are in a new world of doing business. Now that we have transcended into the fifth industrial revolution and the third stage of AI, we are at a crossroads with our own humanity. Our soul and creativity are man's alone. We are the captains of how we protect and guide humanity. This chapter goes into the wonderful technology that we are on the forefront of bringing into fruition. However, it is also a warning and a message to remember what is most important to our species. We have the potential to create a new enlightenment.

INTRODUCTION

In times of change, learners inherit the Earth, while the learned find themselves beautifully equipped to deal with the world that no longer exist. - Eric Hoffer

We are at an interesting time in the history of our planet. Our technology is moving at a faster rate than ever, and we have entered the Fifth Industrial Revolution. This is a time when Artificial Intelligence (AI) changes everything we know about the workforce, and creates even more turbulence. It is the time for disruptive leadership. As these changes take place, it is also the time when we need to focus on the creative economy. When moving into the next industrial revolution a heightened creativity and disruptive leadership will serve business and communities well. With this, our society will be prepared to excel in the sixth industrial revolution.

DOI: 10.4018/978-1-7998-3416-8.ch011

To succeed in these two new industrial revolutions an understanding of agility and absorption is important to have the resources so that we can move quickly and have the advantage of being able to see and implement new strategies and take advantage of new opportunities. Through heightened creativity, absorption and agility we will thrive. As with any struggle, perseverance will lead to a new modern enlightenment.

Elon Musk in 2014 warned us about artificial intelligence, saying it could be more dangerous than nuclear weapons. The late Stephen Hawking feared the third stage of artificial intelligence might be the ruin of humankind. These deep concerns by Hawking were over superhuman artificial intelligence and its ability to replicate human intelligence processes. In other words, the ability to expand intelligence without human support. Hawking's caution was over-thinking machines might modify themselves and independently design and build more capable systems.

At this time, humans would then be tragically outwitted. Hawking was one person who could have benefited from the advancement of artificial intelligence, which could have helped him cope with his neurological disease. However, Hawking wrote about the need for serious research to explore what impact AI would have on humanity, from the workplace to the military, where he expressed concerns about sophisticated weapons systems "that can choose and eliminate their own targets" (Molina, 2018). Hawking wrote, "Once such super human's appear, there are going to be significant political problems with the unimproved humans, who will not be able to compete, and will most likely die out, or become unimportant. Instead there will be a race of self-designing beings who are improving themselves at an ever-increasing rate" (Molina, 2018).

The Fifth Industrial Revolution

As we transcend into the fifth industrial revolution, we transcend into the era of turbulence. The fifth industrial revolution is characterized by the third stage of Artificial Intelligence (AI), which challenges all our current systems, from manufacturing processes, new materials, and new technologies. With the advent of the third stage of artificial intelligence, our current workforce will change drastically. Past and present, we have been warned by great minds such as the late Steven Hawking and Elon Musk, that this may be a time when our technology presents a great risk to humankind. One important issue remains given, and that is we are entering a time of great change on many fronts, and no one really knows what the future holds. The fifth industrial revolution may be about humanity, with machines and humans bonding, an equation used at the 2019 World Economic Forum: Blockchain+AI+Human = Magic. It was stated this magic and will not only help humankind, but that AI will increase human labor productivity, and Blockchain will help give access to banking and capital. Robots will help humans get returns on investments (Fink, 2018).

The fifth industrial revolution is so new that experts across the world are trying to define what it will be. The futurist George Muir argues it will be the AI revolution, Eva Kaili thinks it is all to do with the potential of quantum computing, Genpact believes it is the moment when humans and machines combine in the workplace. However, Salesforce founder and co-CEO Mark Benioff envisions, and that is we are in a crisis of trust with technology. A chief ethical and humane officer is needed (Lindsay and Hudson, 2019). In others words, how can you make the world a better place, not just more efficient. One area it could be better, is that people will be able to work whenever and wherever they want. Jobs can be tailored to the individual (Lindsay and Hudson, 2019).

In the fifth industrial revolution, unpreceded profits are connecting new ways of doing businesses. Capitalism is driving those results, and consumers are demanding sustainability. In this new world, the United Nations Sustainable Development Goals are increasing in stature, and a new matrix for achieving a thriving future is being adopted with UN members (World Economic Forum, 2019). One goal of achieving framework is through public-private partnerships that target private capital. Larry Fink, CEO of Investment Community Bank Blackrock set a standard for practice:

Purpose is not the sole pursuit of profits but the animating force for achieving them, and profits are in no way inconsistent with purpose – in fact, profits and purpose are inextricably linked. Larry Fink (2018)

Beyond funding, brand marketing needs to advance the common good. One example of gaining global attention is the Fifth Element Group's Good Exchange model. A Good Exchange is a marketing framework by which a brand engages its consumers with content activation that unlocks a donation to a cause that matters to both the brand and the consumer. The consumers become the media beacons for brand and cause-connected content, so that a growing portion of brand funds can flow to a cause, rather than to media intermediaries. This creates a bridge where traffic produces key performance indicators and aligned social impact. The Fifth Element Group works with businesses to move from a for-profit to a for-benefit operating model. Collectively, stakeholders become shareholders, but stakeholders are also employees, customers, and the public who will affect the market and workplace. The Fifth Element Group has speculated that even though there are challenges, they can still create a new socio-economic era that closes historic gaps with inclusion and create leaps for humanity (Gauri and Eerden, 2019).

However, patent and design rights will be less enforceable, and with the advent of the 3D and 4D printers, people will have the opportunity to make once highly manufactured products themselves. For example, new building products could transform the entire construction industry. We are currently at the advent of new modern structures being built with materials that allows the homeowner to build their own energy saving smart house (Maxwell, 2014).

The fifth industrial revolution comes at the end of mass production (Marsh, 2014). This new revolution may be a set of converging trends that alter how manufacturers develop, organize structures, and processes. By combining technologies of products, the growing use of global information, and pathways and supply networks, greater opportunities give way to creativity and customized products. This may be the advent where businesses merge manufacturing of products with operating services, environmental awareness, and work together as virtual manufacturers (Marsh, 2014).

This new *distributed manufacturing* may involve many players scattered around the world and create more opportunities for small cluster development. The winners from the new fifth industrial revolution will feature both big and small companies. They will be based in both rich and poor countries. The businesses that succeed in this era will be masters at creativity and collaboration and understand how to realize the wicked opportunities in wicked problems.

An example of a company that illustrates the characteristics of the new fifth industrial revolution is *Trumpf,* based near Stuttgart in Germany. Trumpf is the world's largest manufacturer of laser cutting machines, used in a range of segments, from traffic lights to medical equipment. This company has excelled at developing new technology. Trumpf is the leader in specialized lasers, machine automation, and new materials. Trumpf organizes its global supply chains and information networks while depending on an important group of suppliers (Marsh, 2014). This company is an example of the new creative class that relies on creativity and disruptive leadership through collaboration.

Marcus Weldon, president of Nokia Bells Labs and CTO of Nokia strongly believes that disruptive leaders, not afraid of AI, will guide their organizations focus on 5G wireless technology. Currently, smart phones and mobile internet have delivered convenience, but also distractions that have wasted time and catered to consumers. He feels that 5G will be driven by industry, using 5G to automate physical plant infrastructure, systems, platforms, factories, cities, and beyond (Birritteri, 2019). The consequence of this is that everything becomes local again. With this technology, jobs have to be inside the perimeter of the 5G wireless network so that the experts, the people running repairs and upgrades can perform their duties (Birritteri, 2019). This is the creative economy based on areas within micropolitan areas.

THIRD STAGE OF AI

Deep Learning is a statistical, machine-learning approach that provides the system with training data to enable it to program "itself". In other words, no human program is required. This does not mean that human intelligence was not used to make deep learning possible. The experts in this field are paid higher than programmers because it takes tremendous skill, experience, and experimentation to work with deep learning. Because deep learning has been the revolution in artificial intelligence, tens of billions of dollars are being invested to further develop this technology (Voss, 2017).

Max Tegmark, in his book, *Life 3.0* (2017) explores the future of technology, life, and intelligence. He summarizes his findings into three stages of the development of life:

- Biological stage
- Cultural stage
- Technological stage

In this technology stage today, life is limited in their biological condition, so as we go through this technological stage, life will need to go through a transformation or a final upgrade. The outcome being that man will be the master of his destiny and free of his evolutionary shackles (Tegmark, 2017). This leads to *singularity*, the point where technology overtakes the human, and the human becomes part machine or transhuman. The researchers tout that this will replace tedious and dirty work, and advanced societies will work less hours per week, and only highly skilled people will have work, the rest will get universal basic income or basic support.

Elon Musk in 2014 warned us about artificial intelligence, saying it could be more dangerous than nuclear weapons. The late Stephen Hawking feared the third stage of artificial intelligence might be the ruin of humankind. These deep concerns by Hawking were over superhuman artificial intelligence and its ability to replicate human intelligence processes. In other words, the ability to expand intelligence without human support. Hawking's caution was over-thinking machines might modify themselves and independently design and build more capable systems.

At this time, humans would then be tragically outwitted. Hawking was one person who could have benefited from the advancement of artificial intelligence, which could have helped him cope with his neurological disease. However, Hawking wrote about the need for serious research to explore what impact AI would have on humanity, from the workplace to the military, where he expressed concerns about sophisticated weapons systems "that can choose and eliminate their own targets" (Molina, 2018). Hawking wrote, "Once such super human's appear, there are going to be significant political problems with the unimproved humans, who will not be able to compete, and will most likely die out, or become unimportant. Instead there will be a race of self-designing beings who are improving themselves at an ever-increasing rate" (Molina, 2018).

THE SIXTH INDUSTRIAL REVOLUTION EXPLAINED

Every aspect of our lives is subject to change; innovation and creativity has changed history. The first industrial revolution created manufacturing; the second, the age of steam; the third, the age of electricity; the fourth, technology; the fifth, the rise of singularity and advanced technology and the need to rise to a higher level of humanity. For the sixth industrial revolution the jury is still out, however, it may be the age of sustainability (Silva and Di Serio, 2016). Could this be the start of finding a greater humanity?

Disruptive creative change is often driven the need to be competitive. In recent years, problems with the depletion of natural resources, pollution, natural disasters, traffic, nuclear risk, plus energy and water shortages have given way for the need to create advance technology to solve these problems on a global scale. At the same time, the global society is demanding that companies develop and innovate to accommodate the demands of sustainability. Several green leaders and companies have risen to the challenge, and amazing technology is currently being invented.

Movements and trends in the market suggest that a new wave of advanced innovation is coming, driven by the present environmental and social needs. The inequalities of different societies may have increased the demand for better sustainable solutions (Silva and Di Serio, 2016). These changes may have root in the highly competitive climate that companies have found themselves in and operating in a constant state of turbulence.

In addition, the depletion of natural resources on a global scale is a game changer, where some countries will be able to compete at a higher level than before, and others will lose their competitive advantage. Many developing countries might look forward to high growth based on new advancements in sustainability. Africa has several examples: the Mobile Platform Kiosk in Rwanda, which offers solar charging units for mobile devices; the Saphoians blade-less wind converter in Tunisia, which generates wind-power without blades that harm birds; Twende of Kenya, a car pooling app to counter traffic congestion; and Faso Soap, which repels mosquitoes that carry malaria (Silva and Di Serio, 2016).

As we go forth, we must drink deeper of knowledge. The disruptive creative leader may be a person who leads to create the dreams of the future. If we are entering the age of turbulence, we might be entering the biggest transformation and enlightenment era to occur on our planet. We might be entering the age of global consciousness, where the issues of humankind take priority, and we develop into higher-level human beings with a higher consciousness than before. The next deviation of our evolutionary cycle might be a change of our cognitive and meta-cognitive ability that creates a new disruptive creative leader.

TRADE-OFFS

We often have to make decisions within turbulence while trying to navigate our landscape on autopilot. Often unable to see the unintended consequences, or not considering either implications or unintended consequences. By recognizing that every time we make a decision, we are making a trade-off. A trade-off is dangerous if we are making decisions on autopilot. Technological innovations can change the dynamics of certain trade-offs, thus redefining the parameters and potentially the decision we make.

Never has it been more important to develop the skills of higher-order thinking, divergent thinking and decision-making. Change is now constant. It is important to realize that past decisions may have made perfect sense for the time, but in the current climate, they do not work. Viewing decision-making as plotting a course between trade-offs by consciously selecting a course of action that optimizes for a chosen objective can remove the stress of making decisions. The challenges become a trade-off between second-guessing yourself and steadfastly choosing to believe you have made a good decision. As we go into the 5th and 6th industrial revolutions, what will be the trade-offs? With the current state of the modern world, the trade-offs we make will determine our success.

Agility and Absorption

Research has determined that the best solution to problems often come from unexpected sources. To aspire to nimbleness is to develop organizational agility. Organizational agility is a company's ability to consistently identify and capture business opportunities more quickly than their competitors. Furthermore, agility is the ability to move quickly and effectively shift resources, talent, and attention out of less promising venues to ones that are more attractive.

Absorption is the dexterity with the size, physical strength, and toughness to withstand any punishment. Agility and absorption are complements that balance the shifting changes and the environment. Getting the right mix is important. By getting the right mix, the effectiveness of the two approaches increases during times of risk and uncertainty. Absorption is storing away resources for the right time; it bolsters the company's ability to weather uncertain times. Often our material desires hinder our ability to increase our absorption. Sacrifice is needed to build adsorption. By building adsorption in times of success, an organization will have the resources to be agile to thrive in times of turbulence.

The Modern Era

We are now living in a time when we are transferring into a new geologic epoch. The age of the "Anthropocene"—from *anthropo* meaning "man," and *cene* meaning "new"—because human-kind has caused mass extinctions of plant and animal species, polluted the oceans, and altered the atmosphere, among other impacts. The big question and argument is "have humans really changed the planet?" That seemingly simple question has sparked a new battle between geologists and environmental advocates over what to call the time-period we live in. According to the International Union of Geological Sciences (IUGS), the professional organization in charge of defining Earth's time scale, we are officially in the Holocene (entirely recent) epoch, which began 11,700 years ago after the last major ice age. Some scientists say the human impact cannot be found in the stratification of the earth. However, many recommend starting the epoch with the advent of the industrial revolution in the early 1800s or with the atomic age in the 1950s. In any case, just the idea of a new geologic epoch and man's impact on the earth are reasons for heightened creativity.

As we think about human impact on the planet, the 5th and 6th Industrial Revolutions and the unknowns of artificial intelligence, one might wonder if we are stuck on an unknown path of destruction, and we should fear the future. Not so, all over the world people are coming together with a heightened creativity that has not been seen in a very long time. Our creativity has allowed us to grow and develop the technology for our survival.

A New Enlightenment

Our previous period, "the Age of Enlightenment," was also called the "Age of Reason." The Enlightenment advocated reason as a means to establishing a system of aesthetics, ethics, government, and even religion, that would allow human beings to obtain objective truth about the whole of reality. The legacy of the Enlightenment was enormous and changed the path of the modern world. This group of scholars exposed the corruptness of the church and governments, promoted political and economic liberalism, the belief in progress. In addition, it was a time of science and art. In the Enlightenment, the intellectual framework for democracy and capitalism were created.

The intellectual leaders of the enlightenment regarded themselves as courageous elite who would lead the world into progress from a long period of doubtful tradition, occupying a central role in the justification for the movement known as modernism. Many today look at this age of heightened creativity and learning that paved the way for a 5,000-year leap. The book, *The 5000 Year Leap: A Miracle That Changed the World,* (Skousen, 2006) describes how the (28 Principles of Freedom) our founding fathers said must be understood and perpetuated by every person who desires peace, prosperity, and freedom. The past 200 years has brought about more progress than was made in the previous 5,000 years (Skousen, 2006). This is disruption at its finest.

Today we are calling disruptive leaders the leaders who are changing our world. In education, we are teaching higher order thinking and decision-making skills. We are going back to our culture and heritage with the creative economy. Dr. Niall Ferguson, esteemed scholar and senior fellow of the Hoover Institution, Stanford, and the Center for European Studies, Harvard, feels the world's economy is based on culture. That history has proven economics is not all-powerful. Culture, leadership and morals hold societies together. Culture dominates the outcome of history (Ferguson, 2019).

Leadership studies is now taught in most state universities and private colleges. New technologies are being invented daily, and the human conscious is rising around the planet at a much higher level than 20 years ago. We are going away from materialism; we are back bartering on the internet and social media. Collaborative scholarship is becoming the norm, where arts and science are working together to solve many of the complex issues the modern world is facing. We are at a new modern era, the age of turbulence, an age where heightened creativity is needed to be developed to once again ignite an enlightenment.

The first Age of Reason sought to establish stability in a world of chaos. Today the new age of reason can provide stability in a modern world of turbulence. The creative economy can be a part in the new era, to remind us of our culture, heritage, and values, while maintaining human equality and freedom. This age of reason can give us a new social contract, one that is not only about humanity, but also our planet.

The following case studies are examples of our future and disruptive leadership. Task and Purpose is an organization started by military veterans to serve and help veterans find jobs specific to their unique skill sets. This is done using advanced technology and networking within the military community. The final case study is called "The Calvary". Not everyone mentioned in this case study would want to be referred to as the cavalry, but they are. This is a group of disruptive leaders who decided to build the creative economy in their town and change the face of their community. They are not only stimulating economic development but also they are preparing the community for the future.

CASE STUDY 1: TASK AND PURPOSE

In 2007, while still on active duty, he testified before the United States Senate about the need to protect Iraqi refugees, especially translators and others who put their lives in danger to help US forces. He also had a highly entrepreneurial military career during which he helped build the first successful Iraqi military unit in Iraq's Al Anbar province and a number of elements within the Marine Corps' Special Operations Command including the Recruiting, Screening, Assessment, and Selection pipeline.

He is the founder, former executive director, and current chairperson of a nonprofit mental healthcare company. The Headstrong Project, which manages and provides care for veterans suffering from trauma and suicidality. He is also the CEO/Founder of Task and Purpose and its affiliated military veterans' employment site Hirepurpose.com. In 2010, he directed the documentary film, *The Western Front*, which screened at the Tribeca Film Festival. In 2013, he was a member of the Team USA Triathlon group and participated in the 2013 ITU World Championships in London. In 2017, he received Exeter Academy's John Phillips Award.

Cody Kasselman is the Head of Revenue at Task & Purpose. She is primarily responsible for driving profitable growth and establishing a brand voice in the competitive market. Day to day, she manages sales strategy and business analytics and oversees marketing operations and customer success. Cody previously managed $20 million dollars of accounts from both agency and publisher vantage points.

Task & Purpose Backstory

During his time in the Marines, Zach was moved and impressed by the quality people he met during his military service. Marines who would place themselves in physical danger for their comrades and people they did not even know. Military families made incredible sacrifices during long deployments and time apart from loved ones. It was clear this community represents the best of America.

Every business starts with a problem. Companies were and are currently struggling to find good talent. Military service members were struggling to transition to meaningful employment, despite being the best and brightest of a generation. Zach was fortunate to then meet Steve Amsden, an experienced HR and recruiting sales executive. Together, along with employee #1, Katie Dexter (an Iraq war veteran), they went on to launch Hirepurpose.com in January of 2014.

Shortly thereafter, the team brought aboard Brian Jones and Lauren Katzenberg to operate the website's blog. They named it Task & Purpose after the two components of the mission statement given as part of the military's five-paragraph order. The quality of the work Brian and Lauren did spoke for itself. It soon became apparent that there was a need for a voice like Task & Purpose in the military space - an irreverent and rebellious voice for those who were actually fighting today's wars. With both Brian and Lauren's conviction, Task & Purpose began taking on hard-hitting stories and developed a leadership sharing space.

Fast forward, a few years and the growing portfolio of brands had the opportunity to acquire MilSpouse Festivals. Military spouses have the toughest job in America, and they often find it hard to meet new friends and build community during constant moves over the course of a military career. These events enable them to make new friends, network, and be empowered with information they need to successfully navigate their daily lives and the challenges they face.

Task & Purpose quickly grew into the leading brand for military-related content, advertising, and employment. An employee and veteran-owned business, its mission is to improve the lives of the military community and ensure those shouldering the burden of today's wars have a voice. Task & Purpose serves as a conduit to the military community and its unique needs. The team offers firsthand insights and a close understanding of the military community through content that is authentic, entertaining, informative, and newsworthy. Through its extensive corporate B2B solutions, Task & Purpose can connect advertisers, marketers, and employers with service members, veterans, and their spouses. As the group of companies evolved, what was once the websites blog became the lead brand in the portfolio. Hirepurpose.com essentially became a subsidiary of Task & Purpose, as did MilSpouse Festivals

Market Context

Task & Purpose is fundamentally a media company, with a business model that foresees, through advertising solutions that help brands reach the military market. Whether brands are interested in marketing products or services, hiring, or building deep authentic relationships with our community, Task & Purpose have solutions to support them. Through Task & Purpose's brand studio, they can help companies build authentic branded content and advertising campaigns targeting the military consumer. Through Hirepurpose.com, Task & Purpose operates the only career platform owned and operated by veterans, designed specifically for the military community. They can help employers hire excellent, military-experienced talent exiting the military or already in the workforce. Moreover, through MSF, they can help companies build meaningful, in-person relationships with spouses. Task & Purpose managed to be a disruptive leader by maintaining our authenticity. The military is a tribe and tight knit community that unites many different types of people from across the United States. That cannot be faked.

CASE STUDY 2: THE CALVARY

When thinking about what we can control about the future, we can start in our own communities. In Fort Smith, Arkansas, a special group of people have come together to reinvent their community, and most likely save it. This group of individuals are self-made; all love their community, and are currently investing their time and money to bring back the historical romantic history of Fort Smith's past into the modern world.

It started with a disruptive leader named Steve Clark. The historic Friedman-Mincer building in downtown Fort Smith, Arkansas, was in ruins. It was purchased by Clark's company, Pro Pak, and restored. This action led Clark to urge stakeholders in Fort Smith's future to take charge of the city, and it led Clark to start 64.6 Downtown, the non-profit group responsible for bringing "The Unexpected" contemporary public art festival to downtown Fort Smith. More community festivals have been added: the Steel Horse Rally, Peace Maker Music and Arts Festival, and the Ales for Trails craft beer festival. The Unexpected event is now internationally renowned with over fifteen million views on social media. Clark went on to establish and help fund the Future School of Fort Smith, a tuition-free, public charter high school.

When people ask me why I do The Unexpected, my answer is 'Because that is the kind of city I want to live in.' If you want to live in a city that has trails, that celebrates the arts or music and anything that makes the city rich in culture – if you're waiting on someone to do that, stop. Find a way to get engaged and plugin' - Steve Clark

The support staff for 64.6 Downtown, John McIntosh, Claire Kolberg, and Talicia Richardson, work tirelessly with other organizations to move forward with further downtown development including building trails and urban parks. In addition, they are committed to building vibrant places in

Fort Smith. Their latest project is restoring a historical community theater, performing arts and educational campus.

The support staff are disruptive leaders in their own right. John McIntosh is responsible for developmental funding of The Unexpected each year as well as securing mural installation locations. He is responsible for making all production arrangements prior to and during the festival, and that the artists have all the paint and materials on hand each day they are creating art.

Claire Kolberg is The Unexpected Festival and media director and works directly with the artists and curator teams leading up to and during the festival. She is the social media director and primary contact for other arts organizations, like the Crystal Bridges Museum and Arkansas Parks and Tourism.

Talicia Richardson is working directly with the City of Fort Smith to help guide and implement the Propelling Downtown Forward master plan. She provides a thoughtful connection for downtown merchants, investors, and downtown property owners. She leads the fight for the experience of downtown customers.

Why this case study is called, The Calvary goes beyond Steve Clark and 64.6 Downtown support staff; it also encompasses the 64.6 Downtown board of directors:

- Steve Clark, Founder and CEO Pro Pak
- Trent Goins, Vice President, CEO, OK Foods
- Mitch Minnick, Secretary, Director for Fort Smith Housing Authority
- Sam T. Sicard, Treasurer, President, First National Bank
- Judy McReynolds, CEO, ArcBest, CEO
- Rodney Ghan, Owner, Ghan & Cooper Properties
- Tim Allen, President, Fort Smith Chamber of Commerce
- Griffin Hanna, Development, Hanna Oil & Gas
- Talicia Richardson, Executive Director, 64.6 Downtown

This group of disruptive leaders not only lead successful companies, but one, Sam T. Sicard, recently offered interest-free loans for people who needed to repair or re-build their homes or property after a historic flood. A disruptive leader has heart, the heart of their community, and the people that live and work there. These leaders have come together to revitalize Fort Smith, with their own time and money, and they demonstrate to us not only a commitment to build a vibrant community, but a community that will withstand times of turbulence.

REFERENCES

Birritteri, A. (2019). Weldon on 5G and the 4th industrial revolution. *New Jersey Business, 65*, 56. Retrieved from https://0-search-proquest-com.libcat.uafs.edu/docview/2183515085?accountid=14481

Ferguson, N. (2019). Finance and Economy. *Niall Ferguson*. Retrieved from, http://www.niallferguson.com/

Gauri, P., & Van Eerden, J. (2019). *What the Fifth Industrial Revolution is and Why It Matters*. World Economic Forum.

Lindsay, J., & Hudson, A. (2019). What is the fifth industrial revolution and how will it change the world? *Metro*. Retrieved from, https://metro.co.uk/2019/06/10/fifth-industrial-revolution-will-change-world-9738825/

Marsh, P. (2014). The New Industrial Revolution – all is explained. *Peter Marsh, Observations and Opinions*. Retrieved from, http://petermarsh.eu/the-new-industrial-revolution-all-is-explained/

Maxwell, I. A. (2014). The Fifth Industrial Revolution, Technology. *Academia*. Retrieved from, https://www.academia.edu/7319133/The_Fifth_Industrial_Revolution?auto=download

Molina, B. (2018). Stephen Hawking Warns that AI, "Superhuman" Could Wipe Humanity in Posthumous Book. *USA Today*. Retrieved from, https://www.usatoday.com/story/news/nation-now/2018/10/15/stephen-hawking-warns-superhumans-ai-posthumous-book/1645963002/

Silva, G., & Di Serio, L. C. (2016). The Sixth Wave of Innovation: Are we ready? *IMR, Innovation & Management Review*. Retrieved from, http://www.revistas.usp.br/rai, http://dx.eoi.org/10.10.16/j.rai.2016.03.005

Skousen, W. C. (2009). *The Five Thousand Year Leap*. The American Documents Publishing.

Chapter 12
Conclusion

ABSTRACT

Our future may be as simple as our own ability to be disruptive, creative, and persistent; not to allow failure to define us, but define ourselves by our ability to shift our life path and paradigm through a heightened creativity. Creative economies form organically and often with a disruptive leader who is self-directed and sees a need in the community. They form groups who become disruptors themselves and they work together to ignite the creative economy in their area. They find a way, when others tend to give up, to succeed. In the process, they create a sense of place. This is being done all across America and globally. This chapter explores this.

INTRODUCTION

Really, the only thing that makes sense is to strive for greater collective enlightenment. -Elon Musk

Communities and state governments can pass laws, enact programs, award grants, and collaborate with local and state economic development agencies to encourage disruptive creative entrepreneurs. In recognizing the benefits of the creative economy, a community and state can revitalize itself, attracting young professionals and families seeking a better quality of life.

DOI: 10.4018/978-1-7998-3416-8.ch012

The Role of Collaboration

Universities and community colleges provide valuable resources to these initiatives. Collaboration between business, academia, governmental agencies, foundations, and non-profits launch projects that have lasting value to the overall creative economies. Universities provide knowledge and learning activities. In addition, they provide an infrastructure of essential knowledge. Often, universities are the toolkits used developers to teach the skills needed for entrepreneurs to succeed. Through education, creativity can be cultivated with exposure to the visual arts, performing arts, arts, literacy arts, technology, science and business.

Universities stimulate disruptive ideas through higher order thinking and decision-making (HOTS). Society has blamed universities of indoctrinating the young, instead of teaching students to think on their own. Indoctrinating them to think according to the professor's ideology. Indoctrination is not HOTS. HOTS is teaching students to think on their own. To drink deeply of the knowledge they are receiving, to think critically and use their own intellect to come to understandings of the world's complex issues. The importance of HOTS is that it helps students and society to understand ambiguity, and help them make important decisions through deep thought and understanding. Without this, many will not thrive. They will live confused and not be able to make critical decisions about their own lives. Emotional intelligence grows through knowledge and experience. We do not want a stunted, confused and angry society.

Motivation to be Disruptive

The question to ask is, "What motivates some to be creative and disruptive more than others?" According to Vandor and Franke (2016), immigrants are almost twice as likely to become entrepreneurs than native-born U.S. citizens. Of the new entrepreneurs, 29.5% were immigrants. More than 20% of new and established business owners in the U.S. were immigrants in 2014. The total immigrant community is 13.2% of the U.S. population. In addition, one fourth of all technology and engineering companies started in the U.S. between 2006 and 2012 has at least one immigrant cofounder (Kosten, 2018). Individuals are more likely to migrate to countries of greater opportunity (Vandor and Franke, 2016).

Another study, looking from a different perspective, concluded entrepreneurs mixing cross-cultural products, services and communication differences, developed a higher capability to stimulate their creativity and could better identify promising business ventures (Kosten, 2018). They become disruptive.

However, the same could be said of many entrepreneurs who have come from poverty and no opportunity, but have become successful business leaders and very wealthy. Living poorly is hard and full of despair. Individuals of poverty are desperate to survive not wanting to live in shelters or on the streets. They are barely living with nothing to lose. They need hope! Despair is a terrible feeling, and you want to do everything possible to get rid of it. To change your life one has to take action and never give up. That very despair fuels their motivation, creativity and passion to succeed. Their despair creates disruptiveness.

Howard Schultz is a notable example of someone who was born poor. He was born in Brooklyn, N.Y. He was awarded a football scholarship to Northern Michigan University. He paid for his college with government loans and part-time work. He was a first generation college graduate. He had various jobs in sales and marketing after graduating from college. Then he got interested in the coffee business. After visiting Italy, he saw the coffee business in a new light. Being an employee for Starbucks, he later went on to buy the company. Because of his hard work, and real estate savvy Starbucks became the giant it is, and Schultz became a billionaire (Schultz, 2011).

Rural America and crime ridden urban cores are motivated by quality of life and economics to change and be disruptive. By igniting their creative economy, they bring back a sense of place, capitalize on their culture, and change the environment to attract young families. These young families want better schools and to advance their quality of life. Igniting the creative economy is done with disruptive leadership along with the support of local business, academia, government, and non-profits all collaborating to achieve these goals.

The Future

We are now in the fifth industrial revolution and are coming into the third stage of AI. It is at this time we have to learn to be the captains for humanity, and keep technology and science ethical. At the same time seeing the benefits that future can provide for us. This will take higher order thinking and decision-making, and higher order humans. We do not want a society of haves and have-nots. We want a society where social justice prevails, and ethical conduct is prized in all disciplines.

Disruptive leaders not only change traditional business practices, they change the accepted norms of behavior. Self-disruptive leaders change accepted norms. Furth describes disruptive leaders as, "These are the most ambitious people on the planet and often push ethical and legal boundaries in their unrelenting drive to get what they want," (Furth, 2019, p.29). True leaders are powerful, knowledgeable, and self-aware, and the great leaders are able to modify their behaviors when needed.

Even though these individuals can be complex and contradictory they are also visionary, goofy, nerdy, solution-oriented, introverted, critical, intellectual, nonlinear, chaotic, restless, laid-back, and perfectionist (Furth, 2018). Disruptive leaders are often controversial. These leaders are important for the development of our society; they think divergently and often change a generation's view of ethical behavior. This can be for good or bad. The disruptive leader needs a healthy ego, which is not always well thought of. However, to overcome resistance, it is necessary. Truly great leaders understand the importance of keeping their egos in check, and remain open-minded. Great leaders replace ego with confidence and knowledge (Furth, 2018).

President Franklin D. Roosevelt famously said, "You have nothing to fear, but fear itself." Fear is a waste of time and energy. It alters our reality, clouds our judgement, and affects the way we make decisions. Even highly educated people can be convinced to simply give up because of fear. Disruptive leaders understand the difference between fear and failure. We all have failures, but it is the ability to go back to moments of greatness, be disruptive and leave painful events behind. Disruptive leaders use these failures to become better leaders and higher order humans. Fearlessness is life enhancing, and this can build a better world for our future.

The importance of disruptive leaders in building the creative economy is the fearlessness that they possess. They see the future, and have a clear vision of what is needed. They have well thought out plans, great market research and excellent branding. They know when to frame and re-frame, but most of all they develop other disruptive leaders. They create a movement! This is a group of dedicated professionals. They forget their differences, and work to ignite the creative economy to build a healthy community.

I hope after reading this book, you strive to become disruptive, and look for ways to build the creative economy. Our history should not be forgotten, even the unpleasant part of it. The bad teaches why we changed and what we still need to work on to be higher functioning humans. The good teaches us what was important, what worked and that we should not forget. Our history formed our unique cultures in the communities where we live. Hard working Americans, who deserve to have their legacies live on, formed these cultures. Let us hope that our decedents see our hard work and disruption as making the world a better place.

REFERENCES

DeVol, R., & Wisecarver, S.J. (2018). *Micropolitan Success Stories from the Heartland.* The Walton Family Foundation.

Furth, J.F. (2018). *Owning Tomorrow: The Unstoppable Force of Disruptive Leadership.* Indie Books.

Kosten, D. (2018). *Immigrants as Economic Contributors: Immigrant Entrepreneurs.* National Immigration Forum.

Schultz, H. (2011). *Onward: How Starbucks Fought for Its Life Without Losing Its Soul.* Howard Schultz.

Vandor, P., & Franke, N. (2016). Why Are Immigrants more Entrepreneurial? *Harvard Business Review.* https://hbr.org/2016/10/why-are-immigrants-more-entrepreneurial

Related Readings

To continue IGI Global's long-standing tradition of advancing innovation through emerging research, please find below a compiled list of recommended IGI Global book chapters and journal articles in the areas of business leadership, entrepreneurship, and business management. These related readings will provide additional information and guidance to further enrich your knowledge and assist you with your own research.

Abalkhail, J. M. (2018). Arab Gulf Women and the Labyrinth of Leadership. In E. Al-A'ali, M. Al-Shammari, & H. Masri (Eds.), *Arab Women and Their Evolving Roles in the Global Business Landscape* (pp. 26–50). Hershey, PA: IGI Global. doi:10.4018/978-1-5225-3710-6.ch002

Abe, E. N., & Abe, I. I. (2019). Integrating Multiculturalism in the Design and Implementation of Work-Life Balance Strategies. In S. Atiku (Ed.), *Contemporary Multicultural Orientations and Practices for Global Leadership* (pp. 100–120). Hershey, PA: IGI Global. doi:10.4018/978-1-5225-6286-3.ch006

Abe, I. I., & Abe, E. N. (2019). Dynamics of Human Resource Strategies and Cultural Orientations in Multinational Corporations. In S. Atiku (Ed.), *Contemporary Multicultural Orientations and Practices for Global Leadership* (pp. 80–99). Hershey, PA: IGI Global. doi:10.4018/978-1-5225-6286-3.ch005

Ak, R., & Bingül, B. A. (2018). Kuwait. In S. Ozdemir, S. Erdogan, & A. Gedikli (Eds.), *Handbook of Research on Sociopolitical Factors Impacting Economic Growth in Islamic Nations* (pp. 276–292). Hershey, PA: IGI Global. doi:10.4018/978-1-5225-2939-2.ch014

Akkoyunlu, P. F. (2016). Assessing the Effectiveness of Vocational Education and Training in Economic Development: A Comparison between Turkish and German Education Systems. In M. Erdoğdu & B. Christiansen (Eds.), *Handbook of Research on Comparative Economic Development Perspectives on Europe and the MENA Region* (pp. 127–151). Hershey, PA: IGI Global. doi:10.4018/978-1-4666-9548-1.ch007

Akram, M. U., Chauhan, C., Ghosh, K., & Singh, A. (2019). Knowledge Management, Sustainable Business Performance and Empowering Leadership: A Firm-Level Approach. *International Journal of Knowledge Management, 15*(2), 20–35. doi:10.4018/IJKM.2019040102

Al-Alawi, A. I., Husamaddin, S., Mejeran, F. K., & Madan, F. K. (2018). Bahraini Women Engineers: Factors Influencing Their Career Success Ladder. In E. Al-A'ali, M. Al-Shammari, & H. Masri (Eds.), *Arab Women and Their Evolving Roles in the Global Business Landscape* (pp. 178–208). Hershey, PA: IGI Global. doi:10.4018/978-1-5225-3710-6.ch008

Al-Yafi, K., Hindi, N. M., & Osman, I. H. (2016). A User-Centric Evaluation of e-Government Services in the GCC Region: Case of State of Qatar. *International Journal of Electronic Government Research, 12*(4), 15–34. doi:10.4018/IJEGR.2016100102

Alfantookh, A., & Bakry, S. H. (2017). The State of People and Knowledge in the GCC Countries per a New Index and the Future Ahead. *International Journal of Knowledge Society Research, 8*(4), 34–74. doi:10.4018/IJKSR.2017100103

Alkhuraiji, A. I. (2018). The Influence of the Top Management Characteristics on the Success of the Enterprise Information System. In A. Borchers (Ed.), *Technology Management in Organizational and Societal Contexts* (pp. 1–26). Hershey, PA: IGI Global. doi:10.4018/978-1-5225-5279-6.ch001

Alkraiji, A. I. (2016). Cross-Case Analysis of Top Management Characteristics and Enterprise Information System Success. *Journal of Cases on Information Technology, 18*(3), 40–58. doi:10.4018/JCIT.2016070104

Alraouf, A. A. (2018). A Holistic Assessment of Education City in Doha: The Borderless Knowledge Hub. In A. Alraouf (Ed.), *Knowledge-Based Urban Development in the Middle East* (pp. 228–247). Hershey, PA: IGI Global. doi:10.4018/978-1-5225-3734-2.ch012

Asiri, M. (2017). The Interaction of Pharmaceutical Regulations in Saudi Arabia With the Presence of FDI: Facilitating FDI in Saudi Pharmaceutical Industry. In B. Christiansen & G. Koc (Eds.), *Transcontinental Strategies for Industrial Development and Economic Growth* (pp. 132–145). Hershey, PA: IGI Global. doi:10.4018/978-1-5225-2160-0.ch008

Atiku, S. O. (2019). Institutionalizing Social Responsibility Through Workplace Green Behavior. In S. Atiku (Ed.), *Contemporary Multicultural Orientations and Practices for Global Leadership* (pp. 183–199). Hershey, PA: IGI Global. doi:10.4018/978-1-5225-6286-3.ch010

Atiku, S. O., & Fields, Z. (2019). Global Psychological Capital and Sustainable Competitive Advantage. In S. Atiku (Ed.), *Contemporary Multicultural Orientations and Practices for Global Leadership* (pp. 145–164). Hershey, PA: IGI Global. doi:10.4018/978-1-5225-6286-3.ch008

Atsan, N. (2019). Utilizing Social Networks in Social Entrepreneurship. In N. Iyigun (Ed.), *Creating Business Value and Competitive Advantage With Social Entrepreneurship* (pp. 232–250). Hershey, PA: IGI Global. doi:10.4018/978-1-5225-5687-9.ch011

Ayandibu, A. O. (2019). Green Transformational Leadership and Organizational Behavior Effectiveness. In S. Atiku (Ed.), *Contemporary Multicultural Orientations and Practices for Global Leadership* (pp. 225–244). Hershey, PA: IGI Global. doi:10.4018/978-1-5225-6286-3.ch012

Bartens, Y., Chunpir, H. I., Schulte, F., & Voß, S. (2017). Business/IT Alignment in Two-Sided Markets: A COBIT 5 Analysis for Media Streaming Business Models. In S. De Haes & W. Van Grembergen (Eds.), *Strategic IT Governance and Alignment in Business Settings* (pp. 82–111). Hershey, PA: IGI Global. doi:10.4018/978-1-5225-0861-8.ch004

Bayarçelik, E. B., & Taşel, F. (2019). Social Entrepreneurship for Sustainable Economic Growth. In N. Iyigun (Ed.), *Creating Business Value and Competitive Advantage With Social Entrepreneurship* (pp. 251–270). Hershey, PA: IGI Global. doi:10.4018/978-1-5225-5687-9.ch012

Bayik, M. F. (2019). Social Innovation and Social Entrepreneurship. In N. Iyigun (Ed.), *Creating Business Value and Competitive Advantage With Social Entrepreneurship* (pp. 92–114). Hershey, PA: IGI Global. doi:10.4018/978-1-5225-5687-9.ch005

Ben Hamida, L. (2016). Building R&D Capabilities Abroad and the Role of Reverse Knowledge Transfer in Explaining MNCs' Productivity. In M. Erdoğdu & B. Christiansen (Eds.), *Handbook of Research on Comparative Economic Development Perspectives on Europe and the MENA Region* (pp. 219–235). Hershey, PA: IGI Global. doi:10.4018/978-1-4666-9548-1.ch011

Bergeron, F., Croteau, A., Uwizeyemungu, S., & Raymond, L. (2017). A Framework for Research on Information Technology Governance in SMEs. In S. De Haes & W. Van Grembergen (Eds.), *Strategic IT Governance and Alignment in Business Settings* (pp. 53–81). Hershey, PA: IGI Global. doi:10.4018/978-1-5225-0861-8.ch003

Bergethon, K. P., & Davis, D. C. (2016). Emotional Leadership: Leadership Styles and Emotional Intelligence. In A. Normore, L. Long, & M. Javidi (Eds.), *Handbook of Research on Effective Communication, Leadership, and Conflict Resolution* (pp. 63–77). Hershey, PA: IGI Global. doi:10.4018/978-1-4666-9970-0.ch004

Bhattacharya, P. J. (2018). Managing IT to Innovate and Strategize in the Higher Education Sector: Role of Enterprise Systems. In A. Borchers (Ed.), *Technology Management in Organizational and Societal Contexts* (pp. 27–50). Hershey, PA: IGI Global. doi:10.4018/978-1-5225-5279-6.ch002

Butt, T. A., Iqbal, R., & Kehal, M. (2019). Social Internet of Vehicles: A GCC (Gulf Cooperation Council) Perspective. In Z. Zhang (Ed.), *Global Information Diffusion and Management in Contemporary Society* (pp. 172–188). Hershey, PA: IGI Global. doi:10.4018/978-1-5225-5393-9.ch007

Camillo, A. A., & Camillo, I. C. (2016). The Ethics of Strategic Managerial Communication in the Global Context. In A. Normore, L. Long, & M. Javidi (Eds.), *Handbook of Research on Effective Communication, Leadership, and Conflict Resolution* (pp. 566–590). Hershey, PA: IGI Global. doi:10.4018/978-1-4666-9970-0.ch030

Carlos, V. S., & Rodrigues, R. G. (2016). The Use of Online Social Networks in Higher Education and Its Influence on Job Performance. In A. Normore, L. Long, & M. Javidi (Eds.), *Handbook of Research on Effective Communication, Leadership, and Conflict Resolution* (pp. 330–353). Hershey, PA: IGI Global. doi:10.4018/978-1-4666-9970-0.ch018

Cavusoglu, T., & Onal, D. K. (2016). The Role of Institutional Quality on Total Factor Productivity: A Comparative Analysis on the CEE and MENA Economies. In M. Erdoğdu & B. Christiansen (Eds.), *Handbook of Research on Comparative Economic Development Perspectives on Europe and the MENA Region* (pp. 98–126). Hershey, PA: IGI Global. doi:10.4018/978-1-4666-9548-1.ch006

Chen, E. T. (2016). Virtual Team Management for Higher Performance. In A. Normore, L. Long, & M. Javidi (Eds.), *Handbook of Research on Effective Communication, Leadership, and Conflict Resolution* (pp. 298–310). Hershey, PA: IGI Global. doi:10.4018/978-1-4666-9970-0.ch016

Clark, C., & Stowers, G. (2016). Speaking with Trunks, Dancing with the "Pink Elephants": Troubling E-Racism, E-Classism, and E-Sexismin Teaching Multicultural Teacher Education. In A. Normore, L. Long, & M. Javidi (Eds.), *Handbook of Research on Effective Communication, Leadership, and Conflict Resolution* (pp. 78–97). Hershey, PA: IGI Global. doi:10.4018/978-1-4666-9970-0.ch005

Clarke, M., Hall, J. G., & Rapanotti, L. (2017). Enterprise Architecture: A Snapshot from Practice. In S. De Haes & W. Van Grembergen (Eds.), *Strategic IT Governance and Alignment in Business Settings* (pp. 237–255). Hershey, PA: IGI Global. doi:10.4018/978-1-5225-0861-8.ch009

Cockburn, T., & Smith, P. A. (2016). Leadership in the Digital Age: Rhythms and the Beat of Change. In A. Normore, L. Long, & M. Javidi (Eds.), *Handbook of Research on Effective Communication, Leadership, and Conflict Resolution* (pp. 1–20). Hershey, PA: IGI Global. doi:10.4018/978-1-4666-9970-0.ch001

Cockburn, T., Smith, P. A., Martins, B. M., & Valles, R. S. (2016). Conflict of Interest or Community of Collaboration?: Leadership, SME Network Dialectics, and Dialogs. In A. Normore, L. Long, & M. Javidi (Eds.), *Handbook of Research on Effective Communication, Leadership, and Conflict Resolution* (pp. 210–232). Hershey, PA: IGI Global. doi:10.4018/978-1-4666-9970-0.ch012

Connolly, R., & Kenny, G. (2016). Dataveillance and Information Privacy Concerns: Ethical and Organizational Considerations. In A. Normore, L. Long, & M. Javidi (Eds.), *Handbook of Research on Effective Communication, Leadership, and Conflict Resolution* (pp. 606–626). Hershey, PA: IGI Global. doi:10.4018/978-1-4666-9970-0.ch032

Cross, D. E. (2016). Globalization and Media's Impact on Cross Cultural Communication: Managing Organizational Change. In A. Normore, L. Long, & M. Javidi (Eds.), *Handbook of Research on Effective Communication, Leadership, and Conflict Resolution* (pp. 21–41). Hershey, PA: IGI Global. doi:10.4018/978-1-4666-9970-0.ch002

Dahlberg, T., Kivijärvi, H., & Saarinen, T. (2017). IT Investment Consistency and Other Factors Influencing the Success of IT Performance. In S. De Haes & W. Van Grembergen (Eds.), *Strategic IT Governance and Alignment in Business Settings* (pp. 176–208). Hershey, PA: IGI Global. doi:10.4018/978-1-5225-0861-8.ch007

Davis, D. C., & Scaffidi-Clarke, N. M. (2016). Leading Virtual Teams: Conflict and Communication Challenges for Leaders. In A. Normore, L. Long, & M. Javidi (Eds.), *Handbook of Research on Effective Communication, Leadership, and Conflict Resolution* (pp. 196–209). Hershey, PA: IGI Global. doi:10.4018/978-1-4666-9970-0.ch011

Duarte, M., Baptista, A., & Pinto, G. (2018). Learning in the Laboratory: Accessing Videos With Quick Response Codes. In A. Borchers (Ed.), *Technology Management in Organizational and Societal Contexts* (pp. 117–138). Hershey, PA: IGI Global. doi:10.4018/978-1-5225-5279-6.ch006

Durgun, Ö. (2018). United Arab Emirates. In S. Ozdemir, S. Erdogan, & A. Gedikli (Eds.), *Handbook of Research on Sociopolitical Factors Impacting Economic Growth in Islamic Nations* (pp. 253–275). Hershey, PA: IGI Global. doi:10.4018/978-1-5225-2939-2.ch013

El-Kholei, A. O., & Al-Jayyousi, O. (2018). Cities of GCC in Post-Hydrocarbon Era: Challenges and Opportunities. In A. Alraouf (Ed.), *Knowledge-Based Urban Development in the Middle East* (pp. 248–270). Hershey, PA: IGI Global. doi:10.4018/978-1-5225-3734-2.ch013

Ellis, B., & Normore, A. H. (2016). Effective Engagement and Communication between First-Line Police Supervisors and Police Officers. In A. Normore, L. Long, & M. Javidi (Eds.), *Handbook of Research on Effective Communication, Leadership, and Conflict Resolution* (pp. 479–493). Hershey, PA: IGI Global. doi:10.4018/978-1-4666-9970-0.ch025

Erdoğan, S., & Gedikli, A. (2018). The State of Qatar. In S. Ozdemir, S. Erdogan, & A. Gedikli (Eds.), *Handbook of Research on Sociopolitical Factors Impacting Economic Growth in Islamic Nations* (pp. 212–252). Hershey, PA: IGI Global. doi:10.4018/978-1-5225-2939-2.ch012

Ertemel, A. V. (2019). Lean Approach to Social Entrepreneurship. In N. Iyigun (Ed.), *Creating Business Value and Competitive Advantage With Social Entrepreneurship* (pp. 115–139). Hershey, PA: IGI Global. doi:10.4018/978-1-5225-5687-9.ch006

Ezziane, Z., & Al Shamisi, A. (2017). The Impact of IT Governance Compliance on Enhancing Organizational Performance in Abu Dhabi. In S. De Haes & W. Van Grembergen (Eds.), *Strategic IT Governance and Alignment in Business Settings* (pp. 209–236). Hershey, PA: IGI Global. doi:10.4018/978-1-5225-0861-8.ch008

Farrag, N. A., & Ezzat, A. M. (2016). The Impact of Corruption on Economic Growth: A Comparative Analysis between Europe and MENA Countries. In M. Erdoğdu & B. Christiansen (Eds.), *Handbook of Research on Comparative Economic Development Perspectives on Europe and the MENA Region* (pp. 74–97). Hershey, PA: IGI Global. doi:10.4018/978-1-4666-9548-1.ch005

Fernandes, V. (2016). Reframing Continuous School Improvement in Australian Schools. In A. Normore, L. Long, & M. Javidi (Eds.), *Handbook of Research on Effective Communication, Leadership, and Conflict Resolution* (pp. 98–124). Hershey, PA: IGI Global. doi:10.4018/978-1-4666-9970-0.ch006

Fernández, M. T., & Pablo-Marti, F. (2016). Industrial Competitiveness in MENA Countries: Current Strategic Directions of Industrial Policy. In M. Erdoğdu & B. Christiansen (Eds.), *Handbook of Research on Comparative Economic Development Perspectives on Europe and the MENA Region* (pp. 152–171). Hershey, PA: IGI Global. doi:10.4018/978-1-4666-9548-1.ch008

Fındıklı, M. A., & Yozgat, U. (2019). The Individual and Behavioral Factors of Social Entrepreneurs. In N. Iyigun (Ed.), *Creating Business Value and Competitive Advantage With Social Entrepreneurship* (pp. 69–91). Hershey, PA: IGI Global. doi:10.4018/978-1-5225-5687-9.ch004

Genty, K. I. (2019). Interpersonal Relationship and Global Leadership Mindset. In S. Atiku (Ed.), *Contemporary Multicultural Orientations and Practices for Global Leadership* (pp. 165–182). Hershey, PA: IGI Global. doi:10.4018/978-1-5225-6286-3.ch009

Gomes, J., & Romão, M. (2017). Aligning Information Systems and Technology with Benefit Management and Balanced Scorecard. In S. De Haes & W. Van Grembergen (Eds.), *Strategic IT Governance and Alignment in Business Settings* (pp. 112–131). Hershey, PA: IGI Global. doi:10.4018/978-1-5225-0861-8.ch005

Gul, S. (2016). Alternative Dispute Resolution: A Legal Perspective. In A. Normore, L. Long, & M. Javidi (Eds.), *Handbook of Research on Effective Communication, Leadership, and Conflict Resolution* (pp. 126–143). Hershey, PA: IGI Global. doi:10.4018/978-1-4666-9970-0.ch007

Güler, B. K. (2019). Human Resources Management in Social Entrepreneurship. In N. Iyigun (Ed.), *Creating Business Value and Competitive Advantage With Social Entrepreneurship* (pp. 161–185). Hershey, PA: IGI Global. doi:10.4018/978-1-5225-5687-9.ch008

Gupta, D. S., & Biswas, G. P. (2018). On Securing Cloud Storage Using a Homomorphic Framework. In A. Borchers (Ed.), *Technology Management in Organizational and Societal Contexts* (pp. 99–114). Hershey, PA: IGI Global. doi:10.4018/978-1-5225-5279-6.ch005

Huda, M., Qodriah, S. L., Rismayadi, B., Hananto, A., Kardiyati, E. N., Ruskam, A., & Nasir, B. M. (2019). Towards Cooperative With Competitive Alliance: Insights Into Performance Value in Social Entrepreneurship. In N. Iyigun (Ed.), *Creating Business Value and Competitive Advantage With Social Entrepreneurship* (pp. 294–317). Hershey, PA: IGI Global. doi:10.4018/978-1-5225-5687-9.ch014

Igbinakhase, I., & Naidoo, V. (2019). Global Leadership Competencies and Orientations: Theory, Practice, and Future Implications. In S. Atiku (Ed.), *Contemporary Multicultural Orientations and Practices for Global Leadership* (pp. 59–79). Hershey, PA: IGI Global. doi:10.4018/978-1-5225-6286-3.ch004

Inglezakis, I. (2016). Surveillance of Electronic Communications in the Workplace and the Protection of Employees' Privacy. In A. Normore, L. Long, & M. Javidi (Eds.), *Handbook of Research on Effective Communication, Leadership, and Conflict Resolution* (pp. 591–605). Hershey, PA: IGI Global. doi:10.4018/978-1-4666-9970-0.ch031

İyigün, N. Ö. (2019). Context of Social Entrepreneurship and Background: Definitions, Related Terms, and Characteristics. In N. Iyigun (Ed.), *Creating Business Value and Competitive Advantage With Social Entrepreneurship* (pp. 1–20). Hershey, PA: IGI Global. doi:10.4018/978-1-5225-5687-9.ch001

Jackson, K., & Rasheed, R. (2016). Communication, Culture, and Discord: A Lesson in Leadership Failure. In A. Normore, L. Long, & M. Javidi (Eds.), *Handbook of Research on Effective Communication, Leadership, and Conflict Resolution* (pp. 182–195). Hershey, PA: IGI Global. doi:10.4018/978-1-4666-9970-0.ch010

Kabadurmus, F. N., & Lahiri, S. (2016). Competition and Product Innovation by Turkish Firms. In M. Erdoğdu & B. Christiansen (Eds.), *Handbook of Research on Comparative Economic Development Perspectives on Europe and the MENA Region* (pp. 469–491). Hershey, PA: IGI Global. doi:10.4018/978-1-4666-9548-1.ch019

Kaidalova, J., & Seigerroth, U. (2017). Contemporary Demands on Business and IT Alignment: How Can Enterprise Modeling Help? In S. De Haes & W. Van Grembergen (Eds.), *Strategic IT Governance and Alignment in Business Settings* (pp. 132–175). Hershey, PA: IGI Global. doi:10.4018/978-1-5225-0861-8.ch006

Kalitanyi, V. (2019). Global Business Environment. In S. Atiku (Ed.), *Contemporary Multicultural Orientations and Practices for Global Leadership* (pp. 1–24). Hershey, PA: IGI Global. doi:10.4018/978-1-5225-6286-3.ch001

Karaca, M., & Biçkes, D. M. (2019). Social Entrepreneurship: Constraints and Suggestions for Future Researches. In N. Iyigun (Ed.), *Creating Business Value and Competitive Advantage With Social Entrepreneurship* (pp. 318–332). Hershey, PA: IGI Global. doi:10.4018/978-1-5225-5687-9.ch015

Kariuki, P. (2019). Monitoring and Evaluation Leadership Through Technology: The South African Public-Sector Perspective. In S. Atiku (Ed.), *Contemporary Multicultural Orientations and Practices for Global Leadership* (pp. 121–144). Hershey, PA: IGI Global. doi:10.4018/978-1-5225-6286-3.ch007

Karnaukhova, O., & Nekrasova, I. (2016). The Role of Securitization Market in the Post-Crisis European Economic Recovery. In M. Erdoğdu & B. Christiansen (Eds.), *Handbook of Research on Comparative Economic Development Perspectives on Europe and the MENA Region* (pp. 511–523). Hershey, PA: IGI Global. doi:10.4018/978-1-4666-9548-1.ch021

Kayser, I. (2018). Who Benefits From Regional Economic Integration?: The Case of ASEAN. In A. Özer (Ed.), *Globalization and Trade Integration in Developing Countries* (pp. 97–115). Hershey, PA: IGI Global. doi:10.4018/978-1-5225-4032-8.ch005

Keil, L. J., & Jerome, A. M. (2016). Leadership in a Time of Crisis: Jim Tressel's Ousting from The Ohio State University. In A. Normore, L. Long, & M. Javidi (Eds.), *Handbook of Research on Effective Communication, Leadership, and Conflict Resolution* (pp. 162–181). Hershey, PA: IGI Global. doi:10.4018/978-1-4666-9970-0.ch009

Khoury, G. C., & McNally, B. (2016). The Role of the Leadership Style in Creating Conflict and Tension in a Higher Education Institution. In A. Normore, L. Long, & M. Javidi (Eds.), *Handbook of Research on Effective Communication, Leadership, and Conflict Resolution* (pp. 233–247). Hershey, PA: IGI Global. doi:10.4018/978-1-4666-9970-0.ch013

Kirstein, K. D. (2016). Developing Trust within International Teams: The Impacts of Culture on Team Formation and Process. In A. Normore, L. Long, & M. Javidi (Eds.), *Handbook of Research on Effective Communication, Leadership, and Conflict Resolution* (pp. 385–404). Hershey, PA: IGI Global. doi:10.4018/978-1-4666-9970-0.ch021

Long, L. W., Javidi, M., Hill, L. B., & Normore, A. H. (2016). Credible Negotiation Leadership: Using Principled Negotiation to Improve International Negotiation. In A. Normore, L. Long, & M. Javidi (Eds.), *Handbook of Research on Effective Communication, Leadership, and Conflict Resolution* (pp. 430–455). Hershey, PA: IGI Global. doi:10.4018/978-1-4666-9970-0.ch023

Maes, K., De Haes, S., & Van Grembergen, W. (2017). A Business Case Process for IT-Enabled Investments: Its Perceived Effectiveness from a Practitioner Perspective. In S. De Haes & W. Van Grembergen (Eds.), *Strategic IT Governance and Alignment in Business Settings* (pp. 1–23). Hershey, PA: IGI Global. doi:10.4018/978-1-5225-0861-8.ch001

Maher, C. (2019). Public Services Procurement: Third Sector Social Enterprises Perspectives. In N. Iyigun (Ed.), *Creating Business Value and Competitive Advantage With Social Entrepreneurship* (pp. 352–373). Hershey, PA: IGI Global. doi:10.4018/978-1-5225-5687-9.ch017

Manzoor, A. (2017). Accelerating Entrepreneurship in MENA Region: Opportunities and Challenges. In P. Zgheib (Ed.), *Entrepreneurship and Business Innovation in the Middle East* (pp. 57–73). Hershey, PA: IGI Global. doi:10.4018/978-1-5225-2066-5.ch004

Manzoor, A. (2017). Womenpreneurs in Mena Region. *International Journal of E-Entrepreneurship and Innovation*, *7*(1), 16–28. doi:10.4018/IJEEI.2017010102

Manzoor, A. (2018). High-Growth Entrepreneurship in the MENA Region. *International Journal of ICT Research in Africa and the Middle East*, *7*(1), 54–65. doi:10.4018/IJICTRAME.2018010104

Marois, T. (2016). State-Owned Banks and Development: Dispelling Mainstream Myths. In M. Erdoğdu & B. Christiansen (Eds.), *Handbook of Research on Comparative Economic Development Perspectives on Europe and the MENA Region* (pp. 52–73). Hershey, PA: IGI Global. doi:10.4018/978-1-4666-9548-1.ch004

Mishra, K. E., Mishra, A. K., & Walker, K. (2016). Leadership Communication, Internal Marketing, and Employee Engagement: A Recipe to Create Brand Ambassadors. In A. Normore, L. Long, & M. Javidi (Eds.), *Handbook of Research on Effective Communication, Leadership, and Conflict Resolution* (pp. 311–329). Hershey, PA: IGI Global. doi:10.4018/978-1-4666-9970-0.ch017

Mitchell, R. J., & Von Zoller, K. (2016). The Link between Communicative Intelligence and Procedural Justice: The Path to Police Legitimacy. In A. Normore, L. Long, & M. Javidi (Eds.), *Handbook of Research on Effective Communication, Leadership, and Conflict Resolution* (pp. 456–478). Hershey, PA: IGI Global. doi:10.4018/978-1-4666-9970-0.ch024

Moner-Colonques, R., & Sempere-Monerris, J. J. (2016). R&D Competition, Cooperation, and Microeconomic Policies. In M. Erdoğdu & B. Christiansen (Eds.), *Handbook of Research on Comparative Economic Development Perspectives on Europe and the MENA Region* (pp. 195–218). Hershey, PA: IGI Global. doi:10.4018/978-1-4666-9548-1.ch010

Mukonza, C., & Swarts, I. (2019). Examining the Role of Green Transformational Leadership on Promoting Green Organizational Behavior. In S. Atiku (Ed.), *Contemporary Multicultural Orientations and Practices for Global Leadership* (pp. 200–224). Hershey, PA: IGI Global. doi:10.4018/978-1-5225-6286-3.ch011

Nour, S. S. (2016). Characteristics of Innovation in the Arabic Countries. In L. Al-Hakim, X. Wu, A. Koronios, & Y. Shou (Eds.), *Handbook of Research on Driving Competitive Advantage through Sustainable, Lean, and Disruptive Innovation* (pp. 614–655). Hershey, PA: IGI Global. doi:10.4018/978-1-5225-0135-0.ch025

Nylund, P. A., Arimany-Serrat, N., Ferràs-Hernández, X., & Corral-Marfil, J. A. (2018). Home Bias in Innovation Ecosystems: Relying on Local Users for Knowledge. In A. Borchers (Ed.), *Technology Management in Organizational and Societal Contexts* (pp. 78–97). Hershey, PA: IGI Global. doi:10.4018/978-1-5225-5279-6.ch004

Öncer, A. Z. (2019). Performance Measurement in Social Enterprises: Social Impact Analysis. In N. Iyigun (Ed.), *Creating Business Value and Competitive Advantage With Social Entrepreneurship* (pp. 205–231). Hershey, PA: IGI Global. doi:10.4018/978-1-5225-5687-9.ch010

Önder, I., & Uckac, A. (2016). Opportunities and Challenges for Development. In M. Erdoğdu & B. Christiansen (Eds.), *Handbook of Research on Comparative Economic Development Perspectives on Europe and the MENA Region* (pp. 36–51). Hershey, PA: IGI Global. doi:10.4018/978-1-4666-9548-1.ch003

Oniku, A., Emmanuel, A. A., & Adetunji, O. (2017). Ethical Leadership, Ethical Selling, and Financial Services Performances: A Case of Nigerian Market. *International Journal of Sustainable Economies Management*, *6*(4), 21–34. doi:10.4018/IJSEM.2017100103

Oz, S. (2016). Diffusion of Technology via FDI and Convergence of Per Capita Incomes: Comparative Analysis on Europe and the MENA Region. In M. Erdoğdu & B. Christiansen (Eds.), *Handbook of Research on Comparative Economic Development Perspectives on Europe and the MENA Region* (pp. 236–264). Hershey, PA: IGI Global. doi:10.4018/978-1-4666-9548-1.ch012

Ozer, M., & Yeldan, A. E. (2016). The Relationship between Current Account Deficits and Unemployment in Turkey. In M. Erdoğdu & B. Christiansen (Eds.), *Handbook of Research on Comparative Economic Development Perspectives on Europe and the MENA Region* (pp. 492–510). Hershey, PA: IGI Global. doi:10.4018/978-1-4666-9548-1.ch020

Ozer, S. K., Taglioni, D., & Winkler, D. (2016). Turkey's Participation and Economic Upgrading in Global Value Chains. In M. Erdoğdu & B. Christiansen (Eds.), *Handbook of Research on Comparative Economic Development Perspectives on Europe and the MENA Region* (pp. 418–468). Hershey, PA: IGI Global. doi:10.4018/978-1-4666-9548-1.ch018

Park, H. J. (2016). Recasting Strategic Opportunities and Challenges for Development in Saudi Arabia. In M. Erdoğdu & B. Christiansen (Eds.), *Handbook of Research on Comparative Economic Development Perspectives on Europe and the MENA Region* (pp. 406–417). Hershey, PA: IGI Global. doi:10.4018/978-1-4666-9548-1.ch017

Pereira, R., Mira da Silva, M., & Lapão, L. V. (2017). IT Governance Maturity Patterns in Portuguese Healthcare. In S. De Haes & W. Van Grembergen (Eds.), *Strategic IT Governance and Alignment in Business Settings* (pp. 24–52). Hershey, PA: IGI Global. doi:10.4018/978-1-5225-0861-8.ch002

Perez-Montoro, M., & Sanz, S. (2016). Communities of Practice in Organizational Learning Strategies. In A. Normore, L. Long, & M. Javidi (Eds.), *Handbook of Research on Effective Communication, Leadership, and Conflict Resolution* (pp. 249–266). Hershey, PA: IGI Global. doi:10.4018/978-1-4666-9970-0.ch014

Popovic, M. (2016). Causes of Growth of MENA and East European Countries: Comparative Analysis. In M. Erdoğdu & B. Christiansen (Eds.), *Handbook of Research on Comparative Economic Development Perspectives on Europe and the MENA Region* (pp. 293–350). Hershey, PA: IGI Global. doi:10.4018/978-1-4666-9548-1.ch014

Pyle, A. S. (2016). Surviving the Conflict of Self-Inflicted Organizational Crises. In A. Normore, L. Long, & M. Javidi (Eds.), *Handbook of Research on Effective Communication, Leadership, and Conflict Resolution* (pp. 144–161). Hershey, PA: IGI Global. doi:10.4018/978-1-4666-9970-0.ch008

Radzuan, N. R., & Kaur, S. (2016). Engineering Students' Communication Apprehension and Competence in Technical Oral Presentations. In A. Normore, L. Long, & M. Javidi (Eds.), *Handbook of Research on Effective Communication, Leadership, and Conflict Resolution* (pp. 371–383). Hershey, PA: IGI Global. doi:10.4018/978-1-4666-9970-0.ch020

Rafay, A., & Khan, A. (2018). Synergy for Sustainability in the Upcoming Telecommunications Revolution: The Case of a Developing Economy. In A. Borchers (Ed.), *Technology Management in Organizational and Societal Contexts* (pp. 51–76). Hershey, PA: IGI Global. doi:10.4018/978-1-5225-5279-6.ch003

Rahim, E., & Duncan, T. (2019). Examining the Evolution of Creating Sustainable Leadership. In S. Atiku (Ed.), *Contemporary Multicultural Orientations and Practices for Global Leadership* (pp. 44–58). Hershey, PA: IGI Global. doi:10.4018/978-1-5225-6286-3.ch003

Ramraj, A. B., & Amolo, J. (2019). Leadership Across the Globe. In S. Atiku (Ed.), *Contemporary Multicultural Orientations and Practices for Global Leadership* (pp. 25–43). Hershey, PA: IGI Global. doi:10.4018/978-1-5225-6286-3.ch002

Razzak, W. A., Laabas, B., & Bentour, E. M. (2016). The Dynamics of Technical Progress in Some Developing and Developed Countries. In M. Erdoğdu & B. Christiansen (Eds.), *Handbook of Research on Comparative Economic Development Perspectives on Europe and the MENA Region* (pp. 172–194). Hershey, PA: IGI Global. doi:10.4018/978-1-4666-9548-1.ch009

Rivlin, P. (2016). Stabilization and Liberalization in the Israeli Economy. In M. Erdoğdu & B. Christiansen (Eds.), *Handbook of Research on Comparative Economic Development Perspectives on Europe and the MENA Region* (pp. 524–540). Hershey, PA: IGI Global. doi:10.4018/978-1-4666-9548-1.ch022

Ruffin, T. R., Hawkins, J. M., & Lee, D. I. (2016). Organizational Leadership and Health Care Reform. In A. Normore, L. Long, & M. Javidi (Eds.), *Handbook of Research on Effective Communication, Leadership, and Conflict Resolution* (pp. 42–62). Hershey, PA: IGI Global. doi:10.4018/978-1-4666-9970-0.ch003

Sercovich, F. C. (2016). Wither Convergence?: Catching-up in an Era of Diminished Expectations. In M. Erdoğdu & B. Christiansen (Eds.), *Handbook of Research on Comparative Economic Development Perspectives on Europe and the MENA Region* (pp. 1–24). Hershey, PA: IGI Global. doi:10.4018/978-1-4666-9548-1.ch001

Singh, A., Sengupta, S., & Sharma, S. (2016). Empathy and Mindfulness: Potential Antecedents to Authentic Leadership. *International Journal of Human Capital and Information Technology Professionals*, *7*(4), 1–14. doi:10.4018/IJHCITP.2016100101

Smith, P., & Cames, O. (2016). CAMES: An Approach to Project Management Based on Action Research and the Ideal Speech Situation. In A. Normore, L. Long, & M. Javidi (Eds.), *Handbook of Research on Effective Communication, Leadership, and Conflict Resolution* (pp. 531–544). Hershey, PA: IGI Global. doi:10.4018/978-1-4666-9970-0.ch028

Stock, W. G., Barth, J., & Gremm, J. (2019). The Era After Oil: Knowledge-Intensive Cities on the Arabian Gulf. In M. Lytras, L. Daniela, & A. Visvizi (Eds.), *Knowledge-Intensive Economies and Opportunities for Social, Organizational, and Technological Growth* (pp. 63–88). Hershey, PA: IGI Global. doi:10.4018/978-1-5225-7347-0.ch005

Tayşir, N. K. (2019). Value Creation Through Social Change: An Ashoka Fellow Case. In N. Iyigun (Ed.), *Creating Business Value and Competitive Advantage With Social Entrepreneurship* (pp. 333–351). Hershey, PA: IGI Global. doi:10.4018/978-1-5225-5687-9.ch016

Thoburn, J. T. (2016). Trade and Industrial Policy for Development. In M. Erdoğdu & B. Christiansen (Eds.), *Handbook of Research on Comparative Economic Development Perspectives on Europe and the MENA Region* (pp. 25–35). Hershey, PA: IGI Global. doi:10.4018/978-1-4666-9548-1.ch002

Tran, B. (2016). Communication: The Role of the Johari Window on Effective Leadership Communication in Multinational Corporations. In A. Normore, L. Long, & M. Javidi (Eds.), *Handbook of Research on Effective Communication, Leadership, and Conflict Resolution* (pp. 405–429). Hershey, PA: IGI Global. doi:10.4018/978-1-4666-9970-0.ch022

Tuncel, C. O., & Polat, A. (2016). Nanotechnology, Long Waves, and Future of Manufacturing Industry: Comparative Analysis of European Union, East Asian Newly Industrialized Countries, and MENA Region. In M. Erdoğdu & B. Christiansen (Eds.), *Handbook of Research on Comparative Economic Development Perspectives on Europe and the MENA Region* (pp. 351–377). Hershey, PA: IGI Global. doi:10.4018/978-1-4666-9548-1.ch015

Uğurlu, M. (2016). Firm-Level Determinants of Foreign Investment and M&A Activity: Evidence from Turkey. In M. Erdoğdu & B. Christiansen (Eds.), *Handbook of Research on Comparative Economic Development Perspectives on Europe and the MENA Region* (pp. 265–292). Hershey, PA: IGI Global. doi:10.4018/978-1-4666-9548-1.ch013

Ülgen, B. (2019). The Social Entrepreneur: Personality Traits and Motivation Factors in Social Entrepreneurship. In N. Iyigun (Ed.), *Creating Business Value and Competitive Advantage With Social Entrepreneurship* (pp. 48–68). Hershey, PA: IGI Global. doi:10.4018/978-1-5225-5687-9.ch003

Vance, C. M., & Bergin, R. (2019). The Social Expat-Preneur: Examining a Growing International Career Model Supporting Global Social Entrepreneurship. In N. Iyigun (Ed.), *Creating Business Value and Competitive Advantage With Social Entrepreneurship* (pp. 186–204). Hershey, PA: IGI Global. doi:10.4018/978-1-5225-5687-9.ch009

Vatharkar, S., Gao, P., & Fomin, V. (2018). Factors Affecting Business and Information Technology Alignment at the Lower Levels of a Public Organisation. *International Journal of Healthcare Information Systems and Informatics*, *13*(3), 35–48. doi:10.4018/IJHISI.2018070103

Vecchi, A., & Ricci, F. (2016). The Internationalization of the Space Industry: Anecdotal Evidence from an Italian SME. In M. Erdoğdu & B. Christiansen (Eds.), *Handbook of Research on Comparative Economic Development Perspectives on Europe and the MENA Region* (pp. 378–405). Hershey, PA: IGI Global. doi:10.4018/978-1-4666-9548-1.ch016

Venkatesh, R., Mathew, L., & Singhal, T. K. (2019). Imperatives of Business Models and Digital Transformation for Digital Services Providers. *International Journal of Business Data Communications and Networking*, *15*(1), 105–124. doi:10.4018/IJBDCN.2019010107

Yalcintas, M. (2019). Creating Competitive Advantage With Social Entrepreneurship. In N. Iyigun (Ed.), *Creating Business Value and Competitive Advantage With Social Entrepreneurship* (pp. 140–160). Hershey, PA: IGI Global. doi:10.4018/978-1-5225-5687-9.ch007

Yaseen, S. G., Al-Janaydab, S., & Alc, N. A. (2018). Leadership Styles, Absorptive Capacity and Firm's Innovation. *International Journal of Knowledge Management, 14*(3), 82–100. doi:10.4018/IJKM.2018070106

Yıldız, M. L. (2019). Social Entrepreneurial Leadership for a Better World. In N. Iyigun (Ed.), *Creating Business Value and Competitive Advantage With Social Entrepreneurship* (pp. 271–293). Hershey, PA: IGI Global. doi:10.4018/978-1-5225-5687-9.ch013

Yilmaz, A., & Yilmaz, H. U. (2019). Social Value and Sociological Perspective on Social Entrepreneurship. In N. Iyigun (Ed.), *Creating Business Value and Competitive Advantage With Social Entrepreneurship* (pp. 21–47). Hershey, PA: IGI Global. doi:10.4018/978-1-5225-5687-9.ch002

Zinger, D. (2016). Developing Instructional Leadership and Communication Skills through Online Professional Development: Focusing on Rural and Urban Principals. In A. Normore, L. Long, & M. Javidi (Eds.), *Handbook of Research on Effective Communication, Leadership, and Conflict Resolution* (pp. 354–370). Hershey, PA: IGI Global. doi:10.4018/978-1-4666-9970-0.ch019

About the Author

Kristin Tardif is the lead faculty in the Organizational Leadership and Office Management Technology programs at the University of Arkansas – Fort Smith. Prior to her current teaching role, Tardif was a faculty member at both Central Maine Community College and Fort Hays State University. Tardif is a global citizen having lived and traveled in a variety of countries. She went to high school in Maracaibo, Venezuela. After her studies she pursued a private sector career which spanned 30 years. Her work was with multinational corporations eventually securing a variety of leadership roles across business functions including plant management, market head, quality control, project management, natural resource management, corporate affairs and marketing. Her credentials include certifications in geographic information systems, cartography and leadership. Tardif was awarded a PhD in Organizational Leadership from The Chicago School of Professional Psychology. She holds a Master of Liberal Studies in Organization Leadership, a Bachelor of Science in Geosciences and a Bachelor of Art in History from Fort Hays State University. Tardif's research focuses on the global competences needed for international trade and global assignments; and Disruptive Creative leadership's impact on the creative economy, entrepreneurship, economic development in rural states contending with turbulence while transitioning into the 5th and 6th Industrial Revolutions. Supervisors: Dr. Ken Warden, Dean College of Applied Science and Technology.

Index

M

N

O

P

S

T

www.ingramcontent.com/pod-product-compliance
Lightning Source LLC
LaVergne TN
LVHW081323300926
849161LV00008B/1861